PURCHASING, RECEIVING, AND STORAGE:

A Systems Manual for Restaurants, Hotels, and Clubs

Jack D. Ninemeier

CBI

CBI Publishing Company, Inc.
286 Congress Street
Boston, MA 02210

Library of Congress Cataloging in Publication Data

Ninemeier, Jack D.
  Purchasing, receiving, and storage.

  1. Food service management.   2. Restaurant management.
3. Hotel management.   I. Title
TX943.N56   1983   642′.5   82-12934
ISBN 0–8436–2261–X

Printed in the United States of America.

Printed (last digit): 9 8 7 6 5 4 3 2 1

Dedication

This book is dedicated to a man whose name is synonymous with quality in the food service industry. His intense and consistent effort to produce the highest possible quality—in his thoughts and actions, in his students, in his business—never is removed from anything that he does. As a student, I knew his book; it is indeed an honor to now serve with him on the faculty at Michigan State. Thank you, Dr. Lewis Minor, for your confidence, your advice, and your support.

Contents

11 Security Concerns in Purchasing   147

12 Ethical Concerns in Purchasing   159

14   Evaluation of Purchasing   185

15   Purchase of Foods and Beverages   197

Foreword

What Is a Head Purchasing Agent?

1.   A person of *maximum integrity* with introspective power who is keenly aware of the need to maintain good relationships with suppliers, other members of the administrative and operating staff of food service, and the purchasing warehousing and product testing personnel.

2.   One who *practices honesty and truth* in buying and selling and renounces all illicit practices of commercial bribery.

3.   An individual who *buys without prejudice,* while obtaining maximum value based on performance for the money spent.

4.   A person dedicated to *protecting his employer's interests* and policies.

5.   One who *does not seek shortcuts* that may increase profits but eventually cause losses as a result of changes that lower established standards that insure success.

6.   A buyer who *seeks supplier cooperation* with respect to "contract buying," "standing orders," and "market pricing."

7.   Someone who realizes that *purchasing involves much more than buying*, such as when deliveries may be expected, what the quality standards will be, and what price must be paid to assure that satisfactory performance can be maintained on a continuing basis.

8.   A *planner* who uses a basic set of buying policies and procedures to establish a repetitive pattern of quantity and quality to be delivered at scheduled intervals at prices that assure continuing satisfactory performance by the supplier.

9.   A *realist* who knows that actual bargains are rare, and when weighed against factors other than raw price alone including cost of carrying inventory, shelf life, storage space, and energy, the bargain may actually represent a loss.

10.   One who *uses specifications judiciously* and modifies standards or specifications to increase purchasing efficiency whenever justified. It is better to limit specifications and be certain that they are met.

11.   A *tester* who has his testing group evaluate all processed food items to check on standards and/or try comparing them with new items that may perform as well or better for the intended use.

12. A *custodian* of forms and work sheets used in the purchasing system including inventory control, price quote sheets, order sheets, and approved supplier lists to modify, simplify, clarify, combine, or eliminate wherever needed.

13. A *disciplinarian* who refuses to order from a supplier who has consistently ignored specifications, despite repeated warnings, but later reinstates them and thereafter enjoys consistent adherence to standards.

14. A *coordinator* who completes the purchasing cycle by closing the loop with a trained receiving department that is trained to accept only what has been ordered, in excellent condition, with proper weight and count, labeled as purchased, on schedule, etc. When any of the criteria are not met, failures are immediately reported, and the shipment may be refused or a price adjustment made.

15. A *developer* of effective systems based on immediate and long range requirements for supplies that can be used when advantageous buying conditions occur.

16. A *checker* of the condition of products received to determine whether hidden damage, infestation, or deterioration occurred during transit.

17. A *research and development experimenter* who seeks better utilization of his own facility, and cooperates with other departments to achieve development and standardization of new formulas, improved processing and preserving methods, more accurate portion control, and better evaluation of improved products and packaging methods or package sizes.

18. A *student* of market reports, trade journals, and other information sources or associations and conventions that provide a knowledge of cost/quality standards available in supplies.

19. A *scientist* who has technical knowledge regarding standards of quality, varieties, and types of supplies that insure that high standards can be maintained.

20. A *psychologist* who understands people and their potential weakness which leads to pilferage and must be controlled and eliminated by means of a security program that uncovers internal as well as external theft of both supplies and workers' time.

21. An *opportunist* who obtains products and services and simplifies purchasing by contract buying through a reputable supplier who is capable of providing the lowest overall cost—a combination of quality, price, delivery, and technical assistance from a single source that provides warehousing.

22. A *personnel agent* who hires buyers with knowledge and experience who are adept at communications, mindful of the special staff functions required by the job, thorough, creative, systematic, even-tempered, patient, capable of detailed and analytical thinking, public relations minded, and of the highest possible ethical standards.

23. A person who loves to work with other people in a well organized, efficient, safe, clean, and wholesome environment.

Purchasing has been defined by the National Association of Purchasing Agents as a management function organized to buy the proper product or service for the purpose required, making the material available when needed, in the proper amount, and, at the right price. The long range goal in purchasing is efficiency in obtaining a maximum return in goods and services for every dollar spent in procurement. Outstanding among recent developments in the science of purchasing is *systematic value analysis* which influences quantity buying factors that affect inventory control.

Dr. Ninemeier, in this book, emphasizes the management systems aspect of the purchasing function. He tells *how to extend* the purchasing arm of management *beyond efficiency to proficiency.*

L. J. Minor, Ph.D. and **Mr. Robert F. Herron**
Professor in Foods Director of Central Food Stores
HRI Department (Michigan State University,
Michigan State University Retired)
Chief Executive Officer and Consultant to the
L. J. Minor Corporation Foodservice Industry
Cleveland, Ohio

Preface

This manual is written in Standard Operating Procedure (SOP) format. As such it is meant to be *used,* not just read. Food and beverage management, purchasing staff, and other officials, for whom this SOP manual is designed, have neither the time nor, probably, the need to read each section from cover to cover. For this reason an extensive listing of topics has been supplied in the table of contents, permitting the user to refer directly to the information desired. It is not necessary to read through unwanted material in order to find sections that apply to the problems at hand.

Of course, it is not possible to provide purchasing management principles that apply to *every* type (from fast food to gourmet) and size (from $10,000 to $10,000,000 in annual sales) of restaurant, hotel, and club facility in this country. Therefore, not everything written will be relevant to a manager's food and beverage operation all the time. Much of what is written, however, will be of great use. The task in using this SOP manual is to carefully read through and consider those sections that concern problems within the existing operation. Users will find some extremely helpful ideas that will enable them, sometimes with slight modification, to greatly improve their purchasing management systems. The purpose of this manual will be met it if helps those charged with the important task of purchasing to do the job better; that is, to more consistently obtain the *right* product at the *right* time for the *right* price in the *right* quantity and of the *right* quality.

How to Use This Manual

Users with specific problems may refer to the detailed table of contents to determine those section(s) of the manual that cover their area of interest. Within each major section, subsections have been identified and numbered to make the task of locating specific topics as easy as possible.

Other manual users may prefer, instead, to read the material in its entirety, making note of special points within the broad topic of food and beverage purchasing management. Using this approach, many new ideas and insights may be uncovered.

Each topic is presented in a format of procedures that can be utilized to improve application of purchasing management principles in food and beverage operations. To the extent that the manual adequately explains procedures that apply to a specific food and beverage operation, the manager obtains Standard Operating Procedures the facility can adapt for internal use. If some procedures cannot be used, these sections can be "lined through," rewritten, or removed from the manual. If the other procedures can be modified for use, they can be rewritten or additional pages can be inserted in the manual. In these ways, a manager can "personalize" the manual for use by the food and beverage operation.

A Special Note about the Appendix

The Appendix includes blank copies of all forms presented in the manual. Instructions for the use of each form are also included to clarify the specific procedures involved. If a form can be used, it can be withdrawn from the manual and copied at a local printing service. In other cases the forms will suggest ideas to a manager, who can then modify the form before printing.

1

INTRODUCTION
TO PROCUREMENT

Purchased goods and services consume a very large percentage of income collected from product sales by all food and beverage operations. Since this is the case it is very important to design and implement an effective procurement system. Purchased products can not generate sales dollars until they have been received by the property. Many items must also enter storage to await production. Foodservice administrators realize that not only tangible products (such as food, beverage, supplies and equipment) are purchased: contracted services (such as fire equipment maintenance, janitorial, ventilation system cleaning, etc.) must also be "purchased."

Procurement of products and services directly affects the "bottom line": as one dollar is saved through *effective* purchasing, costs are reduced and one additional dollar of profit is made. The need to develop and utilize a system for purchasing necessary products and services is therefore readily apparent. Procedures to properly receive and store incoming products can also be easily defended.

This handbook will lay out simple and practical procedures that can be incorporated into a system to achieve organizational goals important to procurement, receiving, and storage. The property's cost control program, then, begins *before* products are prepared and served. The professional food and beverage manager will go back to the point where plans for purchasing are developed and will control from that point on.

1.1   Definition of Terms

This handbook is not written to present "fine-line" semantic differences between words which, essentially, mean the same thing. The purpose of this section is to expand the more traditional definition of "purchasing" to include a variety of activities that must be incorporated into more effective purchasing.

1.1.1   Purchasing

This term technically refers to three components of the procurement process:

Negotiation for price
Physical aspects of "purchase"
Payment for products received

In the hospitality industry, however, the term conveys the meaning of *every* step in the process by which goods and services are "bought" and brought into the food and beverage operation. This expanded definition, actually meaning the same as the management term "procurement," (Section 1.1.4) will be used throughout this handbook. For all practical purposes, *purchasing means procurement.*

1.1.2 Buying/Ordering

These terms also refer to steps in the procurement/purchasing process.

Buying refers specifically to the exchange of money (or other commodity) for a product or service. When the exchange is not for money but rather for something else the process is sometimes called "trading" or "bartering." The technique of trading is becoming more common in the hospitality field. For example, a restaurant may "trade" $500 worth of meals for a like amount of advertising in a community newspaper.

Ordering refers to the communication which takes place between buyer and seller at the time an agreement to exchange money (or another commodity) for goods and services is made.

1.1.3 Selection

This term technically means to "choose between alternatives." Again, this subtle definition has little place in the language of the busy food and beverage manager. As long as we know what we mean and accept an expanded understanding of the purchasing/procurement process the "label" attached to the word used to define the process is not important.

1.1.4 Procurement

This term, to be used interchangeably with "purchasing" throughout this handbook, refers to an entire system of decision making and implementation of plans that involves:*

Requisitioning necessary products/services by user
departments within the food and beverage operation.

Determining necessary quality requirements.

Assessing quantity needs.

Arranging for delivery.

Selecting suppliers.

Negotiating price(s).

Making the actual purchase decision.

Arranging for payment.

Following up (Expediting) on "orders".

Receiving.

Maintaining necessary records.

Maintaining proper vendor relations.

---

* *This definition of procurement is based upon ideas initially offered by H. Hodges, in* Procurement: The Modern Science of Purchasing *(N.Y.: Harper & Brothers, 1961).*

Dispensing surplus equipment and other items (frying fat, beverage containers, etc.).

Inspection.

Storage.

Inventory control.

Research and study of the needs of the food/beverage operation.

Obtaining information with which to make purchasing decisions.

1.2 The Purchasing/Procurement Process

The discussion above has expanded the tasks involved in "purchasing" to include many duties and responsibilities undertaken both before and after the time that an order is actually placed with a supplier.

For our purposes then, "purchasing" is much more than calling in an order. Each of the tasks involved in an expanded definition of purchasing/procurement will be discussed in great detail in this handbook. The food and beverage manager must consider the job of purchasing to include *all* of the various components in the *system* of purchasing/procurement described in Section 1.1.4.

Several additional background concerns can help the hospitality manager to more fully understand the process involved in purchasing/procurement:

Regardless of whether the operation is "big" or "small," the tasks outlined above must be completed by a staff member. Larger facilities may have specialized buyers or purchasers; small operations may incorporate the tasks into the job of the manager or another official (see Section 2.3). Regardless, however, the primary tasks involved in purchasing must be completed as products and services are purchased.

The industrial purchaser—(who purchases products that are converted into finished products such as raw ground beef that goes into a casserole or a liquor item into a drink product) has special problems and responsibilities that go beyond the physical task of interacting with suppliers. He or she must, for example, help determine *what* products should be purchased. Suppliers must be selected; inventory and cash flow concerns must be matched; supplier delivery schedules must be correlated with in-house needs, etc.

The purchasing task is ongoing. Through experience with the system itself and with suppliers, products, and services the food and beverage operation can develop over time a very effective system to help control costs and to assure that quality requirements are met from the very beginning of the management process (which considers the cyclical aspects of purchasing, including receiving and storage, issuing, production, and service and then additional purchasing, etc.). Since this is the case a purchasing system is not generally developed overnight; rather, procedures are incorporated and systems are modified as conditions warrant action and as changes are proven to be worthwhile.

1.3 Objectives of Effective Purchasing

A purchasing system must be designed to attain stated objectives. It is important, then, that serious thought be given to what is to be accomplished as a purchasing system is designed.

1.3.1 The Primary Procurement Objective

Simply put, the objectives of a purchasing system must involve, at least, "assuming that the *right* product, of the *right* quality, is received at the *right* time. It must be obtained at the *right* price from the *right* supplier." While this objective is easily stated it is not easily accomplished. Much time and effort are necessary to design a purchasing system that will do all these things.

1.3.2 Specific Objectives

Other objectives of the purchasing task can be highlighted. They become important as the purchasing process is centralized within the hospitality operation. Objectives that might be important in individual operations include:

Providing information to user departments. Time must be allowed to search out products and services that will *best* meet the needs of the operation. This research, study, and recommendation aspect of purchasing is very important in food and beverage operations.

Offering specialized advice and assistance to management. Purchasing staff (including personnel in small facilities who perform purchasing functions as only one of many duties) learn many things which might be of help to line managers as they make decisions. For example, purchasers may be alert to trends in seafood prices, new equipment items, and improvements in existing equipment and products. Purchasing personnel, then, can provide much information to management that can be a valuable aid to decision making.

1.3.3 Quality Goals

The food and beverage operation must obtain the *right* quality of purchased products and services. This not always the *highest* quality available. It is not possible to consider the quality aspects of a product without considering its price at the same time. The relationship between the two is referred to as "value." This concept is reviewed in detail in Section 7.3. Quality, expressed in purchase specifications, is considered in Section 5.

1.3.4 Quantity Goals

Products must be purchased in the *right* quantity. If an insufficient quantity of products is purchased, stockouts (running out of items with increased possibility of guest dissatisfaction) can result. When an excessive quantity of products is purchased inventory and cash-flow problems often occur. Quantity concerns in the purchasing process are presented in Section 6.

1.3.5 Price Goals

The *right* price for a predetermined quality of product to be purchased must be assessed; it can often be negotiated. The food and beverage buyer has a responsibility to obtain required quality products at the "best" price; this price is also a function of related services which the supplier provides. Price concerns are discussed in Section 7.

1.3.6 Supplier Selection Goals

It is important that products are obtained from the *right* source. It is not reasonable either to buy from anybody or, conversely, to deal with one source of supply because "we've always purchased from him." The many considerations which are important in the supplier selection decision are noted in Section 8.

1.3.7 Delivery Schedule Goals

Products must be received at the right time. It is incorrect to consider that delivery is beyond the control of the food and beverage operation. While occasional problems must be anticipated, supplier selection (Section 1.3.6) is based, in part, on reliable delivery schedules. Timing concerns are discussed in Section 6.4.

1.3.8 Relationship of Procurement to Other Organizational Goals

Large food and beverage operations frequently have a separate purchasing department. Smaller foodservice operations incorporate purchasing as one of the many tasks of managers. In either case the very important relationship between purchasing and the attainment of other organizational goals must be noted. Economic goals cannot be met if money is wasted through ineffective purchasing. Other goals—such as providing *consistent*, quality products and service to guests—obviously cannot be met if goods are not there when they need to be—and in the proper quality.

Since the food and beverage operation is in business to sell food, beverage, and service there must be an ongoing emphasis on effective purchasing; without proper purchasing it is not possible for most organizational goals to be met. Fortunately, with use of a purchasing system that is composed of simple purchasing procedures, effective purchasing tactics can be used and the benefits from their use can be of immeasurable help to the food and beverage operation.

1.4 Importance of Procurement

The case for a professionally developed, *effective* procurement system has already been made in Section 1.2. Points for further emphasis include the following.

1.4.1 Control of Costs

The beginning phase of cost control considers, of course, the price paid for products and services purchased. The foundation for a successful control-of-costs program must begin with the purchasing process. A cost-control program, then, cannot be successful in the presence of a "sloppy" purchasing system.

1.4.2 Volume of Purchased Products/Services

Food and beverages are just two of the products purchased by food and beverage operations. When one additionally considers paper goods, supplies, capital equipment, etc., it is easy to defend the fact that, by sheer volume, purchasing control is necessary. More sales dollars are used to purchase goods and services than are used for any other purposes; *purchasing is important*.

1.4.3 Effect on Cash Flow

Even large, high-profit food and beverage operations can have cash-flow problems. An important principle of financial management requires that cash be available to pay bills when they become due. The quantity of items purchased, their price, and the timing of their delivery affects, ultimately, the amount of money (cash) that will be required to satisfy payment.

Only management should make decisions about deferring purchases which increase possibilities of stockouts, and eliminate the possibility of quantity purchase discounts. Input from purchasing staff can be helpful as decisions are made. Purchasing can (and should) arrange for deliveries in required quantities at required times. These tactics, along with directives from line management, can help to assure that cash-flow problems do not result from ineffective purchasing practices.

1.4.4 Supply of Information

Section 1.1.4 expanded the purchasing task to include soliciting information, research regarding new products, etc. It is important in the fast-changing business world for managers to keep up with new technology. Purchasing personnel are in constant contact with many suppliers who, in turn, are in contact with manufacturers, other suppliers, and many other food and beverage operations, so they can be a valuable source of information about "what's new." Purchasing staff must collect new ideas and information and pass them on to user departments.

1.4.5 Continuity of Supply

A very important role played by the purchasing department is the provision of necessary items at the right time. The concept of continuous supply is critical to customer satisfaction. Certainly, from the perspective of a user department (food or beverage production), it is the "fault" of purchasing personnel when required products are not available.

Purchasing staff must expand their responsibilities and job tasks to include that of expediting: following up on orders to help assure that suppliers meet contractual requirements regarding quality, quantity, delivery date, etc. Effective purchasing is required to assure a continuous source of supply; for this additional reason, purchasing is important to organizational success.

1.4.6 Purchasing Success Affects Profits

It is obvious that reduced costs brought about by more effective purchasing increase profits. An example that illustrates the very significant impact which purchasing has on profits may be helpful.

Assume two identical restaurants; through effective purchasing, one is able to reduce its food costs by 5 percent.

	Restaurant A		Restaurant B
Sales	$1,000,000		$1,000,000
Minus Food Purchases (40%)	$ 400,000	Minus 95% of 400,000	$ 380,000
	$ 600,000		$ 620,000
Minus Other Costs	$ 500,000		$ 500,000
"Profit" before Tax	$ 100,000		$ 120,000

Note that a 5 percent *decrease* in purchased food costs results in a 20 percent *increase* in profit before tax.

2

A CLOSE LOOK AT THE PURCHASING FUNCTION

The purchasing/procurement task was expanded in Section 1 to include a wide variety of supportive duties in addition to the traditional "ordering" responsibilities that are most frequently associated with purchasing. This section will examine more closely the role of the purchaser and management aspects of the procurement task.

2.1   Duties of Purchasing Personnel

The basic duties of purchasing personnel do not change regardless of whether the food and beverage operation utilizes a full-time purchaser-buyer or the purchasing task is but one of many duties performed by a management employee. Generally, all of the duties must be performed; obviously, the amount of time that can be spent on each task relates to the amount of time available and the priority given to the task. A review of the duties performed by purchasing personnel follows.* To the extent that these tasks identify responsibilities in specific food and beverage operations, they should be incorporated into the job descriptions outlined in Section 2.3.

2.1.1   Managing Basic Information

One broad category of tasks which must be performed by personnel with purchasing duties involves managing information that is essential to completing the job. Examples include:

Filing and processing purchase documents (delivery invoices, purchase orders, purchase records, credit memos, etc.).

Updating current price lists.

Working with inventory and usage records.

Keeping basic information about suppliers.

Maintaining files of product specification information.

Storing other basic information such as product sheets, catalogs, mailed brochures, etc.

2.1.2   Performing Research Activities

Examples of this task include:

Determining the usefulness of new products.

Assessing the acceptability of items currently purchased.

Performing cost studies. Make/Buy Analysis (Section 10.5) and Value Analysis (Section 7.3.2) are examples of these tasks.

---

*The listing of purchasing duties in this section is adapted from a list initially compiled by S. Heinritz, Purchasing: Principles and Applications (N.Y.: Prentice-Hall Inc., 1951).

Evaluating supplier performance.

Developing new sources of supply.

2.1.3 Performing Traditional Purchasing Tasks

This category of basic duties must generally include:

Processing in-house requisitions for purchase.

Securing supplier price quotations.

Analyzing price quotations.

Scheduling deliveries.

Placing orders.

Negotiating prices and contracts.

Issuing purchase orders.

Expediting (following up on orders).

Checking in deliveries.

Verifying delivery invoices.

Communicating with suppliers.

2.1.4 Undertaking Miscellaneous Purchasing Duties

Examples of these tasks are:

Developing minimum/maximum inventory levels.

Evaluating inventory turnover and maintaining inventory stocks at proper levels.

Disposing of scrap, obsolete, and surplus materials.

Consolidating product needs; reducing the variety of purchased products when possible.

2.2 Duties Shared with Other Departments

Generally, the duties described above are performed primarily by personnel with purchasing responsibilities. Additional duties might be performed, in part, by other personnel. In these cases, purchasing personnel may make recommendations to other management officials who make the final management decision. In each case sharing task performance duties requires a great deal of interdepartmental communication and cooperation. Purchasing, it will be seen, does not stand alone. It must depend on personnel in other departments.

2.2.1 Receiving Products

Security concerns suggest that the duties of purchasing and receiving be split (one employee should not purchase and receive products; there is increased opportunity for fraud). In small operations a manager-purchaser may order products; a cook, steward, or other *trained* individual may receive them. In larger operations the distinction is even greater: one department (purchasing) may order products, and a separate department, (such as accounting) may be responsible for product receiving.

2.2.2 Inventory Management

In many foodservice operations orders are placed as stock levels decrease to an "order point" (see Section 6.5). In these cases decisions regarding both when and how much to order are made according to procedures established between the user department (that specifies quantity needs), storage personnel (who are concerned about stockout and inventory turnover problems), and purchasing staff (who must arrange delivery schedules).

2.2.3 Make/Buy Decisions

Only user departments and top management can make decisions about whether products should be prepared on site or whether they should be purchased in a "convenience" form. However, purchasing staff (through research activities noted in Section 2.1.2) can provide much background help in discovering available products and suppliers, soliciting opinions about quality from other foodservice operations, etc.

2.2.4 Product Specification Determinations

Purchasing personnel must work closely with user departments to establish quality purchase specifications for products that will be purchased. This topic is discussed in Section 5.

2.2.5 Product Substitution Decisions

If products become unavailable or if alternative products become available, the research functions of purchasing staff can help user department personnel make decisions. This is another example of the need for purchasing personnel to have clear and complete knowledge about what is available in the marketplace.

2.2.6 Budget Development

While, for example, the food and beverage departments must develop operating budgets, the financial assistance which purchasing staff can provide by obtaining products at the best price is obvious. Decisions about deals, discounts, and other purchasing incentives should then be made jointly.

2.2.7 Other Shared Duties

Other examples which serve to illustrate the relationship which the purchasing department has with other departments can be illustrated by the following:

Selection of capital equipment items. Research efforts of purchasing personnel can help user department personnel determine which item(s) of capital equipment best suit the needs of the food and beverage operation.

Purchase of construction. Top management and affected user departments must make final decisions about the need for facility construction or remodeling. This topic is discussed in Section 19.

Processing of related purchasing documents. This may be a joint undertaking of purchasing, management, accounting, and, perhaps, other officials.

Other duties. There is an additional category of duties which may, or may not, be performed by purchasing personnel. Food and beverage management must decide, based on their own operation, who (*people and department*) are to be responsible for the following tasks:

1. Storeroom security control including inventory procedures.
2. Product receiving and inspection.
3. Food and beverage cost control and assessment.

It is important that management carefully consider "who is to do what" within the operation. Once decisions are made, tasks and responsibilities should be developed in formal job descriptions (Section 2.3) which explain basic duties and responsibilities for each position in the organization.

2.3 Sample Job Descriptions

Job descriptions should formally indicate who is responsible for each task that is considered part of the purchasing function. Sample job descriptions for three purchasing positions follow. Food and beverage managers should amend these samples as necessary to reflect the purchasing duties of each position in their own operation.

2.3.1 Job: Manager of Purchasing*

Job: Manager of Purchasing

Reports to: Vice-President, Administration

Purpose: Responsible for the coordination of all the company's purchases of raw materials, supplies, capital equipment, and contract services. Exceptions: Real estate and Transportation

Major Responsibilities:

1. Engage, transfer, promote, administer, and terminate purchasing employees. Actively participate in company's Manpower Development Program.

2. Initiate purchasing policy for the guidance of personnel in their dealings with suppliers, the public, and other departments of the company and its affiliates.

3. Keep constantly apprised of economic or business situations as they affect purchasing policy; make decisions to adequately meet those changing conditions.

4. Recommend changes in purchasing organization, including personnel, to affiliate and division management; exercise functional supervision over field purchasing personnel; give final approval to purchasing procedures.

5. Initiate and administer manpower development programs.

6. Give final approval to major purchase agreements for those materials, supplies, capital equipment, and contract services within the responsibility of the Purchasing Department.

7. Make final decision on selection of suppliers in the event agreement cannot be reached at the local level.

8. Determine need and timing for national and/or international purchasing business meetings, and conduct such meetings.

9. Visit vendor plants to observe operations and discuss manufacturing practices.

10. Attend and participate in meetings of functional and trade groups, such as National Conference Board and National Association of Purchasing Management.

11. Coordinate effectively with divisions and departments the financing of large-value purchases.

Scope:

1. General supervision over expenditures in excess of 5 million dollars.

2. Indirect responsibility for materials inventories totaling 2 million dollars.

3. Authorize and sign contracts for purchases not to exceed $50,000 and three years.

---

*From G. Aljian, Purchasing Handbook, 3rd ed. *(New York: McGraw-Hill, 1973) pp. 26–28.*

4. Give final approval or disapproval to claims or expenses resulting from actions of employees or suppliers involving faulty materials, mishandling, or breach of contracts.

5. Annual operating expense budget of $75,000 to $200,000—10 directly supervised employees; functional guidance to 20 employees in operating units.

Knowledge and Skill Needed:

B.S. or A.B. degree. MBA desirable. Proven administrative background in sales, finance, or purchasing desirable. Should be perceptive, analytical, with ability to induce cooperation in complex organizational relationships. Knowledge of manufacturing practices, materials, and their use. Understanding of economic and business situations.

2.3.2 Purchasing Agent (Buyer)*

Job: Buyer

Reports to: Purchasing Manager

Purpose: To promote the most effective use of company funds in the acquisition of assigned commodities. Evaluates market conditions and trends. Plans specific short- and long-range commodity objectives. Develops purchasing arrangements, which are communicated to plant locations. Advises headquarters and plant management of supply sources, arranges for procurement on a pooled basis rather than plant by plant.

Major Responsibilities:

1. Develops specific annual purchasing objectives; creates specific short- and long-range commodity objectives with a view to reducing the cost of materials and improving service to user units.

2. Surveys markets for best source or new supply sources. Contacts potential suppliers and negotiates most favorable proposals.

3. Develops most suitable purchasing arrangement for commodities, including contracts, blanket orders, spot purchase orders, and vendor stocking arrangements.

4. Communicates details of purchasing arrangements to user units, i.e., prices, terms, and method of handling requirements based on arrangements made in their behalf.

5. Receives requisitions: analyzes each item for quantity, specifications, and delivery requirements; develops and investigates sources of supply; issues request for quotations for those items not covered by any existing purchasing arrangement. Develops substitutes if commodity is unavailable, or if more economical product might be satisfactory.

---

* *From G. Aljian,* Purchasing Handbook *3rd ed. (New York: McGraw-Hill, 1973), pp. 26–29.*

6. Receives quotations by mail, telephone, or through personal representation of bidders; analyzes quotations and checks specifications, quantities, etc.; compares competitive products for desirability and use.

7. Determines best source by evaluating quotation or by application of an existing purchasing arrangement or by approved procedure; prepares purchase order draft after reviewing requisitions versus quotations. Instructs typists as to what should be shown on formal order.

8. Consolidates annual requirements for commodities common to several use points. Determines adequate definition of commodity; investigates possibility of improving quality without a price increase or of substituting a lower-priced commodity to accomplish the same function.

9. Evaluates vendor performance based on personal knowledge of prices and deliveries and information received from affiliates relative to product acceptability and vendor service. Anticipates and negotiates possible price changes and in general develops thorough knowledge of those commodities assigned.

10. Advises management of industry competitive situations, alternative supply sources, raw material costs, commodity price trends, and supply/demand situations based on knowledge of company's laws.

11. Maintains effective communications between central purchasing and plants.

12. Maintains good relations with supplier personnel, which means courteous, impartial, and objective dealings with suppliers.

Supervision of Personnel:

1. Clerk-stenographer.

Scope:

1. Directly procure approximately 1 million dollars annually of materials and equipment and supplies.

2. Guide and counsel respective plant and buyers at three plants in the procurement of assigned commodities.

3. Assist operations and manufacturing personnel in approximately five affiliates in the development of sources for material and product needs.

4. Assist manager in the development of purchasing procedures.

Knowledge and Skill Needed:

College degree in either business administration or engineering. Thorough knowledge of purchasing procedures and internal controls; specific knowledge and two years' experience in handling of assigned commodities at a company plant or similar outside experience. Good knowledge of United States, European, and Japanese sources of materials, supplies, and equipment. General knowledge as regards monetary and customs matters. Ability to represent company effectively in dealings with suppliers is essential.

2.3.3 Manager with Purchasing Duties

The following job description might be used by food and beverage managers in smaller operations who must combine purchasing with many additional management duties. It will, of course, need to be modified to meet the specific needs of the individual operation. The description below focuses on purchasing tasks and will need to incorporate the other specific duties required of the position, "manager."

Job: Foodservice Manager

Reports to: Owner

Purpose: To effectively and professionally manage all purchasing tasks within the foodservice facility to assure that the following goals are consistently attained.

1. To obtain the right quality of purchased products and services.
2. To obtain the optimal quantity of purchased products.
3. To obtain the best price for products and services purchased.
4. To select the best suppliers for the conduct of business.
5. To establish delivery schedules which minimize stockouts and early deliveries.

Major Responsibilities

1. Coordinates purchase needs with chef, beverage manager, and other affected personnel.
2. Develops procedures for purchase, receiving, and storage of required products and services.
3. Determines quantities of products needed for special catered events.
4. Manages/coordinates filing and processing of all purchase documents.
5. Updates and revises as necessary price lists, inventory, product specification, and other basic information.
6. Performs required research activities (which includes assessing usefulness of new products), performs cost studies, evaluates supplier performance, and develops new supply sources as required.
7. Performs tasks necessary in the actual purchasing process. This includes evaluating supplier quotations, placing and expediting orders, scheduling deliveries, negotiating and otherwise communicating with suppliers.
8. Supervises personnel responsible for receiving and storing delivered items.
9. Performs miscellaneous duties which include management of inventories and disposing of scrap, obsolete, and surplus materials; also involved in developing product specifications, product budgets,

selecting capital equipment, and deciding upon construction purchase needs.

10. Inspects product storerooms for cleanliness, orderliness, stock rotation, security precautions, etc.
11. Employs, trains, and manages personnel with procurement duties.
12. Coordinates harmonious working relationships with all department heads.

Supervision of Personnel:

1. Purchasing/Office staff
2. Receiving personnel
3. Storeroom personnel

Scope:

1. Directly responsible for purchase, receiving, and storage of all products.
2. Responsible for control of costs within budgetary limitations.
3. Must attain profit goals (which are affected by purchase decisions).

Knowledge and Skills Needed:

Must have cooperative attitude. Should be knowledgeable about all phases of procurement. Must understand quality specifications, be honest, and know how to be an assertive negotiator. Must be an *effective* communicator and have supportive college or technical school educational background. Should have "back-of-house" management experience and must know the restaurant, hotel, and club business.

2.4   Required Knowledge, Ability, and Attitudes

There are many tasks involved in the job of purchasing. Minimum levels of knowledge, ability, and attitude are necessary in order to perform each of these varied tasks. Food and beverage managers may wish to review the following list of performance requirements as the "knowledge and skills" aspects of job descriptions are developed.

2.4.1   Necessary Knowledge

Food and beverage personnel with purchasing responsibilities must know:

Required products and how to determine and evaluate required quality in the products.

Required procedures for purchasing (and have ideas about how existing systems can be improved).

How purchasing fits into the organization and how it relates to other functions carried on by the foodservice operation.

The best sources of supply and how to obtain the best prices from them.

How to establish effective purchasing systems.

Ways to best implement all components of the purchasing plan.

Procedures involved in make/buy, cost, and value analysis.

Ways to control inventory.

2.4.2 Necessary Skills

Food and beverage personnel who are involved in purchasing must be able to:

Communicate effectively. This involves interacting with in-house staff and with suppliers. It involves being able to read, write, listen, and speak at appropriate professional levels.

Manage their time. The many tasks included in the purchasing function cannot be performed when time is not effectively managed.

Solve problems and make decisions about procurement.

Manage the purchasing tasks. They must then be in control of other areas of the operation in order to see purchasing in its proper perspective and to be able to define and achieve purchasing and other organizational goals.

2.4.3 Necessary Attitudes

Purchasing personnel must:

Realize the importance of purchasing and assign a high priority to performing required purchasing tasks *at a high-quality level*.

Understand that existing purchasing systems may need to be modified to better attain organizational objectives.

Be flexible and creative in dealing with evolving purchasing problems and concerns.

Realize that their colleagues may have ideas which can help resolve purchasing concerns; their subordinates *and* supervisors should be consulted for input on matters which involve the purchasing task.

Be objective in their dealings with suppliers. They should not show favoritism and must consistently make decisions based upon what is best for the food and beverage operation.

Be ethical in all their relationships. (This topic is discussed in great detail in Section 12.)

Understand that, in the purchasing role, they are providing staff, supportive service, and assistance to *user* food and beverage department personnel. In this capacity, then, they provide technical assistance.

2.5 Limitations of Purchasing Department Personnel

The relationships and shared duties between purchasing and other departments within the restaurant, hotel, and/or club have been identified in Section 2.2. These serve, in part, to define limitations of purchasing. Several additional, specific limitations of the purchasing function can be identified.

2.5.1 Authorization Required

Purchasing is done to provide products and services needed to attain organizational goals. Therefore, an authorization is needed. This can take several forms. For example,

Top management may develop a policy which, in effect, states that when a product inventory level is reduced to a certain point, a quantity of product at a specified quality may be purchased to bring the inventory up to an agreed upon level. (The minimum-maximum inventory system is discussed in Section 6.5.)

A budgetary limitation may be set on the total dollars that can be spent for food, beverage, supplies, and other purchases during a specified period.

A dollar limit on the value of purchases per order or per supplier serves as an example of the limits of authority provided to purchasing personnel.

In food and beverage operations where no formal authorization is established, purchasing personnel should view past experiences regarding quantities and qualities of products to set a limit on actions beyond which top management approval is necessary.

2.5.2 Purchases for Actual/Anticipated Use

The implications of this limitation include:

Only products and services needed for the foodservice operation are to be purchased.

Quantites purchased should, within limitations noted in Section 2.5.1, be for anticipated actual needs. Only top management should make decisions regarding speculative purchasing (as, for example, when decisions are made to buy wines because prices are increasing or not to buy shrimp because prices may decrease).

2.5.3 Responsibility for Quality and Quantity

Purchasing personnel, through research activities noted in Section 2.1.2, make recommendations to user departments regarding products to purchase. However, the ultimate responsibility for products purchased rests with the user department (in its interaction with top management). The user department specifies needed product (often with assistance from purchasing personnel); then it becomes the responsibility of purchasing to obtain required products from the best source.

2.5.4 Budgetary Restrictions

When there is a separate purchasing department, dollars spent for its operation are obviously limited by the budget. Likewise, as noted in Section 2.5.1, dollar or other limits are often placed on purchases.

2.5.5 Other Limitations

Top management may set other limitations on purchasing personnel. Examples include policies regarding reciprocal purchasing (Section 8.4.8) and local purchasing (Section 8.4.9). The point to be made here is there must be a *clear* understanding between top management and purchasing personnel as to *what* purchasing personnel are to do. A basic principle of management then requires that purchasing personnel be delegated the authority and responsibility necessary to carry out required tasks.

2.6   Management of Purchasing

Basic principles of management apply to the conduct of purchasing as well as to any other activity necessary to attain food and beverage department goals. Each of these activities will be reviewed briefly in this section as it relates to purchasing.

2.6.1 Planning

Planning for purchasing can be considered at three different management levels. Examples of planning activities for each planning level are given below. Each level proceeds from the long-range, top management level of planning down to short-range, routine planning which can be performed by subordinate purchasing personnel.

2.6.1.1 Strategic planning.

At this level very broad plans are made.

What *exactly* are the goals of the purchasing task?

How do responsibilities of purchasing personnel relate to responsibilities of other personnel in other departments within the food and beverage operation?

What capital equipment and construction needs must be studied or researched by the purchasing department?

Policies for designing the purchasing system must be established. These include a definition of the limitations noted in Section 2.5.

Determining the initial list of eligible suppliers is an important strategic concern.

Developing purchase specifications is a final example of a strategic plan.

It is very important that top management and purchasing personnel agree on the long-range plans, policies, goals, and parameters for purchasing personnel.

2.6.1.2 Management control planning.

Examples of planning tasks which are included in this intermediate level of planning include:

Developing the operating budget for the purchasing department (and for amounts to be spent on food, beverage, and other products).

Establishing procedures and policies regarding the physical purchase of goods and services.

Planning purchasing staff requirements.

Developing personnel policies.

Defining necessary research and study activities which should be undertaken by purchasing personnel.

Making decisions about capital expenses.

Evaluating the effectiveness of purchasing personnel and the department itself.

2.6.1.3 Operational planning.

This short-range phase of the purchasing planning process involves more routine day-to-day plans such as for:

Hiring, supervising, and evaluating personnel with purchasing duties.

Ordering products and services according to procedures and policies developed as part of the management planning process.

Scheduling deliveries of products.

Designing means to assure compliance with quality control procedures during purchasing, receiving, and storage.

Securing inventory against theft and pilferage.

Evaluating performance of suppliers.

2.6.2 Organizing

The task of organizing involves developing the structure that will be used to attain the plans designed in Section 2.6.1.

In most small food and beverage operations management does the buying. Management might be the owner-manager in very small operations or the head chef or head bartender in somewhat larger facilities. In both instances the tasks and duties to be performed (see Sections 2.1 and 2.2) must be determined. Likewise, plans that accomplish the tasks must be developed (see Section 2.6.1).

In larger food and beverage operations a full-time "buyer" may be hired. As is the case with small operations, there is the same need to both determine tasks to be performed and to design plans which assure that tasks will be done.

In food and beverage operations of any size, personnel (either management or purchasing staff, as size dictates) must be delegated the authority and responsibility necessary to perform required tasks and to attain expected goals. As noted in Section 2.5, limits to the authority and responsibility should also be determined by top management, and then be imposed on purchasing staff.

Personnel at all levels in the organization must know what is going on. They must know "who reports to whom," and "who is responsible for what". This process requires that the organization of the purchasing task consider the most effective means to communicate and coordinate activities between top management, purchasing, and user (food and beverage) departments. The result should be the design of an organization chart that shows the relationship between positions. Likewise, frequent employee meetings, willingness of staff at all levels to communicate with personnel at other organizational levels, and staff training designed to resolve problems which result from departmental differences can be helpful as the organizational concerns are resolved.

It is generally better to have centralized purchasing (in which all products for every department are purchased by the same personnel or by a purchasing department) than to develop a system in which each department (for example, food and beverage) purchases for its own needs. Job descriptions (see Section 2.3) are developed as part of the task of organizing the purchasing process.

2.6.3 Staffing

The process of staffing for the purchasing task includes all related personnel management duties. This means:

Selecting qualified personnel to perform purchasing tasks outlined in the job descriptions. "Qualified" personnel are those who are judged to have minimum levels of knowledge, abilities, and acceptable attitudes as outlined in Section 2.4.

Providing proper training to assure that personnel with purchasing duties can perform all required tasks at minimum levels of acceptable performance.

Providing timely and useful personnel evaluation to assist purchasing personnel to determine how, from management's perspective, they might become more effective in attaining purchasing and organizational goals.

Developing and administering all necessary personnel policies both to assure that consistent and fair procedures are utilized in dealing with purchasing personnel and to explain management concerns about purchasing activities.

Determining ways to motivate and involve staff with purchasing duties. Does the food and beverage operation have a career progression program which permits staff to advance up the ladder of successively more responsible (and higher paid) positions? Are there job rotation, job enrichment, and/or job enlargement activities planned for the staff?

This handbook cannot describe in depth all aspects of personnel management. Management staff must realize that supervision of the employees with purchasing duties is a very important determinant of the eventual success of the purchasing task. This being the case, a high priority should be given to viewing purchasing from the perspective of the staff members who are involved in it daily. How, from their perspective, can the job be improved so that both their goals as employees and the goals of the food and beverage operation can be mutually attained?

2.6.4 Directing

Directing really means the same as "supervising." This task of management involves the day-to-day "people" aspect of the purchasing process.

In small operations where food and beverage management personnel do the purchasing these staff members must supervise employees with and without duties involving purchasing. It is then important (and relatively easy) to assure that all employees are supervised in the same manner.

In large operations which have a purchasing agent this staff member may or may not supervise other personnel. He or she clearly has a boss and it is this supervisor to whom this section is addressed.

Basic principles of directing and supervising include:

Training duties that were noted in Section 2.6.3. It is important that employees with purchasing duties know how to do their jobs. The ability to determine acceptable quality in perhaps hundreds of items purchased by the food and beverage operation can be given as but one example of the need and importance of proper training for purchasing staff members.

There must be incentives provided to encourage proper performance of required tasks. This topic is generally referred to as "motivation." A whole book can be written on topics of leadership styles and their effect on employee work performance; techniques of using "human relations" in supervision; determining and providing what employees desire from their jobs, etc.

Examples of incentives include increases in wages, promotions, better working conditions, etc. It can be very helpful for top management to sit down with employees having purchasing duties and to develop basic procedures to most effectively manage the purchasing task. What are purchasing goals? What activities must be done in order to reach them? What kind of employee can best do them? What do employees want from their jobs, etc.?

Supervising also includes disciplining. In a positive sense this means telling employees about rules and policies they must follow. Negative discipline involves punishing employees who violate rules and policies with which they are familiar. Careful thought must be given to using this supervision task as a way to *prevent* trouble rather than to *dispense* punishment.

Promoting employees is another task of supervision. Advancement opportunities, increased challenges, and responsibilities through additional work assignments, etc., are generally useful ways to motivate employees. When supervisors have good employees, they should work to retain them within the food and beverage operation; recognizing their skills is one way to do that.

Evaluating employees. Purchasing staff must know how their supervisor views their work performance. Staff must know how they can improve before the improvement process can begin. Evaluation of purchasing personnel is considered in Section 14.

The directing task, of course, also involves and requires the supervisor to be available throughout the work shift and at each stage in the procurement process. Giving advice, making decisions, reviewing employees' work, helping with the tasks as required, and otherwise "managing" personnel with purchasing duties is an ongoing and important part of the job of supervisor-manager.

2.6.5 Evaluation

A final management function involves the evaluation of purchasing. To what extent are purchasing goals attained? This topic is so important that Section 14 of this handbook is devoted to purchasing evaluation.

3

OVERVIEW OF THE PROCUREMENT PROCESS

This section provides a step-by-step overview of the purchasing process. This overview will describe:

The sequence of activities involved in an effective purchasing system.

Basic components of the design of a purchasing system.

The handbook section in which the reader can find additional, detailed information regarding each component in the purchasing process.

3.1   General Information

While a purchasing system may evolve over time, in many food and beverage operations a better plan is to purposely design a system that incorporates, as a minimum, components which have been helpful to other hospitality operations. Here are the basic concerns which should be considered as a total purchasing system is developed.

The system should be designed to yield desired results in a simple, practical, and easy manner in the shortest time. Thus, for example, detailed analysis, research, and study may go into the development of purchase specifications in large food and beverage operations with specialized food buyers. This may not be possible in smaller operations in which management personnel perform purchasing as well as many additional duties. However, the *task* of developing specifications is important to both sizes of operations. The amount of input from outside sources, time spent on specification development, and detail expressed in the quality statement will be different.

The point being made here is that each foodservice manager must make individual decisions regarding both the time to be spent on each task, and the expectations required to complete it. He or she must also decide, based upon the unique operation, which of the many procedures outlined in this handbook are and are not necessary. The individual management team must define what a "simple, practical, and easy" system is for their food and beverage operation.

Procedures utilized in the purchasing system must be definite and consistent. The "best" procedures should be designed into the purchasing system and, once included and evaluated, should be utilized consistently. All personnel with purchasing responsibilities should know what their job is, and should also know how best to perform it.

Procedures, once implemented, should be written down. To the extent that procedures outlined in this handbook can be used in the individual property's purchasing system this handbook itself can become the "Standard Operating Procedures" reference for the food and beverage operation.

Responsibility must be fixed for each procedure. Each person in every position must know what he or she is supposed to do. Authority and responsibility levels adequate to perform these required tasks must be delegated. Personnel must be held accountable for performing their tasks to at least a minimum performance level.

There must be some flexibility in the purchasing system to handle unique situations. Not every eventual problem or situation can be anticipated. Time might be ineffectively used to design procedures to "routinely" handle matters which occur only rarely. Rather, purchasing personnel must know the limitations and boundaries of existing policies and procedures and must know when and whom to contact in extraordinary situations.

Procedures must be reasonably priced given what they will produce. The concept of "cost-effectiveness" is very important and, essentially, requires that each procedure which is part of the purchasing task must be "defended"; that is, it must be worth more to the food and beverage operation than it costs.

Procedures incorporated within the purchasing system must facilitate (or at least not hinder) communication and cooperation. The relationship between purchasing and user department personnel is stressed repeatedly in Sections 2 and 4 of this handbook. This concern can perhaps best be addressed by assuring that:

All affected personnel work together in developing and revising procedures for the purchasing system;

Purchasing and user department staff understand each other's duties and responsibilities;

There is agreement as to which responsibilities and duties are undertaken by purchasing and user department personnel and which tasks are shared by both groups of staff.

3.2 Determine Need for Products and Services

The first step in the purchasing process is, of course, to determine the need for the product or service to be purchased.

Someone within each department (food and beverage) must be responsible to define these needs in terms of *what* exactly is needed, *when* it is needed, and *how much* is needed.

Product needs, then, must be defined in terms of both quality and quantity requirements.

Products and services, of course, must also be necessary for managing the food and beverage operation and for attaining operational goals.

The origin of the purchase request may be from several sources. This depends primarily upon the procedures required by the purchasing system utilized by the food and beverage operation.

For example,

> In decentralized purchasing operations each user department purchases what it needs.

> In the more popular and preferable centralized purchasing system a purchase request may originate within a user department but must be processed through a series of procedures by purchasing staff (who may or may not, depending upon size of the operation, have additional, nonpurchasing duties).

In many operations purchasing is done to replenish inventory levels; in these cases the purchase request may be initiated by the storeroom which, in effect, requires an order to build up inventory levels to required maximum levels.

Some items (especially perishable commodities such as dairy products, fresh produce, etc.) are purchased by most operations on an as-needed basis. Thus quantities are determined and purchase requests originate from the production and/or purchasing personnel on the basis of anticipated volume needs and the storage life of products to be ordered.

In other operations the systems require purchasing staff themselves to originate purchase requests. For example, this may occur when storage is under control of purchasing, when "routine" orders of specified size are to be placed on an agreed-upon schedule by purchasing personnel, and when day-to-day orders for items are required on a trial basis.

In each of the instances above note the very close levels of communication and cooperation necessary between purchasing, storeroom, and/or user department personnel. (Details regarding determining the need for purchased products and services are provided in Section 4.)

3.3 Describe Need

The second step in the purchasing process is to accurately describe the item needed.

> The purchasing personnel must know exactly what user departments want and need. This is best done through a procedure in which both purchasing and user department personnel develop purchase specifications. (The final decision, however, should be made by the user department.)

> When purchasing staff are knowledgeable about products to be purchased:

>> They may make suggestions about ways to save money without affecting quality and other product concerns;

>> They will be better able to recognize inadequate specifications (either as they are being developed or as products represented by them are being delivered);

>> They will be better able to guard against user bias in regards to specified products;

They can evaluate newly marketed products for potential suitability for the food and beverage operation.

Careful description of quality needs will be helpful in day-to-day operations. For example, the operation is better assured that products ordered are, in fact, products desired. Unwanted, inadequate products are less likely to be accepted.

Product descriptions—quality purchase specifications—can be developed to translate quality *needs* (noted in Section 3.2) into quality requirements that must be consistently met as products are purchased and re-reviewed.

Quantity and necessary delivery time information are not generally included in purchase specification forms. To do so limits their usefulness since quantity and timing requirements may differ between orders. It is more appropriate to develop quality requirements by stating them on purchase specifications sent to eligible suppliers and considering quantity and timing requirements separately as each order is placed.

Details about developing purchase specifications and other objective factors which describe necessary products are presented in great detail in Section 5.

3.4   Develop and Transmit Purchase Requisition

A purchase requisition system may be used by large food and beverage operations to indicate when and how much product of a specified quality should be ordered by purchasing personnel.

When additional quantities of necessary products are needed, the purchasing personnel are alerted through use of a purchase requisition.

If production and/or purchasing personnel determine quantities of non-inventory items ("directs" such as perishable products), purchasing department staff are instructed about the need for and quantity of necessary purchases through a purchase requisition.

A sample purchase requisition is found in Figure 3.1. A blank copy which can be reproduced and instructions for completing the form are found in Section 22.3.

Smaller food and beverage operations often operate more informally and do not utilize a purchase requisition system. Instead, user department personnel may be responsible to assure that maximum inventory levels are not exceeded. They then have the authority to develop a weekly listing of items which are informally given to the person(s) responsible for purchasing products.

FIGURE 3.1 Purchase Requisition

Needed by ___Catering / Banquet___
                          (Department)

Requisition Number ___100-10___

Date Needed ___7/18/—___   Date ___7/5/—___

Item	Purchase Unit	Number of Units	Specification Number
Sterno	Case (10# cans)	3	N/A
Strip Loins	12 oz	150 only	MBG 1179
Beef Base	Case (16 oz jars)	2	13-402

___Sam Smith - Catering Mgr.___
(signature of authorizing staff member)

These same individuals, sometimes working together with purchasing staff, determine daily, twice-weekly or other time-based needs for perishable products. Again, an informal process is used to identify and report purchase needs to purchasing personnel.

Regardless of the system used or the size of the food and beverage operation it is clear that an effective communication method is necessary to inform purchasing personnel about the quality of products which must be purchased.

Since "quantity needed" depends, in part, on both the frequency of deliveries and the time needed between order and delivery, the timing aspect of deliveries is most important. This concept is reviewed in detail in Section 6.4.

3.5   Negotiate with Supply Sources

At this step in the purchasing process personnel must again formally interact with supplier representatives. (The first time occurs when supplier input about new products, usefulness of existing products, etc., is used to help develop quality purchase specifications.) There are several aspects involved in negotiating with supply sources.

3.5.1   Determine Eligible Suppliers

Purchasing personnel have the responsibility of selecting the best possible suppliers. There are many specific procedures necessary in order to do this. These are discussed in great detail in Section 8.

3.5.2   Negotiate Price and Other Concerns with Eligible Suppliers

Each eligible supplier will have copies of purchase specifications that describe quality aspects of products which the food and beverage operation desires to purchase. As individual orders are placed the buyer will have to determine price, quantity, and required delivery times. These matters (especially price) may need to be negotiated with the supplier. Depending upon the specific situation:

Prices may be set (as with some laws regulating beverage purchases);

Prices may be negotiable with individual suppliers;

Prices may be developed through a formalized bidding process. Details regarding price negotiation are discussed in Section 7.

3.5.3 Other Aspects of Working with Suppliers

It is also necessary, on a routine, recurring basis to:

Evaluate supplier effectiveness (should we continue to do business with the supplier?);

Determine non-price aspects of buying from a supplier (delivery times, payment policies, service, etc.);

Consider multiple and alternate sources of supply. These topics are considered in Section 8.

3.6 Analyze Proposals and Select Supplier

It is obvious that the supplier with the most acceptable proposal should be given the order. What is, however, "most acceptable" to the food and beverage operation?

The quality being offered by suppliers should be the same or similar (since each is aware of quality requirements laid down by the purchase specification).

The mix of price and quality (referred to as "value") then becomes very important. This concept is discussed in Section 7.3.

Other concerns dealing with what the supplier offers in addition to a product of specified quality at a certain price become important. (Supplier services, reputation and experience, payment policies, etc.) These are discussed in Section 8.12.

There are two special procedures which occur *after* the supplier is selected.

3.6.1 The Purchase Order/Purchase Record

Large operations may use a purchase order to formally indicate products, quantities, bidded price, and other important details of the purchase agreement. A copy of the form may actually be sent (or handed to) the supplier/representative.

Small operations may rely on telephone calls, salesperson visits, etc., to place orders. In these instances, an in-house document, called a purchase record, should be used to note quantity, price, etc., which the purchaser has agreed to.

Both documents are needed for product receiving and accounting purposes. (See Section 9.2.) Copies of these forms are found in Sections 22.6 and 22.21.

3.6.2 Expediting/Follow-up

There are occasions when efforts of the purchasing department personnel are needed between the time that an order is placed and when it is received. This effort is referred to as expediting. Examples include:

When deliveries do not come in on schedule;

When changes *must* be made in some aspect of the agreed upon purchase;

When emergency or rush orders are necessary.

In each of these instances purchasing personnel must interact with the supplier to resolve problems.

If problems related to supplier performance occur consistently the buyer must evaluate the continued eligibility of the supplier to do business with the food and beverage operation. If problems relate to internal purchasing system procedures these problems must be investigated and resolved. (Expediting is discussed in Section 8.12.6.)

3.7   Receiving and Inspection

This next task in the receiving process involves several steps necessary to assure that the food and beverage operation gets what it pays for. The receiving process, then, involves much more than signing the ticket and throwing items into storage.

Personnel with receiving duties must be trained and allowed sufficient time to perform required duties.

Purchase order/purchase record information must be available to indicate what *should* be received.

Detailed inspection for product quality, weight/count, and other considerations is important.

In larger food and beverage operations a receiving clerk's report is completed which provides accounting and food/beverage cost control information.

A detailed description of all of the procedures in the product receiving process is presented in Section 20.

3.8   Storage

After products are received they must be quickly placed in storage. Storage tasks essentially involve:

Securing access to storage to only those personnel requiring to enter storage areas.

Developing procedures to control inventory. These concerns deal with
counting, inventory turnover rates, reducing inventory costs, etc.
(Details regarding control aspects of storage are reviewed in Section
21.)

3.9 Processing of Purchase Documents

The final step in the purchasing process involves internal processing of various purchase documents. These procedures are necessary to help prevent fraud and to keep a management and accounting handle on purchases. Purchasing, from an accounting perspective, is discussed in Section 9.

DETERMINING
PURCHASING NEEDS

Section 3 noted that the first step in the procurement process is to determine the need for products and services to be purchased. While this may appear obvious, problems often arise because food and beverage buyers purchase what they *think* is needed rather than what is *actually* needed. This section will expand upon the concern that careful thought must be given to the facility's needs before the purchasing task is undertaken.

4.1   Introduction

The purchasing task begins with the recognition that a product or service is needed. The product may be a food or beverage item needed by, respectively, the food or beverage department. The service may be the performance of tasks which involve specialized personnel or equipment not available to the food and beverage operation, or it may involve tasks (grounds maintenance, interior cleaning, etc.) that management believes might be performed more cost effectively by an outside firm. In either case, there must be an awareness of need by someone within the property before a product or service can be purchased.

There must also be knowledge about the quality and quantity of the required product or service and the time by when it must be delivered or performed. Also, "need" is frequently a function of price; as price increases decisions about alternatives may be made so that a "needed" product is no longer necessary.

Finally, even if a product is needed it may not be purchased. For example, it may already be available in inventory or storage and need only be requisitioned in order to be available for use. Continuous withdrawal from inventory will, of course, eventually require replacement (purchase of product) of storage items at some specified time. Should we order (do we "need" a product) when we have 1, 10, or 100 cases or pounds of product still available? Most food and beverage managers agree that it is not wise to buy items before they are needed. When is this point of need reached?

4.2   Role of Specific Personnel in Determining Need

Personnel with differing responsibilities are involved in deciding what products and services are needed by the food and beverage operation.

4.2.1   Role of Purchasing Personnel

Section 2.2 noted that there are a variety of organizational formats used by many food and beverage operations. Responsibilities for assessing need (viewed as determining required quality and quantity requirements) may be shared between purchasing and other departments. Thus, for example, purchasing staff, as part of their responsibilities may provide help in developing purchase specifications which outline quality needs of products. They may also provide assistance in designing storage and inventory systems which may identify a need to order an additional quantity of an item. In most cases, however, the final decision about need is made by the *user* department.

4.2.2 Role of User Department Personnel

In most foodservice operations the final decision about products to be purchased rests with user department management. For example, while assistance in developing purchase specifications (which define quality requirements) is provided by purchasing staff, the final decision about product needs is still made by those who use the products. Likewise, if a separate department (such as accounting) controls storage, those management officials (*not purchasing employees*) finally decide upon required quantity levels needed in the storage areas.

4.2.3 Role of Top Management

While top-level management has the right to make decisions about need, it most frequently delegates this task to user department managers. Top management *may* make the decision; more frequently these managers provide advice as it is needed.

Top management does, in effect, ultimately determine product need since—probably with assistance from user departments—it determines the menu, which ultimately establishes the type of products needed. (See Section 4.3 for additional information about the role of the menu in determining needed products.)

Top management should also be involved in determining need for several types of purchasing:

Purchase of capital equipment. As noted in Section 17, top management must both approve such purchases and allocate funds to purchase capital equipment items.

Purchase of construction. Section 19 reviews the primary role which top management must play in making purchase decisions regarding construction or remodeling of food and beverage facilities.

Purchase of contracted services. Top management must be involved as decisions are made to go outside the restaurant, hotel, or club to purchase services that might otherwise be performed by employees of the facility. Organizational, staffing, and budget implications are obvious. Therefore, purchasing personnel can locate the best available service *after* the user department and top management agree upon the need for an outside contracted service.

4.3   Menu Determines Products Needed

The basic types of food and beverage products needed are determined by the menu. If, for example, ground beef is not utilized in any menu item, this product is not needed. If Blue Curacao is not used as an ingredient in any beverage prepared at the bar, this beverage item is not needed.

Within this very broad parameter necessary items are those required in items dictated by the menu(s). Quality, quantity, and other concerns about the type of required products must still, of course, be established.

Menus may change. When this occurs products available but no longer needed must be used if food costs are to be controlled. What storeroom does not have dusty and rusty cans and cases which indicate that this principle is violated?

4.4   Other Purchase Needs Must Be Determined

Need for supplies and other non-food and beverage items must be determined by top management and affected departments based upon:

The image of the food and beverage operation. Are paper or cloth napkins required? Fine silver or disposable eating utensils?

Available funds. Capital equipment purchase decisions are frequently determined in large measure on the basis of funds available.

Available storage areas. Quantity needs for supplies may be established on the basis of available space. If primary purchase concerns relate to utilizing space first for storage of food and beverage products in desired amounts, only the space that's left can be used for storage of other items.

4.5   Quality Needs Must Be Assessed

A description or statement of quality needed in all of the products or services that are purchased must be developed. This quality statement is called a purchase specification and is discussed in great detail in Section 5.

4.6 Purchases Needed for Inventory or Immediate Use

Section 4.1 noted that products may not *need* to be purchased if they are available in inventory. What determines whether products are purchased for inventory or immediate use?

4.6.1 Inventory

Few food and beverage operations purchase any items for extended storage. Increased chances of theft, pilferage, spoilage, lack of storage space, and the cost of money tied up in storage are several reasons. Normally, food products turn over at least one time per month. Stated another way, the value of food inventory at any one time is seldom more than one-twelfth of the annual cost of food purchases.

Beverage products generally turn over less frequently than food products. Thus the value of a beverage inventory at any one time may be more than one-twelfth of the annual cost of beverage purchases. Several important points need to be made.

The actual frequency of food and beverage product turnover must be determined by the individual foodservice operation. Those properties with cash flow problems or little available storage space may purchase for weekly (or smaller) needs only. Other operations may wish to take advantage of quantity or other discounts and will purchase in larger amounts.

Some foodservice operations calculate food costs on a daily basis. For daily calculations there are two types of food costs:

Items issued from inventory.

Items purchased as ''directs'' which never ''entered'' inventory in terms of food cost calculations (see Section 4.6.2). Management officials desiring to perform daily food costing must thus determine what items will be a part of inventory for their facility.

Perishable items (bread, milk, eggs, etc.) are not purchased for inventory. They are purchased for immediate use.

Many foodservice operations use a minimum-maximum inventory system (see Section 6.5). With this plan items in inventory are needed (and hence must be purchased) when the level of existing stock decreases to an established minimum point. User departments requisition needed products from inventory; inventory levels are replenished through additional purchases. With this plan, then, purchases increase inventory stock levels; they are not (unless products are considered ''directs'') used for production immediately.

4.6.2 Immediate Use

Some small operations, in effect, "bypass" storage or inventory by purchasing all (or almost all) products on an as-needed basis. As noted in Section 4.6.1, however, many properties purchase some products for inventory and other items for immediate use.

Immediate use items ("directs") generally go directly from the receiving area to user department production areas. There may be a brief storage period—one or two days—but for food costing purposes these items are "expensed" on the day received. Examples of immediate use items may include fresh meats and poultry, produce, milk and bread products, etc.

"Stored" products (which can effectively be stored for relatively long time periods) are generally not "directs"; rather, they are stored and withdrawn from inventory as they are needed. Examples include canned foods, frozen items, cereal products, etc.

4.6.3 Quantity Decisions

The decision about designating a purchase to be for inventory or immediate use affects the quantity of product that will be needed.

If a type of product is purchased for inventory purposes, its "need" is figured in terms of quantity by considering the amount that will build inventory levels back to a predetermined level. Likewise, new products do not have to be purchased until the amount available is reduced to a previously established order point.

If a product is purchased for immediate use, its "need" is assessed in terms of amount/quantity by two factors:

1. The amount judged sufficient to meet scheduled production needs; and,
2. The anticipated storage life of the perishable product before spoilage reduces product quality.

Management must therefore give careful thought to the storage requirements, the food costing plan, and systems that are used to determine quantities of products needed.

4.7 Emergency and Rush Orders

There are occasions, even with the best purchasing system, when emergency and rush orders will occur. Some such orders cannot, however, be justified. Examples include:

When poor inventory management systems do not accurately indicate quantities of product in stock.

When poor food or beverage production planning fails to anticipate needs.

When supplier delivery schedules do not permit effective timing of deliveries.

When lack of concern necessitates frequent emergencies.

These types of orders place burdens and pressure on all affected personnel (user, storage, purchasing, and supplier employees). Generally, normal procedures in the purchasing system must be bypassed in order to receive the products quickly. Expediting, perhaps picking up at the supplier's place of business, etc., can cost the food and beverage operation much in terms of time, effort, and incurred costs.

Thus, when there are frequent rush orders, the existing procurement system should be studied to determine where problems lie so that they can be corrected.

4.8 Special Problems in Determining Product and Service Needs

Several special problems affect the determination of product needs.

4.8.1 Consolidating Needs

When purchasing management is centralized (one department or person purchases all necessary products and services for the entire food and beverage operation) it becomes possible to group similar purchases together. This system has some advantages.

Fewer purchase orders (which cost money) need to be placed.

Minimum delivery poundage or purchase dollar limitations imposed by suppliers are more easily met.

Purchasing personnel can often assist in reducing the variety of purchased products which are needed. Thus, for example, working with user departments, management may determine that only three, rather than more, different sizes of frozen shrimp may be needed for menu items. Efforts and costs are reduced as the variety of items needed by the food and beverage operation is reduced.

In the beverage operation it may be determined that consumption of several "call" brands of Scotch is almost negligible. As this occurs, these brands can be run out and not reordered. Again, associated costs incurred in carrying a larger variety of items than needed are reduced.

4.8.2 Anticipating Future Needs

An effort to anticipate future needs can create another type of special problem. Section 2.5.2 indicated that top management rather than purchasing personnel must make decisions regarding the desire, if any, to purchase products in recognition of future higher or lower prices. Thus, the task of future price speculation should not be part of the purchasing staff's responsibility.

Areas of concern about future needs for the purchasing staff include the following:

Research time is generally necessary to evaluate the usefulness of products, to develop purchase specifications, and to select eligible suppliers. It is, therefore very helpful, and perhaps necessary, for sufficient lead time to be given to employees with purchasing duties to perform these tasks before products are needed.

Study of purchasing practices may reveal that some products are frequently ordered. If, for example, a few items must be ordered from a specific supplier, ordering costs might be reduced by placing a larger order (which then reduces the frequency of orders placed) with the supplier.

Purchasing staff must schedule frequent meetings with representatives of user departments in order to keep up with anticipated changes and plans. They must not assume that user department personnel will contact the purchasing department in advance of product/service needs. (This topic is discussed in Section 4.9.)

User department needs may change. A purchase specification, once developed, is not carved in stone. Thus, for example, a specification for fresh seafood may need to be changed to permit a frozen product when the former is not available locally, if price increases reduce its suitability, etc. Likewise, new products are continually being marketed. Purchasing personnel need to keep up with these to determine their suitability, if any, for the property and to assure that they are purchasing the best products. Purchasing personnel must, therefore, not relax; the assessment of need for quality products is a continual process.

4.9 Communication and Cooperation between User and Purchasing Personnel

By its very definition the role of the purchaser is to provide specialized help regardless of whether one is a full-time buyer or has additional responsibilities.

The manager who must perform purchasing and many other duties is helping food and beverage production personnel by bringing into the facility those items needed to produce meals and prepare drinks. Likewise, the full-time buyer is providing service to user personnel.

In both cases user personnel are involved in purchasing tasks. They help with development of purchase specifications, determine proper quantities of inventory stock, etc. They also are required to make the final decision about these and other activities in which purchasing personnel input has been provided.

It can be seen that effective communication between purchasing personnel and product users is critical. The user must know how purchasing personnel can make his or her job easier. The purchaser must know what the user wants.

Cooperation between affected personnel is also necessary; in fact, it may be a required element in the communication task noted above. Several techniques noted in the organization of purchasing (Section 2.6.2) can be very helpful in assuring a cooperative "we" approach rather than a negative "them versus us" approach.

5

THE PURCHASE SPECIFICATION: AN OUTLINE OF QUALITY REQUIREMENTS

The purchase specification is a statement about the quality requirements for products purchased by the food and beverage operation. It must be developed and presented to suppliers *before* orders are placed so that supplier price quotations will reflect the desired quality of product needed. To do otherwise means that supplier prices may differ because of quality differences; comparison is not then possible—or useful.

5.1   Definition

The definition of two terms will help identify the importance of quality concerns in the purchasing task.

5.1.1   Quality

In simplest terms "quality" means the suitability of a product for its intended use. The closer a product comes to being suitable, the greater its quality is.

Quality, then, does not always refer to "highest possible" quality. For example, perfectly shaped, uniform sized super colossal olives (which are expensive!) are not necessary if olives are to be chopped for salad. A *much* lower priced "broken pieces" product is acceptable; it is the proper quality olive needed.

The term "quality" requires that the product do what it is supposed to do better than any other (quality) product.

5.1.2   Purchase Specification

The purchase specification is a quality statement written for products that indicates what requirements must be met in order for a product to be "suitable" for its intended purpose. After the food and beverage officials determine what is needed (for example, olives) they must describe the quality characteristics of products (olives) that will be acceptable for their operation. There may well be more than one specification written for each product. For example, chopped olives may be needed for salads; stuffed olives might be required for beverage garnishes; and unpitted olives might be needed for another purpose. In this instance three purchase specifications for olives are required. Details about purchase specifications are found later in this section and additional ideas are found throughout Section 15.

5.2   Quality Overview

Several special concerns about the concept of quality must be noted.

5.2.1 Quality and Price

It is not possible to separate price from quality. These factors must always be considered together. In large measure, the purchaser's job is to locate the product of proper quality with the lowest price. (Factors concerning supplier selection in Section 8.0 are also, of course, important.) This may involve making comparisons between similar quality products with differing prices. This introduces the concept of "value" which is discussed in Section 7.3.

5.2.2 Quality Control

The importance of quality control to the food and beverage operation must be emphasized. In order for a desirable product (food or beverage) to be served to guests, quality must be controlled at each step in the food and beverage production system.

Quality control must begin at the time of purchasing. If the proper quality of product is not purchased and received it cannot be served to the guest. Therefore, while control of quality is of large concern to food and beverage production/service personnel, it is likewise of great importance to purchasing staff members.

5.2.3 Quality and Other Factors

Unfortunately, the purchasing task is not as simple as comparing prices charged by several suppliers for the same quality product and making a purchase decision. Other economic and noneconomic factors such as payment policies, service, and dependability of delivery are also important. These are reviewed in Section 8.12.4. It is true, however, that the base of comparison and the start of the purchasing process must begin with a definition of required quality.

5.3 Description of Quality

If quality is important (which it is), it must be properly described. An accurate, consistently used quality description is a necessary first step in a quality control program. There are several ways to describe quality.

Brand or trade name designation. If a purchaser is satisfied with a specific product offered by a supplier, the brand or trade name of the product may be an adequate quality description. An obvious disadvantage is the elimination of suppliers who do not carry the specific product brand.

Purchase specification. This is a written quality statement of factors judged important in quality for the specific product. Purchase specifications are a popular and very useful way to describe quality. They are described in great detail in later parts of this section.

Blueprint. Purchase of construction (Section 19) is often aided with blueprints which illustrate required characteristics of the construction or remodeling project being purchased.

Grades. Food products might, in part, be purchased by quality descriptions referred to as grades. For example, the U.S. Department of Agriculture (USDA) has established quality grades for meats (beef, veal, lamb, pork), poultry, fish and shellfish, eggs, dairy products, and fresh and processed fruits and vegetables. For example, a buyer who specifies an Extra Fancy McIntosh apple of a specified size, is, in effect, requiring a product of definite quality as defined by the USDA in its term "Extra Fancy."

Samples. In some instances samples may be requested from suppliers with purchase decisions to be based, at least in part, upon quality exhibited in the sample lot. In effect, the purchaser is saying that "I will purchase your product with the understanding that the product received will be equal to or better than that of the sample." This method may be necessary with new products and new suppliers on an occasional basis, but it would not be a commonly used quality description.

Trial orders. A small "sample" order may also be placed and, after acceptance, products in the trial order may become the foundation for a quality description of required products. This method, as with samples, is not a commonly used process for defining required quality.

5.4   Responsibility for Assistance in Quality (Specification) Determination

Input for development of quality statements comes from several sources.

5.4.1   Suppliers

Obviously suppliers have *no* responsibility for determining quality requirements for products purchased by the food and beverage operation. They can, however, provide a great deal of technical assistance involving:

What products they have available.

What other food and beverage operations use.

New products that are or will be available.

Objective criticism of proposed specifications.

Suppliers, then, should be asked for comments about purchase specifications as they are developed. Their ideas, along with those from in-house sources, will yield a better quality specification. Specific information about the role of suppliers in the development of purchase specifications is found in Section 15.2 of this handbook.

5.4.2. User Department Personnel

In the final analysis, user department personnel must decide (perhaps with assistance from top management) what required quality will be. Their role in developing a quality specification includes:

Accurately defining product need (which is critical since quality is dependent upon the suitability of the product for intended use).

Providing technical expertise in development of purchase specifications.

Making suggestions about which suppliers and competitors to talk with about ideas.

Evaluating and testing samples and trial order products.

5.4.3 Purchasing Staff

The role of purchasing staff in specification development is one of providing assistance, *not* making a final decision. Purchasing personnel are the ones who might question suppliers and competitors, arrange for sample and trial orders, and otherwise gather information which user department personnel will find helpful as decisions are made.

Purchasing personnel have two other roles in quality determination:

They have some responsibility in product receiving. Since quality inspection is part of the receiving process, they may note problems which would lead to revision of quality specifications.

Purchasing staff may give advice about specifications to user department personnel as quality decisions are made. While not binding, this advice (along with that of top management and other sources) can provide very useful assistance.

5.5 Quality Standardization

As purchase specifications are developed, a standard quality definition is developed.

This standardization will represent quality requirements for a product regardless of its source.

Standardization of quality is an important consideration as decisions about a variety of items are made. In the example about olives presented in Section 5.1.1, there may be advantages to reducing the number of different types of olives which are needed by the property. As this is done, the quality description concerning olives must be expanded to cover the additional number of products in which olives will be utilized.

The need for standardization of quality is critical to the entire purchasing task. Likewise, food and beverage cost standards and, hence, control systems are based upon anticipated product costs which are influenced by quality desired. Therefore, quality standards must be developed and *consistently* used and monitored as the food and beverage program is operated.

5.6 Minimum Requirements for Purchase Specifications

A purchase specification is used to describe quality requirements for products which will be purchased by the food and beverage operation. In order to accurately describe products, certain requirements are necessary.

5.6.1 General Requirements of Specifications

Certain requirements are generally necessary for all purchase specifications.

Specifications must *accurately* describe quality aspects of needed products; this requires specific, observable features of the quality definition.

They must be realistic; quality definitions must not be so stringent that few or no products will be acceptable.

Specifications must be as clear and simple as possible; excessive detail should be avoided.

Specifications should enable suppliers to provide products that are readily available; products needing processing or manufacture to order are much more expensive than readily available products.

Specifications must be written to make it possible for several suppliers to be able to quote prices and supply products.

Specifications must provide some flexibility for both buyer and seller.

5.6.2 Specification Format

All specifications must generally meet the basic requirements noted in Section 5.6.1. Additionally, as specifications are written for individual products detailed information is necessary to adequately describe the product.

5.6.2.1 Specific information required.   As a minimum, specifications must generally include the following information:

Name of product. The standard trade name of each product must be identified.

Name of food and beverage operation for which the specification is written must be included. This is because the specification, after development, will be sent to eligible suppliers. They may well have specifications from other accounts and an identifying name will prevent confusion about "whose specification is this?"

Product use. Since quality means "suitability for intended use," the purpose for which the product is purchased should be included.

Product general description. This section provides a general overall description of the required product.

Detailed description. Specific quality factors should be identified in order to indicate clearly what is needed; this section is important to avoid any communication problems resulting from lack of clarity in the "product general description" section above. Examples of factors to include in a detailed description are noted in Section 5.6.2.2.

Product test procedures. This section should indicate what procedure(s) will be used by the food and beverage operation to assure compliance with quality factors in the purchase specification.

Special instructions and requirements. This section of the purchase specification is utilized to list any additional, special requirements which must be met in the products provided to the food and beverage operation.

5.6.2.2 Sample specification format.   A sample purchase specification format sheet is found in Figure 5.1. A sample copy which can be reproduced and instructions for completing the form are found in Section 22.1.

Recall that the primary purpose of the purchase specification is to indicate clearly the quality expectations of products that are being purchased. Detail necessary to be clear (but not to confuse the reader) helps to assure that the item described will be received. Examples of details which may be helpful to fully describe the required product are included on the format sheet in Figure 5.2.

5.6.3   Other Important Order Information

Section 5.6.1 provided general information that applies to all purchase specifications. Section 5.6.2 listed information that is necessary as individual product specifications are developed. There is another category of information which must be provided to suppliers. One type of information of a general nature is applicable to all orders. Another type of information is applicable only to specific orders.

FIGURE 5.1 Purchase Specification

Ernie's Seafood Shop

(name of food and beverage operation)

1. Product name: _Ground Beef_

2. Product used for: _Hamburger Patties; also for various casserole dishes_

3. Product general description: _Fresh ground; 20% fat content; to meet USDA IMPS req'ts below._

4. Detailed description: _USDA Inspected and Graded; to meet Institutional Meat Purchase Specification (IMPS) #136. Finished grind to be through ⅛" diameter plate._

5. Product test procedures: _Thermometer to test internal temperature of meat. Periodic USDA lab tests will be run to verify fat content and bacterial count._

6. Special instructions and requirements: _Packed in 10# bulk polyethylene bags; twist tied. Internal temperature of meat to be less than 38° when delivered. Bacterial plate count to be less than 100,000 per gram._

FIGURE 5.2 Purchase Specification Format

_____
(name of food and beverage operation)

1. Product name: _____

2. Product used for:

> Clearly indicate product use (such as olive garnish for beverage, hamburger patty for grill-frying for sandwich, etc.).

3. Product general description:

> Provide general quality information about desired product. For example, "iceberg lettuce; heads to be green, firm without spoilage, excessive dirt or damage. No more than 10 outer leaves; packed 24 heads per case."

4. Detailed description:

> Purchaser should state other factors that clearly identify the desired product. Examples of specific factors, which vary by product being described, include:
>
> | | | |
> |---|---|---|
> | · Geographic origin | · Grade | · Density |
> | · Variety | · Size | · Medium of pack |
> | · Type | · Portion size | · Specific gravity |
> | · Style | · Brand name | · Container size |
> | | | · Edible yield, trim |

5. Product test procedures:

> Test procedures occur when the product is received and as or after the product is prepared or used. Thus, for example, products to be at a refrigerated temperature upon delivery can be tested with a thermometer. Portion-cut meat patties can be randomly weighed. Lettuce packed 24 heads per case can be counted.

6. Special instructions and requirements:

> Any additional information needed to clearly indicate quality expectations can be included here. Examples include bidding procedures, if applicable, labeling and/or packaging requirements, and delivery and service requirements.

5.6.3.1 For all orders.

Some general information must be provided to eligible suppliers in addition to purchase specifications for products carried by the supplier. Examples of this general information include:

Delivery instructions (delivery entrance, acceptable days and times for deliveries, etc.).

Authorized personnel (names of persons employed by the food and beverage operation who are authorized to order and receive or sign for products).

General bidding procedures (if competitive, pool or other bidding systems are utilized).

Required qualifications or capabilities of suppliers in order to be deemed eligible to do business with the food and beverage operation.

5.6.3.2 For individual orders.

Some information is applicable only to the specific order and must be provided each time an order is placed. Examples include:

The quantity (count, weight) of product ordered for the specific delivery.

The agreed price of the product for the particular order (it is wise for the buyer to confirm his or her understanding of the price by including it on the purchase order or by noting it in the telephone call or during the on-site visit when the order is placed).

Purchase unit size: If, for example, frozen ground beef is sometimes purchased in 10#, 25#, or other sized packages, the proper sized containers should be noted for the specific order.

5.7 Advantages and Disadvantages to Use of Formal Purchase Specifications*

There are both advantages and disadvantages to the use of formal purchase specifications.

5.7.1 Advantages

There are several advantages to the use of purchase specifications for food and beverage operations. These include:

Time spent in developing specifications often results in a clearer understanding of desired product quality.

---

*This discussion is adapted from information presented in J. Westing, et al., Purchasing Management: Materials in Motion; 4th ed. (N.Y.: John Wiley and Sons, 1976), pp. 5–14.

Product consideration may reduce the variety of each product which is necessary.

Less costly alternative products may be discovered as quality factors are determined.

There may be increased competition (with lower prices resulting) since all suppliers know *exactly* what quality product is desired; all sources of supply will then quote on and provide the same quality product.

Specifications indicate quality required as the receiving inspection process is undertaken.

Specifications add more assurance that the quality of products desired will be attained (since, if they are followed, user department personnel know that the proper quality product is ordered and received).

5.7.2 Disadvantages

Food and beverage operations must consider possible disadvantages to the use of purchase specifications:

Much time and effort are necessary to research and write purchase specifications. They may, therefore, be impractical for many inexpensive, low-volume products.

The task of writing specifications increases the duties of purchasing personnel. Officials with nonpurchasing responsibilities may not be able to assign a high priority to developing specifications because of other ongoing work.

As the detail of quality requirements increases, the time and expertise needed to inspect products for quality compliance also increase.

If specifications are not reviewed periodically, they may not be current indicators of product quality desired.

Minimum quality specifications developed by a purchaser may become the "maximum" quality of products which will be delivered.

5.7.3 Specifications for the Small Foodservice Operation

It is obviously not practical for small food and beverage operations to develop detailed purchase specifications for all products. Management officials who must perform purchasing as well as many additional duties do not have the time necessary to develop and write them.

The food and beverage manager may see an advantage to the use of purchase specifications. If so, he or she may have time available to hasten the process of writing specifications. This might be done by:

Thinking about and writing down several brief statements which describe important quality factors for some products.

Asking supplier(s) who normally provide these products to give additional suggestions and otherwise react to the written statements.

Revising "first draft" specifications to incorporate useful suggestions.

The food and beverage manager may wish to develop specifications for a limited number of items. A priority can be given to:

Expensive items.

Products which are purchased in large amounts at high total dollar value.

Problem items which are of inconsistent quality.

Items currently purchased from only one supply source and for which changes in quality might lead to additional supply sources.

Throughout this handbook the point has been continually stressed that *basic* principles of purchasing management are the same regardless of whether the food and beverage operation is large or small. It has also been noted that in small operations the task of purchasing must fall upon the shoulders of management personnel who have other duties and responsibilities. This creates pressure since not all tasks can be performed to the same degree as when a full-time employee has no other responsibilities besides purchasing. It is therefore up to the management official, knowing *all* the things which must be done to set priorities, to find ways which best utilize available time. A long-range plan to develop and utilize purchase specifications may be the best option. Management personnel realize, however, that things to be done in the future must begin sometime. With daily duties needing priority, long-term activities are frequently ignored. Personnel should carefully consider the possible advantages of purchase specifications in the improvement of the food and beverage operation. Staff members should be encouraged to see that some time should be allocated *now* to beginning the task of purchase specification development to make future ordering more effective.

6

CALCULATION OF QUANTITY TO PURCHASE

Serious thought must be given to procedures used to determine the quantity of products to purchase. Procedures currently in use in the hospitality industry range from "order enough to get us through the week" to, in some large operations, sophisticated computer-generated formulas for determining precise quantities that minimize a wide variety of costs at a preset "stockout" factor.

Basic principles of purchasing management can be used to develop a reasonable, practical, and cost-effective quantity needs assessment system. These are presented in this section.

6.1   Purchase Proper Quantity

Food and beverage managers know that decisions about quantity are important.

6.1.1   When Excessive Quantities Are Purchased

When products are purchased in excessive quantity several concerns must be addressed.

Excessive money is tied up in inventory. Cash flow and other problems arise when cash generated from sales must be used to pay suppliers when it could be used for other purposes.

Food and beverage managers must often pay increased insurance, interest, and storage costs because of improper inventory management.

Potential problems of reduced value can occur when products are purchased at a high cost with later replacement value lowered.

There is a possibility of quality deterioration and product damage that increases with longer storage times.

Risks of theft and pilferage increase.

6.1.2   When Insufficient Quantities Are Purchased

To buy in quantities lower than needed is also not wise.

Stockouts may result; problems with customer dissatisfaction, last-minute changes in production scheduling, and "small batch" cooking (with built-in inefficiencies) may result.

Emergency and rush orders may need to be placed; these take time, cost money, and create anxiety (will the order arrive in time?).

Discounts from volume purchases, which can reduce product costs when used wisely, are lost.

6.2   Inventory Management

Determination of the quantity to purchase is really an inventory management decision. Inventory refers to products that have been purchased and are "in the house" but have not been produced in final form for sale.

6.2.1   Types of Inventory

There are actually four types of inventory in food and beverage operations.

Raw materials: Basic, unprocessed food and beverage supplies. These food products include convenience food items which will be reconstituted or further processed on site.

Work in process: Items withdrawn from inventory and in some stage of production. This includes, for example, products taken out of the freezer for thawing in the refrigerator and items in a preproduction stage for later use (cleaned shrimp, various stocks and basic mixes, etc.).

Supplies: Miscellaneous disposable, linen, chemical, small equipment items, and other expendable products that are used to produce and serve products but do not become part of the product.

Finished products: This type includes, for example, items prepared for future sale (such as dressings made in advance of need, bread products frozen for future use, etc.).

6.2.2   Types of Storage Areas

When we think of storage areas we often think of large (or not so large!) central storage rooms such as those used to store dry food and also beverage products. We also quickly consider walk-in refrigeration and freezer units. There are, however, other areas in which products are stored.

Work center storage areas: Shelving, bench, mobile, and drawer storage areas hold products in production-site storage. Many work centers also have refrigerated or frozen food storage units of various types.

Broken case storage areas: Some food and beverage operations have areas where split cases, opened bags, bales, etc., are stored. They are frequently issued from storage in purchase units (such as cases of six #10 cans, 50-pound bags, etc.), and products not needed for immediate storage are relocated to another storage area.

Off-site storage: Food and beverage operations with inadequate storage space may need to rent storage areas off-site. Frozen food lockers and dry storage warehouses are examples of these options.

6.3   Factors That Affect Quantity

A broad range of factors can affect the quantity of products to purchase. A list is presented here so that food and beverage purchasers can develop a better understanding of specific influences which affect the quantity to purchase decision in their food and beverage operation.

Scheduled need: As a larger volume of product must be produced, a greater quantity of the item must be ordered.

Changing price concerns: Product prices are very important factors in quantity decisions. This topic is discussed fully in Section 7. Two points can be emphasized here:

As prices increase quantities purchased might decrease because of menu changes which reflect higher product costs. Thus, while a steak house must purchase meat, regardless of its price, it does not need to purchase oranges for a garnish; if orange prices increase, this product might be replaced with less expensive garnish ingredients.

If food and beverage officials believe prices will decrease, they may instruct purchasers to buy on an as-needed basis only; conversely, if they believe prices will increase, they may desire to buy for inventory. *Note:* These decisions are made by management personnel, *not* by purchasing personnel.

Available storage facilities: Space may limit the quantity of products which can be purchased.

Storage and handling costs: These costs are not easily identified when on-site storage space is available. They are, however, known when space must be rented. In this instance it is necessary to justify the cost of the off-site storage or to assure that production requirements—related to supplier delivery schedules—demand additional storage space.

Waste and spoilage: Increased spoilage may occur as products remain in storage. Quantities of perishable products then are estimated on the basis of immediate need.

Theft and pilferage: There are opportunities for theft and pilferage even in very secure storage areas. If quantities of products are purchased for long inventory periods, these chances increase.

Additional quantities for emergencies (safety factor): Quantities to be purchased often include a safety factor which extends beyond the actual estimate of quantity needed. This allows for delivery delays, runs on specific products, and similar problems which would otherwise create stockouts.

Market conditions: Irrespective of prices, as products become more or less available, decisions about quantities are affected. Thus, as a popular French wine becomes scarce, additional cases may be secured for inventory and future use.

Level of available inventory: The amount of product available in inventory is a very important consideration in quantity of product to be purchased. This will be again noted in Section 6.4.

Quantity discounts: Discounts for quantity purchases may be worthwhile and, if so, they will influence quantities to purchase. Serious study must be done, however, to assure that this decision is cost effective. (Note, for example, possible problems with purchase of larger than necessary quantities discussed in Section 6.1.1.)

Minimum order amounts: Suppliers sometimes specify minimum order amounts (in dollar value and/or poundage) that must be met in order for deliveries to be made.

Transportation and delivery costs: When suppliers charge separately for transportation and/or delivery, or when food and beverage purchasers consider costs involved in pickup at the supplier's warehouse, it may be more cost effective to increase the quantity of product ordered. This can result in lowered costs.

Standard packaging units: When suppliers will not break up cases of items the standard commercial units of packaging will influence quantities to be purchased. Thus, while only 35# of a cereal product may be desired, 50# (one bag) may need to be ordered.

Order costs: It is difficult to assess costs of placing orders. Purchasers do, however, know that significant expenses are incurred by the time required to perform all tasks in purchasing, receiving, and storage.

6.4 Quantity Needed for Immediate Use or for Inventory

Products can be purchased for inventory or immediate use.

Immediate use: Perishable products, such as fresh produce, bakery, and dairy items must be purchased only in a quantity that can be used within a very short time period.

Inventory: Nonperishable products such as frozen meats, canned grocery, and liquor items can be purchased in quantities which permit longer storage times if this is desirable.

In either instance the quantity to be purchased is found by reducing the quantity needed by the quantity available:

Quantity needed (−) quantity available (=) Quantity to purchase

Stated another way, the quantity of perishable products to be purchased is:

Quantity needed for immediate use (−) Quantity available (=) Quantity to purchase

If 5 cases of lettuce are needed and 2 cases are available in the walk-in refrigerator, 3 cases should be purchased.

(5 cases needed − 2 cases available = 3 cases to purchase.)

Likewise, the quantity of inventory products to be purchased is:

Quantity desired in inventory − Quantity available = Quantity to purchase

If 8 cases (6#10) of canned corn should be in inventory and 5 cases are available in inventory, 3 cases should be purchased.

(8 cases needed − 5 cases available = 3 cases to purchase.)

Procedures, then, must be developed to assess the quantity of items needed for immediate use and for inventory.

6.4.1 Immediate Use

Normally an ongoing routine is utilized to determine the quantities of immediate use (perishable) products needed.

Food and beverage management personnel and purchasing staff know the general usage rates of these products. For example, in an average three-day buying cycle a specific number of cases of various produce, pounds of fresh meat, and number of chicken fryers are used.

If, for example, an order is placed and delivery is made early in the week (when business may be slower), a reduced quantity of necessary items is purchased.

Conversely, the order placed for later week delivery (when business picks up) will require an increased quantity of necessary products.

Purchasers, then, determine the quantity of each product available and subtract it from the quantity deemed necessary (by the process noted above) to determine the necessary amount to purchase.

Routine quantities needed must be adjusted as business volume fluctuates. Thus, for example, additional quantities are needed as celebrations, holidays, conventions in town, and other activities judged to increase business occur during the order period.

Routine quantities needed must be reduced when business will decline during the period covered by the perishable order. Thus, holidays (on which the food and beverage operation is closed) and continuing periods of poor weather also have their negative effects on business.

Perhaps the need to revise forecasting procedures can best be noted when:

Spoilage or waste occurs (suggesting that excessive quantities are being purchased);

Stockouts and "emergency" orders consistently occur (which suggests that inadequate quantities are being ordered).

Generally, through a trial and error process, purchasers can establish a useful, reasonably accurate process to determine the quantities of perishable products they need to purchase.

6.4.2 Inventory

Different procedures are necessary to determine what quantities of nonperishable products to purchase. The problem is different; purchasers can buy in a quantity for short-term use or for inventory—long-term storage.

If purchasers buy nonperishable items for inventory purposes different procedures are necessary to determine needed quantities. A detailed presentation of these procedures is outlined below.

6.5 Minimum-Maximum Inventory System

When nonperishable items are purchased for inventory (storage) they are received, placed into secure storage, and withdrawn from inventory as they are needed. Procedures must be developed to provide an accurate, efficient way to determine the quantities of inventory items to be purchased.

6.5.1 Introduction

The minimum-maximum system is a process of inventory management that can be a useful aid in determining the quantity of nonperishable products to be purchased. While the topic of inventory management policy is considered in Section 21, this section will focus on aspects of inventory management dealing with quantities to order.

6.5.2 Overview

Basically, the minimum-maximum system involves determining, for each product to be included in the system,

The minimum quantity below which inventory levels should not fall;

The maximum quantity above which inventory levels should not rise.

Procedures for determining the quantity of each product to order essentially involve calculating the amount of goods that will bring the present inventory level back up to maximum point at the time the order is received.

6.5.3   Conditions for Use

The minimum-maximum system can best be used in these conditions:

For food and beverage products that are standardized; for example, quality characteristics do not change between orders; products are readily available from more than one supply source.

When prices are relatively stable.

When products are used in essentially consistent quantities.

For products that are costly.

For products purchased in large quantities.

When products will continue to be used in the future.

When products do not have a limited shelf life.

When reasonable maximum quantities do not present storage space problems.

Stated another way, there is little practical need to utilize procedures in a minimum-maximum system for inexpensive, low-volume, nonperishable items that do have a long storage life. As these types of products are withdrawn from inventory they can be reordered; there is less concern for lead time before they are needed.

6.5.4   Definition of Terms

Before going through an illustration of the process it will be helpful to define the terms that describe the components of the minimum-maximum system.

Purchase unit: The size of container or package in which the product is normally purchased. A purchase unit may be a case (for example, of six–#10 cans), a pound (as in fresh meat), a drum (as in a 30# cannister of deep fry fat), etc.

Usage rate: Quantity expressed in terms of the number of purchase units used per order period. For example, if six cases of applesauce are normally used from the time of one delivery to the next, the usage rate is six cases. The usage rate depends on production requirements and is generally developed by trial and error procedures which, over time, help the manager to estimate quantities of products used.

Lead time: Quantity expressed in terms of the number of purchase units used from the time the order is placed until it is delivered. For example, if three cases of applesauce are normally used between order and delivery times, the lead time is three cases.

Safety level: Quantity expressed in terms of the minimum number of purchase units that must remain available in inventory. *Safety level = minimum level*. This safety factor is established to allow for late deliveries, unexpected increased use of products, and to otherwise help prevent stockouts.

Order point: Quantity expressed in terms of the number of purchase units that indicates when an order should be placed. The order point, then, represents the sum of the number of lead-time units and the number of safety-level units. It can be seen that when products are ordered at the order point, the quantity will be reduced to the safety/minimum level by the time the order is received.

Assume: Lead time = 8 cases
Safety level = 8 cases

Order-point units (=) Lead-time units used (+) Safety-level units required

16 =   8   (+)   8

Additional quantities of product are ordered at the order point (16 cases). By the time the order is received only 8 cases (the safety/minimum level) will remain:

Order-point units		Lead-time units used		Safety-level units required
16	(−)	8	(=)	8

Maximum level: Quantity expressed in terms of the number of purchase units that represent the maximum number of purchase units which are permitted to be in inventory. The maximum level represents the sum of the safety level and the usage rate. Since usage rate is equal to the quantity of the product used during the order period, it can be seen that this quantity plus the safety level (which represents minimum inventory level) can represent the maximum inventory quantity.

6.5.5 Establishing the Minimum Level

The minimum (safety) level is the point below which product levels in inventory may not decrease. It must be set by considering:

The lead time for reorders. As the frequency of delivery decreases, the number of lead-time units increases. When delivery timing and schedules are not predictable, minimum inventory levels must also be increased.

The usage rate for products. As the volume of product usage increases, the safety levels may have to increase. It is more likely to expect greater runs on high-volume items than on lower-volume items; likewise, more guests will be dissatisfied with stockouts of high popularity items (obviously the goal must be to reduce or eliminate stockouts so that *no* guest will be dissatisfied).

The minimum-maximum system must attempt to establish a safety level that minimizes the possibility of a stockout without the need to carry excessive quantities of a product in inventory.

6.5.6 Establishing the Lead Time

Lead time is the number of purchase units used from the time the order is placed until it is delivered. There are two ways that it can be set:

The amount of lead time required for an "average" order.

The amount of time required for the longest order period.

If the usage and safety levels incorporate a margin or "cushion" to compensate for unanticipated problems, a small variance in length of lead time is not critical; as these figures are closely calculated, more concern about lead time is warranted.

Several special conditions cause special problems:

When suppliers are not dependable (this should be a factor in continuing to do business with a supplier);

When there is only one supplier;

When the food and beverage operation is in a remote location (and, hence, long delays are more possible);

When market conditions, distribution channels, etc., cause erratic conditions that can affect the availability (and hence, need) to backorder some products.

In these instances the food and beverage manager must increase allowable lead times for product delivery.

6.5.7 Examples of Minimum-Maximum System Process

Illustrations of the process which incorporates the components of the minimum-maximum system are presented below:

Assume:

Purchase unit—case

Usage rate—2 cases per day

Order period—monthly (30 days)

Monthly usage rate: 2 cases per day × 30 days = 60 cases

Lead time = 4 days

$$4 \text{ days at 2 cases per day} = 8 \text{ cases}$$
$$\text{Safety level} = 8 \text{ cases}$$

Order point
$$\text{Lead time} + \text{Safety level} = \text{Order point}$$
$$8 \text{ cases} + 8 \text{ cases} = 16 \text{ cases}$$

Maximum level
$$\text{Usage rate} + \text{Safety level} = \text{Maximum level}$$
$$60 \text{ cases} + 8 \text{ cases} = 68 \text{ cases}$$

6.5.7.1 Quantity to buy at order point. If an order for a product is to be placed at the time the order point is reached, the following process is used:

Order at order point	16 cases
(see 6.5.7 above)	
Order monthly usage rate	+60 cases
Total cases will equal	76
However, during time from order to delivery (lead time), daily usage rate has continued; deduct lead time units	(8)
Maximum stock level is thus maintained	68

6.5.7.2 Quantity to buy before order point. If any order is to be placed *before* the order point is reached (as would occur when an order of many products is being put together for price quotations from suppliers) the following process is used:

Assume 25 cases in storage.
$$\text{Excess over order point} = \text{Amount in storage} - \text{Order point}$$
$$9 \text{ cases} = 25 \text{ cases} - 16 \text{ cases}$$
$$\text{Amount to order} = \text{Usage rate} - \text{Excess over order point}$$
$$51 \text{ cases} = 60 \text{ cases} - 9 \text{ cases}$$
The decision to order 51 cases can be proved:

Order 51 cases	=	51 cases
Amount available	= +	25 cases
Total		76 cases
Less lead time		(8) cases
Maximum inventory level		68 cases

6.5.8 Advantages and Disadvantages

As with most purchasing management systems food and beverage operations can find both advantages and disadvantages to use of the minimum and maximum system.

6.5.8.1 Advantages.   Several advantages to use of the system can be cited.

Excessive stock buildup is less likely; a maximum inventory level has been established.

The minimum stock level provides a cushion against stockouts.

The system is easy to understand, explain, and use.

Actual performance can be monitored against standard performance.

Analysis of inventory levels required by the minimum-maximum system may yield effective changes in the quantity of orders which would otherwise not be made.

6.5.8.2 Disadvantages.   Negative features of the minimum-maximum system include:

The system may not be the optimal way to calculate required quantities (there are computer-assisted systems which provide a more detailed and accurate plan of "when to purchase how much").

The assumptions built into minimum safety and lead-time calculations may decrease the system's accuracy; stockouts can still result.

Quantity discounts may not be possible when maximum inventory quantities cannot be exceeded.

Some time is necessary initially to calculate safety and lead-time estimates.

6.5.9   Minimum-Maximum System for Small Operations

It would appear that many of the procedures in the minimum-maximum system described above can be useful to small food and beverage operations. Perhaps management officials in these operations can implement a system for selected products. Examples of those which might be selected include:

Expensive food items
Frequently used food items
Liquor items
"Problem" products where stockouts seem to occur frequently

6.5.10   Summary

Recall that a minimum-maximum system is one component in a total inventory management system (which is described completely in Section

21.0). Attention provided to the process of determining the quantity of nonperishable products to be purchased can be very helpful in attaining a primary purchasing objective: to order enough without running out before the time of the next delivery.

6.6 Other Methods of Determining Purchase Quantities

There are other, probably "special situation" methods that can be used to determine the quantities of products to purchase. These are reviewed in this section.

6.6.1 Definite Quantity Contracts

Large-quantity buyers may wish to enter into an agreement with a supplier to provide a definite quantity of product(s) in a specified number of deliveries. With this plan:

Purchasers must estimate the total quantity required for the period covered by the contract.

The amount to be delivered is generally a function of production volume, available storage space, and delivery charges, if any, imposed by the supplier.

The method may have merits when quantity discounts are involved, when a source of supply can be assured, and when purchasing time and effort should be minimized.

6.6.2 Requirements Contracts

This method is similar to definite quantity contracts (Section 6.6.1) except that the quantity to be purchased is not fixed. It may, however, need to fall within a stated minimum and maximum limit.

Advantages of the requirement system to the food and beverage operation are similar to those of the definite quantity contracts. Additionally, the food and beverage operation is somewhat more flexible; only a range of quantity needs rather than a fixed quantity needs to be estimated.

6.6.3 Open Market Purchasing

For products purchased in small quantities and of minimal value, calculation or estimation of exact quantity needs is less important. A workable procedure for these items may involve a periodic inventory (such as monthly, when food-cost analysis is done for accounting purposes) with subsequent purchases in sufficient quantity as need dictates.

6.6.4 Exact Requirements System

This plan involves purchasing the exact quantity needed for a specific function. Thus, for example, a special catered event may be planned with an entree item not generally available at the food and beverage operation. In this instance the exact quantity judged necessary for the catered event would be ordered.

6.6.5 Cyclical Ordering System

This process is perhaps the most popular method to determine the quantity of products necessary in food and beverage operations. Essentially, a periodic review is made of quantities of available products in inventory. If experience suggests that the available quantity will not be sufficient to meet production needs for the time covered by the order, additional quantities are purchased.

Frequency of inventory review varies according to the frequency of ordering. If, for example, grocery supplies are ordered biweekly, inventory review would need to be done before the order is placed.

Inventory review can be done by physical inspection or by study of perpetual inventory records (see Section 21).

Several disadvantages to use of the system can be noted.

Since all items must be counted, time is consumed.

A minimum quantity may need to be utilized to compensate for fluctuating production usage (if this is the case, the system begins to approach the minimum-maximum system discussed in Section 6.5.).

Stockout and other inventory management problems may occur if the quantity review process is not done carefully.

6.6.6 Cooperative (Pool) Buying

Cooperative buying is the process that involves several food and beverage operations combining orders for like quality products and submitting one order rather than separate orders to a supplier. Multiunit companies are most likely to utilize this system, although it can also benefit a group of smaller operations who might not be able to meet suppliers' minimums otherwise.

Cooperative (pool) purchasing may not, by itself, have a direct impact upon the quantity of products to be purchased; however, participants in the system may be required to meet minimum quantity purchases to remain members of the pool.

PURCHASING
AT THE RIGHT PRICE

7

PURCHASING
AT THE RIGHT PRICE

Buyers and sellers are concerned about the prices of purchased goods and services. Frequently there is a range of prices within which compromise is possible. Buyers want to spend at the lower end of that price range; paying less is to their benefit. Sellers want to sell at the higher end of that price range; collecting more is to their advantage. Food and beverage purchasers are *not* doing their jobs effectively when they simply ask the price and then pay it. Frequently, price negotiation is possible. This section considers the concept of price, a most important component in the purchase process.

7.1 Definition of the Right Price

An objective of purchasing is to buy at the "right" price. What is the right price? It depends, of course, upon whether the question is answered by the buyer or the seller.

7.1.1 Price: The Buyer's Perspective

Holding quality constant, the buyer wants to pay as little as possible; however, there is an upper limit to what a buyer will pay. It is affected by these factors:

How badly the buyer wants the product. The range of price which will be paid increases for necessities and decreases for optional purchases. Thus, the steak house will buy meat regardless of price; however, there is even an upper limit here. At *some* point, decided by the buyer based upon financial analysis of the operation, the steak house will charge market price for steaks and begin to feature seafood or other lower cost items.

An optional purchase, such as a replacement dishwasher, might be deferred by the steak house during times of high meat prices; cash must be reserved for higher necessity items.

How much other suppliers charge. Competition is a great equalizer of prices. Over a long period of time a buyer will not pay a supplier more for a product than he or she must pay elsewhere. Recall, however, that a buyer is paying not *only* for product, but also for service, dependability, etc. Factors that affect the willingness of a buyer to pay the supplier's price are noted in Section 8.4.

7.1.2 Price: The Seller's Perspective

The seller, obviously, wants ro receive as much as possible for products he or she sells; however, there is a minimum limit to the amount a seller will accept. It is affected by:

What prices other suppliers are charging for a similar quality product. The supplier *knows* that buyers make purchase decisions based upon prices charged by all suppliers.

Whether the buyer is price conscious. This topic is discussed in Section 7.2.

Supplier costs. Suppliers must generally at least cover their cash costs for the product being sold.

Supplier overhead and profit requirements. Suppliers also want to generate funds for associated overhead costs and profit requirements. Their definition of a "fair" price would obviously be one that contributes a reasonable amount of funds to these purposes.

Their control of the market. When a seller has few competitors prices will be set at a rate that is favorable ("fair") to the supplier. When a supplier has many competitors and, hence, wants a larger share of the market, he or she will adjust prices downward.

Generally, prices are based upon what the market will bear. Buyers who are price conscious can, however, influence the price that they are charged.

7.2   The Price-Conscious Purchaser

While all purchasers are concerned about price some purchasers emphasize price concerns above quality, service, and other aspects of purchasing decisions. Conversely, other buyers may emphasize non-price aspects, especially quality, of the purchases made. A third group of buyers may adopt either concern depending upon the product being purchased.

Since buyers can influence supplier's prices this suggests that all purchasers should be price-conscious if this means attempting to obtain an optimal, fair, and reasonable price from the buyer's perspective.

Price must always be considered in the context of quality; this concept is discussed in Section 7.3. It is noted here, however, to remind the food and beverage purchaser that price reductions that result from lowered quality will probably not result in a fair and reasonable price if quality falls below the level noted in the purchase specification (see Section 5).

7.2.1   Procedures to Reduce Purchase Price

Buyers can use many procedures to reduce purchase price. These are reviewed in this section:

Negotiate with the seller. The art of negotiation can be a most effective procedure to reduce purchase price. This topic is discussed in detail in Section 7.4.

Consider lower quality products. If the purchase specification (Section 5) accurately describes current quality requirements the base of quality needs is established. To purchase products of lower quality in order to reduce the purchase price may not be in the best interests of the food and beverage operation. If, however, current quality needs have evolved through a subjective process without serious consideration in a process yielding an objective purchase specification it is possible that a higher than necessary quality product is being purchased. Lowered quality demands may yield reduced prices.

Evaluate your need for an ordered product. Perhaps some products being purchased should be made in total or partially on-site. The concept of "make-buy" is discussed in Section 10.

Discontinue some supplier services. For example, prices may be decreased if delivery is discontinued; food and beverage operation employees may pick up products at the supplier's warehouse. Likewise, payment time deadlines, services such as on-site visits by salespersons, etc., can be curtailed. Purchasing personnel can explore cost-saving implications of these and similar alternatives.

Combine orders. If fewer suppliers are used with each supplier getting a larger volume of the purchaser's orders, prices may be decreased.

Purchase in larger quantities. Suppliers may provide discounts for volume purchases. Careful study may indicate that these discounts benefit the food and beverage operation.

Reevaluate the need for high-cost items. As the prices of optional items (garnish ingredients, menu items which do not need to be offered, etc.) increase, creative judgment may suggest that lower cost products can substitute for these high-price items.

Pay cash, when possible, to provide an incentive for a supplier to reduce prices. He or she may have cash-flow problems and this alternative can frequently benefit both buyer and supplier.

Speculate about purchase price trends. If the buyer anticipates rising or falling prices quantities of purchased products may be, respectively, increased or decreased to take advantage of likely future price changes. This, however, must be a management, *not* a purchasing decision.

Change purchase unit size. Price per pound, quart, etc., may decrease as larger packaging units are purchased. Thus, for example, one pound of flour may cost less when purchased in a 100-pound sack than when bought in a 10-pound sack.

Use a new kind of buying. For example, cooperative (pool) purchasing was noted in Section 6.6.6. This plan, which involves combining needs from several properties in order to increase purchase quantities, may yield cost savings because of volume purchase discounts.

Use competitive bidding procedures, whether formally or informally. These can be very effective price reduction techniques. Too many food and beverage purchasers get comfortable with a supplier and fail to get competitive prices for needed products. This topic is reviewed in Section 7.5.

Enter into creative price agreements with suppliers. For example, some suppliers, assured of the business, will agree to a price markup based on changing wholesale market prices. Another possibility includes long-term commitments at lower prices for purchases in a predetermined quantity. Some suppliers may exchange products at a certain value with a like value of meal and beverage charges at the food and beverage operation. The practice of bartering is increasing in many locations.

Take advantage of promotional discounts (such as for new or slow moving products) and "opportunity buys" (as when discontinued products or damaged products—which are usable—are offered at reduced prices).

Bypass the supplier and purchase directly from a distributer/manufacturer/grower if you are a large-volume purchaser. Cost savings from eliminating the middleman can be significant.

7.2.2 Cooperate with the Supplier: A Cost Savings Necessity

Food and beverage purchasers who maintain a "them versus me" relationship with suppliers cannot, in the long run, be effective. Rather, buyers must be willing to work with suppliers in a process that yields a fair price from the perspective of both parties. Some principles which should be practiced include:

Be truthful; if you lie (about competitors' prices, for example) the supplier will soon realize it.

Practice basic principles of effective supplier relations (these are reviewed in Section 12.5).

Consider how you would feel if you were the supplier reacting to a purchaser who does what you do. Your feelings and reactions might well mirror how your supplier will respond.

Realize that both buyer *and* seller must benefit from the transaction. The seller must receive a fair price to meet expenses and profit goals; you must buy at a fair price to maintain control of costs and to generate required profits. To attempt to place a supplier in an "I win—you lose" relationship cannot work over the long run (and probably not in the short run either).

7.3 The Concept of Value

Value, simply defined, is the relationship between price and quality. The two components cannot be separated in any purchase decision.

7.3.1 Price and Quality Relationship

To clarify, from the *buyer's* perspective:

If price increases and quality stays the same, value decreases.
If price increases and quality goes up accordingly, value stays the same.
If price increases and quality decreases, value decreases.
If price decreases and quality stays the same, value increases.
If price decreases and quality goes down accordingly, value stays the same.
If price decreases and quality goes up, value increases.

It is the purchaser's task to receive optimal value in purchases made. (This, by the way, is the identical concern to guests of the food and beverage operation; they want to receive value—quality relative to price—for the purchase of products, service, and atmosphere in the food and beverage facility!)

7.3.2 Value Analysis

Unfortunately for the food and beverage buyer value cannot be easily measured by comparing AP (as purchased) prices of many required products with a quality standard in order to measure or to compare value as purchase decisions are made. For example,

A gallon of floor cleaner may cost less from one supplier than another; however, the cleaning cost per square foot may be more for one brand (since a larger quantity of the product must be used to clean a reduced number of square feet).

The food cost per portion of beef stew may be higher when a convenience food product is utilized than when an item is prepared "from scratch"; however, *total* cost, which includes labor and energy, may be less for the prepared product. If quality is constant this fact puts new light on the purchase decision.

These two examples illustrate the principle that more than "up front" costs need to be considered; rather, the bottom line calculation of what it will actually cost to use the product must be determined. If this can be done the *value* of a product can be more accurately determined because quality aspects will relate to the total price *not* to the purchase or initial price.

7.3.2.1 What products should be studied.   Food and
beverage purchasers should give priority to value analysis study for items which:

Represent a large dollar cost;
Are purchased in great volume;
Have created quality concerns;
Are complex and require additional on-site labor or expensive equipment.

7.3.2.2 The value analysis process. Procedures used to perform an analysis of products which are identified in Section 7.3.2.1 include the following tasks.

Obtain all required information about the product; for example,

What is its AP price?

What is it supposed to do?

Is the product needed?

Are there "better" alternatives?

If so, why are they "better"?

Can the product, or procedures to handle it, be modified to make it "better"?

Is the product of proper quality?

Can a lower quality product be used?

Is special equipment required?

Is packaging acceptable?

Are there problems with continuity of supply?

Are there storage problems?

Does the product cost more than it is worth?

When basic questions about the product have been asked and information is assembled, food and beverage purchasing staff, user department personnel, and management officials should consider *answers* to the questions. For example:

What are the *real* problems with the product?

What are its *real* alternatives?

What purpose does the product really serve?

How well does the product perform relative to how well we want it to perform?

At this point the value analysis process becomes very helpful. Concentrated study of the above and similar questions can provide meaningful answers. In the examples cited in the beginning of this section:

Real costs incurred in the use of floor cleaner and beef stew can be determined.

Quality descriptions included in purchase specifications can be modified to incorporate newly discovered quality requirements (for example, the floor cleaner will be evaluated on the basis of effective usage cost per square foot).

Alternative products which provide necessary quality at a cost effective price can be discovered and evaluated.

In the case of food and beverage products, quality can also be subjectively measured from the perspective of the customer (by involving regular guests in sample testing, for example).

A final step in the value analysis process involves considering whether the products judged as acceptable do actually meet the concerns of

> Consistent, necessary quality;
>
> Acceptable performance;
>
> Proper reflection of the food and beverage operation's standards to the public.

7.3.2.3 Conclusion   The objective of the value analysis process is to help the food and beverage purchaser define what a product *really* costs and what standard of quality exists at the point of product use (as opposed to point of purchase). If this can be done the "price" charged by a supplier can be considered in relation to the product's usefulness to the facility and its acceptance by the customer. It will also be easier to make more realistic comparisons of "fairness" and "reasonableness" of each supplier's prices.

7.4   The "Art" of Negotiation

It is true that purchasers can influence the prices paid by the food and beverage operation to suppliers for required products. Many techniques were listed in Section 7.2.1. The practice of negotiating prices must be high on the list of potentially useful tactics to obtain low prices.

7.4.1   Definition

Negotiation is, simply, a process used to reach agreement on all matters important to a purchase. Examples of concerns include product specifications, delivery times, and price. In terms of price, the purchaser, through the negotiating process, attempts to obtain a final cost that is most favorable to the food and beverage operation.

Both buyer and seller must give and take in the process of reaching agreement. The objective of both buyer and seller in price negotiation is to show that the best interests of both parties are served when they move closer to meeting each other's objectives.

7.4.2   Basic Principles

Many basic principles of negotiation can help the food and beverage purchaser become an effective "persuader." These include:

> The purchaser must know his or her limitations. Can he or she obligate the food and beverage operation? Are there price or total cost limitations beyond which top management input is required? There are generally legal implications to the purchasing agent's responsibilities and duties (*see* Section 13).

Almost all purchases should involve some price negotiation. Major purchases which involve significant costs certainly deserve the effort. Likewise, small-cost items which are routinely purchased represent large-dollar values over an extensive time period.

Within these restraints, of course, the extent of negotiation will relate to the potential dollars that can be saved.

The food and beverage buyer must know that he or she is negotiating with the proper supplier official. While salespersons might be authorized to make minor price adjustments, major price negotiations will need to be conducted with the sales manager or another officer of the company.

A formal meeting should be held for discussing major price items. Rarely can a hallway chat or telephone conversation be adequate for large dollar concessions.

Purchasers should know in advance what they will initially offer and the highest price they can accept. They should likewise attempt to consider, from the supplier's perspective, what concessions he or she is likely to make. Other aspects of the purchase agreement should be thought out. For example, will the purchaser accept reduced services of a specified type for a lower price?

The conversation should not become emotional; it should remain calm, professional, and friendly.

Areas of agreement should be highlighted. Also, when the supplier concedes a point the next one brought up by the purchaser should be one that the buyer doesn't mind losing.

The agreement, once made, should be summarized in writing.

The purchaser should not lie or make threats he or she can't live with. For example, to lie about "the other guy's prices" or to suggest that "I can take my business elsewhere" (if this can't be done) are not signs of an effective negotiator.*

Suppliers must be able to predict the effect of their negotiation; they should understand that they will get the order if their price is low and, conversely, that they will not obtain an order if their price is high.

The purchaser should be concerned about major points important in the negotiation; he or she shouldn't get wrapped up in details unless and until it is necessary.

A buyer should negotiate for the long, not the short, term. He or she should be alert to the need to make short-term concessions that might lead to an increased advantage over the long run. For exam-

---

Many purchasers also believe that it is unethical to indicate another supplier's prices with the intent to have a second supplier reduce prices below this point.

ple, to pay a slight bit more for a product when it is plentiful may prompt the supplier to give the buyer first priority when the supply is limited.

The purchaser should be sure that all information and facts on hand are correct.

7.4.3 Buying without Negotiated Prices

Generally, price negotiation is important before order decisions are made. There are several times, however, when negotiation is not or cannot be used for specific orders:

When requirements contracts, definite quantity contracts, or other purchasing methods have established definite prices in advance of the specific order (see Section 6.6).

When small and/or petty cash purchases are in order.

When there is only one source of supply.

When prices are fixed by law.

When published catalog prices showing discounts have been printed, negotiated price reductions are less likely (but still possible).

When emergency, rush, and special orders must be placed.

When a formal competitive bid purchase system is to be used (see Section 7.5.2). If an informal system (Section 7.5.1) is used negotiation can take place before the price is quoted.

7.4.4 Conclusion

Food and beverage purchasers must be aware that they can affect the price paid for products through effective negotiation with suppliers. This process, used informally before the supplier formally quotes a price, is one of the true measures of a purchaser's skill in performing his or her job. In addition to the obvious advantage of lower prices, effective negotiation can yield other benefits:

It promotes better understanding; the buyer better knows the needs of the seller; the seller better understands the buyer's situation.

It can generate suggestions which can be helpful to the buyer; for example, suggestions regarding what might be done to reduce the price may result.

The agreement, when made, is more likely to benefit both parties; this is important in any long-term relationship.

7.5 Competitive Bidding

The concept of competitive bidding incorporates the basic principle that price differences will occur when more than one supplier quotes a price on a similar product. The purchaser can, then, accept the lowest quoted price which will result in cost savings to the food and beverage operation.

Competitive bidding will help assure the food and beverage purchaser of the lowest price when:

The order is large enough to justify the time and expense that is involved;
Specifications are clearly known by all suppliers;
There are several suppliers desiring to quote prices on the order.

Competitive bidding can be done in two ways: through formal and informal processes.

7.5.1 Informal Process

This method is, in effect, done when one "calls around" for prices. (Note the quotation-call system and other techniques for selecting suppliers for specific orders in Section 8.12). When this process is used some informal negotiation (Section 7.4) might also be possible. Thus, for example, when prices are being obtained from suppliers, the process might be preceded with an attempt to secure a lowered price quotation before the price is given to the buyer.

Basic principles in an informal bid purchasing system include:

The quoted price and other terms of the agreement must be clearly understood; a purchase decision will be made on the basis of the understanding between the buyer and seller at the time of the price quotation.
It is important that the price quoted by the supplier remain "firm" for the length of time needed by the purchaser to make an order decision.
It is important that all suppliers quote a price on the same quality product and otherwise agree to comply with the same terms of the order.
All eligible suppliers should be allowed to quote on the order.
Purchases should be distributed between suppliers whenever possible in order to keep several supply sources interested in dealing with the food and beverage operation.
A purchase order, return telephone call, or other procedure is necessary in order to confirm the agreed price and other terms under which the order will be placed.

7.5.2 Formal Process

A formal process of competitive bidding is rarely, if ever, used by small food and beverage operations. It is more likely to be used by large, operations. This process involves use of sealed bids submitted by suppliers who are invited to bid prices on a detailed, written prospective order. Bid bonds may be required.

Most food and beverage operations will improve their purchasing success by utilizing an informal, rather than formal, competitive bidding process.

7.6 Payment Policies

Prices paid for products purchased can be affected by the method of payment. Likewise, payment procedures must be of concern to the purchaser even though these decisions are made by top management.

7.6.1 General Principles

Basic principles can guide the design of an effective payment policy.

Bills should be paid when due; it is not to the advantage of the food and beverage operation to pay bills before they are due.

Suppliers do not like to deal with "slow payers." Thus, any bargaining or negotiating advantage is lost when the food and beverage operation has the reputation of paying bills late.

If there is a discount for prompt payment the operation should take it if cash flow permits. (If there is not a discount offered, bills should be paid when due.)

Payment terms should be negotiated *after* the price is agreed on (so that discounts aren't added to the price before it is quoted).

If there is a problem paying a bill the purchaser should discuss it with the supplier. Don't try to hide it or make excuses. Most suppliers are willing to work out payment terms with food and beverage operators who are honest and professional in their dealings with suppliers.

Generally, bills should be paid by check. This helps provide an "audit trail" of purchases from the time the order is placed (or before in the case of request for price quotations) until it is paid. Likewise, internal security (theft) problems are minimized when cash is not routinely used for payment of purchases.

There may, however, be times when cash payments are in order.

7.6.2 Petty Cash Funds*

It is often wise to set up a petty cash system for payment of small purchases.

It has been already indicated that, *with few exceptions,* checks should be written to pay for all incurred expenses. Checks are easier to control, expenses are easier to categorize for accounting purposes, and audit trails are more available (since sales are deposited intact as opposed to paying bills out of the cash register and depositing only the remaining funds). There are, however, some minor expenses which can best be paid by cash. Examples might include "emergency" food

---

*Section 7.6.2 is adapted from J. Ninemeier, Food and Beverage Security: A Systems Manual for Restaurants, Hotels, and Clubs (Boston, Mass.: CBI Publishing Co., 1982).

supplies from a local grocery store, payment of parcel post charges, and purchase of miscellaneous small hardware supplies. These minor expenses can frequently be best administered through use of a petty cash fund. Petty cash funds can be misused, so security controls are necessary.

7.6.2.1 Security of petty cash funds   Security precautions include:

The petty cash fund should be set up on an imprest (cash advance) system.

With this plan, an amount (for example, the value of petty cash purchases for a two- or four-week period) is established. A check charged to "petty cash" is written. At any point in time the actual value of the petty cash fund (cash and vouchers invoices) should be equal to the original amount of money allocated to petty cash. The fund will thus contain cash and petty cash vouchers for all purchases. When the petty cash fund must be replenished a check is again written to "petty cash" and is equal to the value of vouchers in the fund. This check, converted to cash, will restore the fund to its original value. A sample of a petty cash voucher is found in Figure 7.1. A blank copy which can be reproduced and instructions for completing the form are located in Section 22.2.

Definite policies should be set in terms of items which can be purchased, frequency of purchases, and maximum dollar value of transactions from petty cash funds.

The responsibility for keeping the petty cash fund secure and authorizing its use should be vested in one person.

No item should be purchased without the approval of the management official charged with responsibility for the fund.

All purchases must be supported with receipts; if a notation is needed to identify the product(s) purchased, it should be written on the receipt. The receipt should be attached to the applicable petty cash voucher.

The petty cash fund should be kept secure at all times; money should not remain in an unlocked, easy access area.

Petty cash funds should not be mixed up with cash register or cash bank funds.

If necessary, a statement should be signed by the employee receiving cash from the fund to make a purchase in order to assure agreement about the amount of money for which he or she is responsible (cash plus sales receipt).

Unless the employee responsible for the petty cash fund is the owner or manager, the fund custodian should not be permitted to write the check used to replenish the fund.

The check to replenish the fund should be made out to "petty cash" rather than to "cash" or to the employee responsible for the fund.

FIGURE 7.1 Petty Cash Voucher

```
Date:  8/1/—              No.  3072

Amount:  2.15

Purpose:  purchase special light
          bulb for emergency exit sign.


Authorized by:  CDB



                  Attach receipt
```

7.6.2.2 Other procedures.   Other concerns in use of a petty cash system include:

There should be no long-term, unauthorized borrowing from the petty cash fund. It is generally not a good practice to permit any cash advances to employees to originate from this fund.

When the fund must be reimbursed to its approved level all receipts should be examined to assure their legitimacy.

Petty cash funds should be "spot checked" to assure that funds remain intact at all times. The spot check should reveal that the total amount in the fund (cash and vouchers) is equal to the authorized amount of the fund.

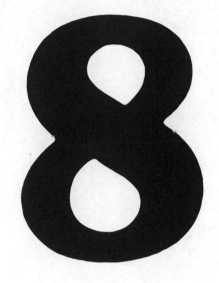

SUPPLIER SELECTION PROCEDURES

It will do little good for hotel, restaurant, or club managers to develop detailed purchase specifications, calculate systematically the quantity of food to purchase, and otherwise design and implement a professional procurement system if competent suppliers cannot be found.

This section presents background information and specific factors that should be considered as suppliers are determined "eligible" to do business with the facility and as their performance is subsequently evaluated.

8.1 Importance of Proper Supplier Selection

Experienced foodservice managers realize that not every supplier who carries the product should be permitted to do business with the operation. They realize that quality, price, service, dependability, and other concerns require that careful thought be given to selecting the best sources of supply.

As potential suppliers are considered, decisions are being made that will very quickly determine whether food and beverage operating goals are attained. Considerably more attention to supplier selection is needed than to just "buy from the guy we always use" or to "call around for the best price."

It is important to select the best possible suppliers because the foodservice operator needs to

Purchase products at a fair price (from the perspective of both the foodservice operator and the supplier).

Consistently obtain the quality and quantity of product desired.

Receive ordered products on a timely basis.

Develop a relationship with suppliers that will maximize the amount of information and other assistance which the supplier can provide.

In general, be able to work with the supplier as day-to-day business transactions occur.

Further, in larger businesses which have a separate purchasing department supplier selection is important for an additional reason. When the purchasing department selects suppliers with resulting "supply" problems, interdepartmental friction, morale problems, and lack of cooperation can occur; the user department blames (often rightfully) the purchasing department for problems which occur in the provision of necessary products.

It is also interesting to note that the external contacts which buyers have with suppliers can affect the good will which the foodservice operation enjoys in the community. Its image is affected by all outside company relationships, including those with its suppliers. Therefore, even the way in which a supplier is informed that he or she is or is not on the eligible supplier's list or will or will not receive an order can influence the foodservice operation's reputation.

These elements should reinforce the fact that supplier selection decisions are very important to the foodservice manager. There are some basic procedures that should be followed to help assure that "good" suppliers are chosen to furnish products and services to the foodservice operation.

8.2   Definition of a "Good" Supplier

The foodservice manager will, when possible, want to deal with "good" suppliers. Therefore the selection decision will be in large measure based upon the individual perception of what a "good" supplier is.

The following list of characteristics might be included in the description of a good supplier. The supplier will:

Be honest and fair as he or she does business with the foodservice operation.

Know the product, the market, and the needs of the foodservice operation.

Consistently be able to meet quality and quantity needs for products on a timely basis.

Operate with and be able to maintain a sound financial position.

Offer fair, reasonable prices.

Desire to continue to improve products and services.

Offer services which the foodservice operation believes to be important.

Be accessible. It will be easy to contact him or her about problems, to negotiate any concerns, etc.

Be careful. The supplier will take care in delivery of products and in after delivery followup.

Both foodservice managers and suppliers should realize that their own interests are best served when they work together to develop a cooperative relationship; for the foodservice management to insist on something which will hurt the supplier or for the reverse to occur obviously cannot be good for the relationship.

Even price conscious foodservice officials must understand that it is more than offering the cheapest price which makes a supplier "good." The product purchased at a low price which does not arrive when it is needed or the supplier in a "shaky" financial position with its own suppliers cannot be helpful to the foodservice operation.

8.3   Source of Information about Suppliers

In order to select a supplier, it is first necessary to identify those who are available to provide the needed products and services. One approach to supplier selection, then, is first, to identify potential suppliers, and, second, to select from this preliminary list suppliers who are "eligible" to do business with the foodservice operation. This section presents techniques which can be used to identify possible sources of supply. Section 8.4 will then present factors that might be utilized to determine which of the identified suppliers will be most useful to the foodservice operation.

The need to identify as many sources of supply as possible is very important. Foodservice operators who are currently in business obviously know some suppliers who can provide necessary products and services. However, they may not be aware of all, or even the best, sources of supply. Foodservice officials currently planning new facilities must learn about possible suppliers. Techniques which can be used to identify possible sources of supply follow.

8.3.1 Consider Past Experience

The experiences that foodservice officials have had with suppliers who are currently used (or not used) are probably among the most available and popular methods used to identify eligible suppliers. If a supplier has been acceptable in the past, it is likely that the relationship will continue. The reverse may also be true: unless significant changes occur within a supplier's operation (such as new management) there is little reason for a foodservice manager to believe that past unsatisfactory relationships will be changed.

8.3.2 Ask Salespeople

Good salespersons know who their competition is. Many also have at least some familiarity with other suppliers with whom they do not directly compete. It would not be unethical, for example, to ask a seafood supplier representative about "any good produce companies you have come across."

8.3.3 Supplier Catalogs

Catalogs are frequently provided by, for example, foodservice equipment dealers, paper and disposable goods companies, grocery (especially "one-stop") shopping outlets—see Section 8.10—and others. These printed materials will indicate what types of products are available from the supplier and may also provide important general information about the supplier.

8.3.4 Trade Journals and Papers

The many advertisements in hospitality industry trade publications can be very good sources of information about "who carries what," and the printed material received in response to the ads can provide additional useful information about suppliers.

8.3.5 Yellow Pages

The local telephone directory should not be overlooked as a very handy, helpful source of supplier information.

8.3.6 A File of Mailing Brochures

If foodservice officials have maintained a file of mail advertisements on a by product basis, this can likewise help to identify possible suppliers of selected products.

8.3.7 Trade Shows

Exhibits manned by representatives attending various local, state, and national shows are additional sources of supplier information. Foodservice officials who attend these shows and talk with exhibitors about their products can frequently determine whether a supplier and his or her products can be useful.

8.3.8 Talk to Your Competition

Foodservice officials can talk with their competitors at trade shows and professional meetings (or even by calling them!) about their experiences with suppliers and for ideas about new sources of supply.

8.3.9 Other Sources of Information

Foodservice managers can learn about possible suppliers through other sources. These include:

Employees of the foodservice operation itself.
Buyer's guides (frequently published in popular trade journals).
Professional industry associations.
Directives furnished by Chambers of Commerce.
Sales literature distributed by suppliers.

8.4 Factors to Consider in Supplier Selection

After possible suppliers have been identified, foodservice officials must evaluate them according to specific, selected factors. This is done in order to select from the preliminary list the suppliers who, in the judgment of foodservice management, can be most helpful to the foodservice operation.

Generally, at this point the process of supplier evaluation must involve an analysis of each supplier's ability to consistently provide necessary products and services at the desired quality, price, and quantity. In the context of Section 8.2, foodservice management must determine who the good suppliers will be. There are a number of factors which should help management with these decisions.

8.4.1 Location of Supplier

A close location shortens delivery time and transportation costs and reduces the possibility of accidents and other problems that cause delays.

8.4.2 Visit to Supplier's Facility

This trip can help a foodservice manager assess sanitation levels (important when food and beverage products are being purchased), procedures used to process orders, variety and quantity of items in current stock, morale levels, expertise of employees, etc.

8.4.3 Financial Stability

A good supplier does not go out of business, nor does he or she have difficulty obtaining products from suppliers because of poor credit management. The Dun and Bradstreet credit service provides, at little cost, valuable information which indicates the financial soundness of potential suppliers.

8.4.4 Technical Ability of Supplier's Staff

Good salespersons are more than just people who take orders. They will *know* their products and should be able to tell foodservice officials whether the products will or will not meet their needs.* They should be on the alert for ways that current products might be adopted for use by the foodservice facility and for new products that may interest the foodservice operation.

8.4.5 Reasonable Prices

The supplier can only offer reasonable prices if he (or she) knows all of the costs, operates efficiently, and is satisfied with a fair (rather than exorbitant) profit. Foodservice buyers can issue a request for price quotation with accompanying specifications (see Section 5) to assess the current prices charged by the supplier. This should be done as foodservice officials seriously consider several suppliers. However:

Foodservice managers should not play one supplier's price against another's (as occurs when a foodservice official says "Joe will sell me the product for $1.35 per pound; what is your price?").

Foodservice managers should be aware that some suppliers will quote low prices initially to obtain new business; then they will gradually increase prices as the foodservice operation gets comfortable with them.

In order to do this it is obviously necessary for foodservice management to provide a clear needs description to salespersons.

Some suppliers will quote a low price with the intent of providing a product of lower quality than that required by the specification.

A low price for a product may be offset by lessened service (such as shorter time allowed for payment or less consistency in meeting delivery schedules). Section 7 provides detailed information relating to price concerns.

8.4.6 Compatible Attitudes

Mutual working relationships between the foodservice operator and the supplier are enhanced if their business attitudes are compatible. Does the supplier encourage the foodservice manager to cheat or deceive the public? Are attitudes toward ethics (discussed in Section 12) agreeable? To a large extent, buyer and seller must be able to think alike.

8.4.7 Honesty and Fairness

It is easy and obvious to say that a "good" supplier will be honest and fair. It is much more difficult to determine that, in fact, a supplier does have these traits. Every foodservice manager should understand that these characteristics cannot be assumed; they must be *seen* in the business practices of the supplier.

8.4.8 Reciprocal Purchasing

Reciprocity occurs when suppliers are, in part, chosen because they are also customers of the foodservice facility. For example, a supplier might do extensive entertaining of other customers or may have employee parties at a restaurant or country club where he sells products.

Top management must set policy regarding use of reciprocity as the sole determinant in supplier selection. While this practice may not effectively reduce costs (and hence not increase profits) it might be assumed that, *when all other things are equal*, it may make good business sense to buy from a supplier who is also a customer.

Seldom, however, are all things equal. This is why decisions about reciprocal purchasing must be made by high-level management. These officials are the only personnel in a position to assess whether the practice will lead to increased profits that might generally be the basis upon which this decision *should* be made. An objective analysis is not difficult. For example: (a) If the foodservice operation generates a 10 percent profit on sales; and, (b) If a supplier spends $500 a month in the foodservice operation, then the facility realizes a $50 monthly profit from the supplier ($500 × 10% = $50). If the cost to purchase products from the supplier-customer are more than $50 higher than from a competitor supplying a similar quality product, the reciprocal arrangement cannot be justified on a profit increase basis alone.

8.4.9 Local Purchasing

Many foodservice officials desire to purchase from local sources when possible. This relates to a good will, community relations concern. Advantages include:

Close locations of buyer and seller may provide greater degrees of cooperation.

Delivery problems are lessened; lead times for order placement can be decreased; emergency, rush orders are more likely to be filled.

Community relations are enhanced.

Possible disadvantages can include:

Prices may be higher since local companies may not be able to purchase in large quantities with resulting discounts.

Local suppliers may not have the degree of technical expertise of larger, state or nationwide companies.

8.4.10 Conclusion: Selection Factors

The foodservice buyer essentially wants four things from a supplier.

Prompt delivery

Adequate quality

Reasonable prices

Service

These are the primary concerns that influence the supplier selection decision. Foodservice officials must attempt to determine the factors which are most helpful to anticipate these four qualities in prospective suppliers. These concerns and factors become important not only when suppliers are selected, but also when chosen suppliers are evaluated (Section 8.11). Thus supplier selection becomes a cyclical process; the experience which a buyer has with a chosen supplier affects the desire to continue in the buyer-seller relationship. This concept is explored in greater detail in Section 8.5.

8.5 Supplier Selection and Past Experience

The importance of a buyer's experience with a supplier was briefly noted in Section 8.3.1. It is not practical, or even desirable, to develop a comprehensive, preliminary list of possible suppliers over and over again. Once the list is developed, and after eligible suppliers are selected, the business relationship begins. The importance of selecting the best possible supplier(s) has already been noted (Section 8.1). The objective of the selection process must be both:

To find the best possible source of necessary products and services; and,

To be able to use the sources for future purchases of the same products and services.

Several points must be considered as experiences with suppliers are reviewed:

The real test of supplier selection involves not the *process* but the actual experience that foodservice managers have with the supplier.

Buyers should be careful to avoid getting too comfortable with a supplier. This occurs when, for example, a foodservice official thinks that "we've always done business with Joe; there's no need to check his prices" (or the quality of his products).

Buyers should have several possible suppliers for each product they purchase whenever possible; each should be contacted for price and quality decisions and proposals of each should be reviewed before purchase decisions are made.

When there are supplier problems, judgment should assure that there are not factors within the foodservice operation which contribute to them. Should suppliers be blamed when rush orders do not always arrive on schedule (why must frequent "emergency" orders be placed?) or when there is a "communication problem" which might, in part, be caused by a foodservice official?

Most suppliers recognize that effective, professional foodservice operators are constantly checking quality and prices, reviewing supplier performance, etc. Foodservice managers should take on these tasks as important, ongoing parts of their jobs.

Buyers must realize that ongoing relationships between buyers and suppliers can only be maintained when both parties gain from the relationship.

Ethical considerations (see Section 12) greatly influence the type of experiences that buyers have with suppliers.

Most suppliers are concerned about their reputation. Their reputation is, of course, a function of the individual experiences that they have had with all of their other customers. It is quite possible that other foodservice groups have had similar good or bad experiences with a supplier. This point emphasizes the usefulness of asking other foodservice officials about possible suppliers.

8.6 Supplier Selection for One-Time or Major Purchases

Special concerns and precautions are important when a one-time and/or major purchase is being made. There is a great deal of difference in the process used, for example, to purchase one case of green beans versus a $25,000 dishwashing unit. Many of these are reviewed in Section 17. Several special concerns, however, relate directly to the supplier selection process.

Among the most important considerations in selecting a supplier for a major expense item are:

Supplier's reliability. This is an expression of several things. The supplier
> will be there when needed,
>
> will do what he says he will do,
>
> has a proven reputation of honesty and fairness.

Supplier's cooperation. The supplier should both provide necessary technical assistance (type and placement of equipment, suggestions regarding usefulness of options for the equipment, etc.) and help with before- and after-purchase transaction details.

Competitive prices. If the foodservice buyer specifies name brand and standard stock equipment (rather than customized items built specifically for the individual facility) reputable suppliers should be able to quote reasonable, competitive prices.

Repair service. The supplier must be able to repair what he or she sells; alternatively, arrangements with a local service company are necessary. The concept of acceptable service implies technically competent service people, availability of parts, and the service aspect of timely assistance.

Acceptable prior experiences. Past, positive experiences with a supplier are a definite ''plus'' in the supplier selection decision for a one-time or major purchase.

While it is true with the purchase of all foodservice products and services, it is extremely important that much more than just the lowest price be considered as the basis for supplier selection decisions for buying major items.

8.7 Factors Limiting Supplier Selection

There are times when it is not practical to identify and evaluate possible suppliers through the use of techniques described in Sections 8.3 and 8.4 of this handbook. This selection will identify some of these situations.

8.7.1 Small Volume Purchases

Management must spend its limited time on the matters most important to attaining foodservice goals. When items are purchased in small quantities at small costs, detailed procedures to identify and select suppliers cannot be justified. Few foodservice managers could justify extensive study leading to selection of suppliers of toothpicks or swizzle sticks, for example.

8.7.2 Exclusive Sales Territories

If an operator wants a certain brand of a canned item, liquor, or foodservice equipment, for example, it may be that only one supplier will carry the required items. This is why buying by brand is a limiting factor (for supplier, price, and availability reasons).

8.7.3 Personal Friendship

Although friendship (or kinship!) should not affect supplier selection decisions, it obviously might. It is much better for purchase and supplier selection decisions to be made on the basis of the best interests of the company rather than because of friendship. As with reciprocal purchasing (see Section 8.7.4) company policies determined by top management are necessary.

8.7.4 Reciprocal and Local Purchasing

Requirements that purchasing be done on a reciprocal or local basis limit the supplier selection decision. Refer to Sections 8.4.8 and 8.4.9 for information about these concerns.

8.7.5 Personality Conflicts

The human element of personality can often affect or limit supplier selection decisions. While it is difficult to do business with someone you don't like, this may well be what is best for the foodservice operation. Being objective and nonbiased is the best way to get the job done.

8.7.6 Large Quantity Purchases

Foodservice buyers needing large quantities of product may not be able to purchase from small suppliers without storage, capital, or other requirements necessary for handling large orders. Buyers who are reviewing identified suppliers must be assured that any large quantity needs can be handled.

8.7.7 Type of Supplier

There may be times when a foodservice manager can buy directly from the manufacturer rather than through a distributor-supplier. If this alternative exists, the foodservice buyer must consider possible cost savings against advantages of good will from local buying and the need to purchase other items from a distributor-supplier.

8.8 Special Concerns in Dealing with New Suppliers

Factors to consider as relationships are established with new suppliers are not very different from those used to evaluate the worth of current or known suppliers as selection decisions are made. Essentially, the foodservice buyer will do well to assure that:

There will be no surprises. Buyers should talk with foodservice officials in other properties to learn something about the new supplier.

The supplier currently sells items similar to those to be purchased (ask the supplier *what* he or she sells and to whom).

Dependable transportation methods will be used to transport items from the supplier's site to the buyer's place of business.

The supplier enjoys stable labor relations. If a supplier has a history of union troubles, it may well be that such trouble, which obviously will affect the buyer, will continue. The reverse is also true; an absence of such labor difficulties is a clue that problems are less likely to develop.

Proposed purchase and sale transactions are in the long-term best interests of the supplier. A supplier may make short-run "deals" to sell overstocks, discontinued products, etc. But the buyer who is interested in a long-term relationship with the supplier would do well to ask "if I were the supplier and concerned about long-run best interests, would I make the deal?" If the answer is "no," the buyer should be suspicious.

8.9 Single and Multiple Sources of Supply

Wise purchasers know that there is a general need to have more than one source of supply for each required item. The advantage to this plan primarily concerns the need to constantly check on price and quality differences between suppliers.

There may be cases where the quality of a product may be vastly superior to competitor's suppliers (fresh meat or produce may be an example) and, therefore, foodservice buyers believe it is best to utilize a single supply source.

There may be other selected advantages to use of a single supply source.

It is not feasible to check on the price and quality of inexpensive or infrequently used items.

There may be greater assurance of supply during times of shortage.
Suppliers may give priority to selling items to their best customers.

Service, price, and other considerations *may* accrue to the buyer who is a regular customer of the supplier.

Generally, however, the advantages to use of multiple supply sources are greater. They include:

There is greater assurance that products at the best prices and at proper quality are being purchased.

There are fewer delivery interruptions; if one supplier is out of stock of a product, there is some likelihood that another supplier will have the necessary product available.

Buyers can benefit from the technical expertise of each supplier with whom business is done.

8.10 One-Stop Shopping—A Special Note

The concept of one-stop shopping—in which a supplier adds an increasing variety of products to available lines—is growing more popular. For example, a canned goods or grocery supplier may begin to offer common varieties of fresh produce, popular frozen meats and, perhaps, small equipment items. The buyer, it is suggested, can benefit from reduced paperwork, lessened time spent in purchasing tasks, and other possible advantages cited to use of single supply sources noted in 8.9.

Disadvantages to use of one-stop shopping were likewise noted in Section 8.9. Suppliers who sell popular items at a competitive price may need to sell other products at a higher markup. Therefore, if many items are purchased from one supplier, there is a greater likelihood that some of these unattractively priced items will be purchased as well.

Within reason, then, the objectives of purchasing may be best met by purchasing fairly marked up items from each supplier without spending more than can be saved by use of multiple suppliers. Smaller foodservice operations which can save time through use of one-stop suppliers perhaps have the most to gain. This is especially so if the time saved is spent on other important areas of foodservice management.

8.11 Evaluation of Suppliers

Should a foodservice operation continue to deal with a supplier? That question is best answered when an objective system is used to evaluate the supplier's performance.

8.11.1 The Process of Evaluation

The buyer must decide what is desired from a supplier. This decision is then used both to select and, subsequently, to evaluate a supplier. Generally, a buyer desires:

Adequate quality. This may be evaluated by noting the number of times deliveries are rejected because quality specifications are not met. Likewise, storage and/or processing problems relating to inferior quality products can be observed.*

Delivery performance. Late deliveries can be noted. (Excessively early deliveries are also of concern since payment will be due earlier than planned and inventory costs will be higher). Foodservice officials might identify two types of late deliveries:

Those in which expediting resolved the matter.

Those which resulted in stockout problems.

The latter problems are much more serious and may well require changing suppliers.

Reasonable prices. Foodservice officials can judge the fairness of prices by reviewing prices for similar quality products quoted by other suppliers.

Service factors. The quality of service provided (technical assistance, followup on problem orders, payment requirements, etc.) must be subjectively evaluated by the foodservice buyer. Perhaps this is most easily (but not necessarily most accurately) done by comparing the experiences a buyer has with a supplier with his or her relationship with other suppliers (even if different products are involved). Each supplier, for example, should be able to provide expert technical assistance regarding his product, should quickly follow up on problems, should offer acceptable payment plans, etc. In other words, the question arises: "Does it appear through his actions that the supplier desires or appreciates my business?"

Food and beverage buyers should routinely evaluate the performance of all suppliers with whom they do business. The evaluation should consider the same factors as each supplier's performance is assessed. A supplier performance rating sheet is found in Section 22.4. Instructions for its use can provide consistency and help in the task of evaluating supplier performance.

8.11.2 Supplier Lists Do Not Change Frequently

Foodservice officials should remain alert to the possible need to change eligible suppliers. In many instances the list of eligible suppliers may remain

---

*It should be noted, however, that products not meeting quality standards should be rejected at delivery and should never be put in inventory. See Section 20.3.

almost constant (with the only changes occurring as supplier businesses change hands or products requiring selected suppliers are added to or deleted from the foodservice menu). Occasionally, however, there may be a need to reconsider eligible suppliers. This is best accomplished by a formal process of supplier evaluation done, for example, on a semi-annual or annual basis (rather than just when "we're having trouble" with a supplier).

8.12   Supplier Selection for Specific Orders

Procedures reviewed in this section thus far have concerned selecting suppliers generally "eligible" to supply products to the food and beverage operation. When possible, there should be several suppliers qualified to provide each type of needed product to the foodservice facility. This section, then, concerns procedures used to determine which and when eligible suppliers should be selected for specific orders.

8.12.1   Background

After purchase specifications are developed (Section 5) which describe quality requirements of products to be purchased, copies should be distributed. They should be sent to all suppliers who are determined to be eligible through the process described in Sections 8.1–8.7.

> This quality description should be used as the basis for any price quotation given in response to a purchase order from the food and beverage purchaser. For example, while the purchase order may specify only "applesauce," suppliers will know in advance of the order the quality of applesauce required; it will be spelled out in the purchase specifications which the supplier has received.

> Generally, routine schedules are developed for assembling information and analyzing and placing orders. For example, perishable products may be ordered on Monday for Tuesday delivery, and on Thursday for Friday delivery. Grocery items may be ordered twice monthly (midweek) for delivery on Monday of the following week.

> Large operations may have some flexibility in setting up order and delivery schedules which best suit their needs.

> Small foodservice operations must frequently accept the order and delivery schedules of their eligible suppliers (although the definition of "eligibility" may be affected by inconvenient timing of these requirements).

8.12.2 Contact with Supplier

After the quantity of products to be ordered is known (see Section 6), contact must be made with all eligible suppliers. This may be done in two ways:

Informally—Purchasers in small operations may call in for order information, meet with suppliers' representatives in their weekly or other visits to the facility, or use standing orders (this is generally not a good practice; see Section 6.5.9).

Semi-formally—Some food and beverage operations use a quotation-call system to determine supplier prices. With this system type and quantity of products to be ordered are determined and eligible suppliers are called to obtain prices. Prices quoted are recorded on the quotation-call sheet and subsequent analysis determines the supplier with the lowest price (by item or total for the entire order), who then receives the order.

Figure 8.1 shows a sample of a quotation-call sheet. A blank copy which can be reproduced and instructions for completing the form are found in Section 22.24.

Formally—Large food and beverage operations may use a formal request for price quotation form to obtain information about suppliers' prices. A sample copy of a request for price quotation is found in Figure 8.2. A blank copy which can be reproduced and instructions for completing the form are found in Section 22.23.

8.12.3 Consideration of Price

With quality held constant (dictated by the purchase specification provided to eligible suppliers), price *relative to quality* (value) becomes very important. The concepts of price and value are considered in Section 7.3.

8.12.4 Consideration of Other Factors

Price and quality concerns are not the only factors that indicate which supplier should be awarded an order. Other factors include:

Knowledge about late deliveries, substitution of lower quality items, excessive back orders, etc., give the supplier a bad reputation and may affect the buyer's desire to award the order. These practices should also affect the buyer's consideration of the supplier as an "eligible" source of supply; perhaps price quotations should not even be solicited from suppliers with poor reputations.

Payment policies, extension of credit, billing cycles, and other economic concerns may affect the purchase decision.

FIGURE 8.1 Quotation-Call Sheet

Date: 4/17/—

Needed Product	Amt.	Supplier			
		Jones Co.	ABC Supply	Oand G Pro	Smith Co.
Lettuce, Iceberg	1 co.	17.50	17.00	17.40	18.10
Spinach	1 co.	21.80	22.00	21.50	21.50
Cucumbers	20#	7.85	9.10	7.95	8.15
Carrots	35 #	12.10	12.10	13.50	12.00
TOTAL:		215.80	205.40	222.55	224.60

FIGURE 8.2   Request for Price Quotation

Date __4/17/–__   Request Number __10 71–10__

To

Adams Meats	
1410 Elm Street	
Anytown, LA 70001	

(supplier/address)

Please quote your price and delivery on the following products. Return to this office by _____

__4/22/–__

Product Description	Quantity			Price	
	Unit	Total		Per Unit	Total
Ground Beef (IMPS 136)	10#	17			
Rib, Bone in (MBG #110 712)	#	170			
Bottom Sirloin Butt (MBG #118612)	#	85			

Date of Delivery __4/24/–__   Request by

Price Valid for _____   _Jones Family Rest._
                (number of days)   (company)

Signed _____   _1382 Sunny Rd._

                (supplier)   _Anytown, LA_

_____   _70001_
                (address)   (address)

_____   _J. Jones_
        (authorized signature)   (authorized signature)

The supplier who provides high quality technical help to the buyer may be given an order even if his or her price "is a little high."

Suppliers who help out with emergency, rush, and small orders might be given some priority as proposals are analyzed.

8.12.5   Order Acceptance Procedures

After considering price and factors discussed in Section 8.12.4, the decision to order from a supplier is made. The order acceptance procedure can be:

Informal—Small operations may merely call the supplier or tell the supplier's representative during a visit that the order has been accepted. Even when this approach is utilized, it is important for the purchaser to have an internal record of what was ordered. Information can be posted to a purchase record (see Section 22.21). This form serves at least three purposes.

It "reminds" buyers about price and other agreements made with suppliers.

It is used at time of product receiving (see Section 20.3).

It is used as a source document in the accounting process (see Section 9).

Formal—Purchasers in large food and beverage operations may use a formal purchase order to indicate products, quantities, and other information about products to be ordered. A purchase order serves the same three purposes as a purchase record (see immediately above). A sample copy of a purchase order form is found in Figure 8.3. A blank copy which can be reproduced and instructions for completing the form are found in Section 22.6.

8.12.6   Order Followup Procedures (Expediting)

Purchasing personnel should take responsibility for orders from the time they have been placed until they are received. The followup process is referred to as expediting. Followup is often necessary:

When deliveries are not made as scheduled.

When there are problems (such as improper quality or quantity) with orders that are delivered.

When rush/emergency orders are made.

When orders are placed with new suppliers (the buyer has no experience with the supplier, and he or she does not want to take any chances).

When orders are placed with "problem" suppliers (as when there is no other source of supply).

If frequent followup is necessary with some suppliers these sources might be withdrawn from lists of eligible suppliers.

FIGURE 8.3 Purchase Order

Purchase Order Number ___10776___   Order Date ___8/1 -___

Payment Terms ___30 days___

To ___ABC Foods___   From/Ship to ___Ernie's Seafood Shop___
  (supplier)   (Name of foodservice)
___1600 Locust Street___   ___1365 Lakefront Drive___

___Anywhere, LA. 70127___   ___Anywhere, LA 70126___
  (address)   (address)
                                  Delivery Date ___8/8/-___

Please Ship

Quantity Ordered	Description	√	Units Shipped	Unit Cost	Total Cost
3 Cases	Applesauce (6 - #10)			18.50	55.50
5 Cases	Peaches (6 - #10)			22.65	113.25
2 - 50#	All-Purpose Flour			13.55	27.10
10 - 30# cans	XYZ Brand Deep Fry Fat			26.75	267.50

Total Cost ___$463.35___

IMPORTANT: This Purchase Order expressly limits acceptance to the terms and conditions stated above, noted on the reverse side hereof, and any additional terms and conditions affixed hereto or otherwise referenced. Any additional terms and conditions proposed by seller are objected to and rejected.

___Ernie J. Smith___
(authorized signature)

Procurement:
The Accounting
Perspective

The role of the accounting department deserves special attention since, of course, all goods ordered by the purchasing department must be paid for. Designing a system that makes the accounting function an integral part of the purchasing task is very important.

9.1   Introduction

In small food and beverage operations the owner and manager may be both the purchaser and the bill payer. As operations become larger, these tasks are split between operations and accounting (or bookkeeping and "office") personnel. As food and beverage operations grow bigger still, the purchasing responsibilities for receiving and/or storage may be assumed by the accounting department in an increased effort to separate duties. This result is desirable to reduce the possibilities of theft and fraud which are otherwise more feasible when one official is responsible for everything. Note that the procedures for receiving and storage (Sections 20 and 21) are identical regardless of which department—purchasing or accounting—has the responsibility for the tasks.

It is clear that, when possible, personnel who purchase products should not pay for them (unless that official is the owner). When a manager is hired by an owner for a small operation, a bookkeeper or other part-time employee with accounting, clerical, and bookkeeping duties should be considered.

This section concerns the role of the accounting department (or bookkeeper) in the purchasing process. The topic can best be explained first by reviewing the flow of documents leading to an order and a bill to be paid; and, second, by looking at the bill-paying process.

9.2   Purchasing Documents

Personnel with accounting or bookkeeping responsibilities generally pay the bills. To do this effectively they must work with a system which assures them at the time of payment that the items to be paid for were, in fact, ordered and received. Such procedures are discussed in this section according to the size of the business.

9.2.1   Small Food and Beverage Operations

In a small food and beverage operation the following procedures might be used to *prepare* bills for payment.

Quantities of products to be ordered are determined through a visual observation of what's available in storage and through study of perpetual inventory records.

Quantities, prices, etc., are entered on a purchase record form (Section 22.21) when the order is placed; a copy is sent to the employee(s) with receiving duties.

When the products are received, incoming items are accepted only if they have been noted on the purchase record form.

Incoming products are compared against the accompanying supplier delivery invoice which is signed *only* if it agrees with the purchase record (and if product quality meets requirements of the purchase specifications).

At the end of the day or shift the purchase record forms and delivery invoices are forwarded to the manager or bookkeeper. If an absentee owner hires a manager, it is preferable for these two documents to be sent directly to the bookkeeper. If this is not practical then the system should be amended so that the supplier sends a duplicate copy of the delivery invoice directly to the bookkeeper.

The bookkeeper has several tasks to perform. He or she must:

Assure that there are no differences in quantity and/or price between items ordered (purchase record) and received (delivery invoice).

Assure that arithmetic extensions on the delivery invoice are correct. (The special process of handling credit memos is noted in Section 9.3.)

File the invoice with the purchase record attached for payment.

Pull the invoice or statement at the appropriate time and ready it for payment. These steps are detailed in Sections 9.5 and 9.6.

9.2.2 Large Food and Beverage Operations

Procedures are modified by larger commercial operations:

The purchase requisition (Section 22.3) may be used by storeroom personnel to indicate when additional products must be purchased.

Request for price quotations (Section 22.23) and purchase orders (Section 22.6) may be utilized to order products formally. A copy of the purchase order is sent to the receiving and accounting departments.

When products are accepted, the receiving clerk must assemble the purchase order and delivery invoice. Additionally, a receiving clerk's daily report (Sections 22.7 and 22.8) is completed.

Each of these forms, completed for each order received, is forwarded to the accounting personnel.

The accounting-bookkeeping staff perform the same basic functions as listed for the personnel in Section 9.2.1. One additional duty is the need to match up the documents with the receiving report.

9.3 The Credit Memo Process

When a problem is noted at the time of delivery, a formal correction must be made on a credit memo. Examples of these problems include:

Wrong price charged.

Back order—product not delivered or sent in smaller than required quantity.

Items rejected—unacceptable quality.

Short weight or count.

In these and similar instances a credit memo is required to adjust the delivery invoice to reflect the actual amount of the bill. Often the delivery person has a form to be used for this purpose; otherwise it can be supplied by the food and beverage operation. A sample copy is found in Figure 9.1. A blank copy which can be reproduced and instructions for completing the form are found in Section 22.22.

Essentially, the credit memo informs the supplier that the bill for the food and beverage operation must be adjusted (credited) downward to reflect the value of the products actually received.

Special concerns in processing of credit memos include:

The delivery person *must* sign and receive a copy of the form.

It is wise to call the supplier to confirm that no processing problems exist and that the credit will be reflected on the next current statement of the food and beverage operation.

When the invoice is processed and filed for payment the adjustment required by the credit memo must be made on the specific delivery invoice.

A system must be established to assure that the food and beverage operation does not pay bills until they have been adjusted by any applicable credit memos.

9.4 Methods of Payment

There are generally two methods used to pay suppliers for purchased products: by invoice or by statement.

With the "by-invoice" plan, processed invoices (approved for payment) are filed *by due date*, and they are paid when due. For example, if an approved bill is due on August 10, it may be "pulled" on August 6 and processed for payment (see Section 9.5). It might be signed and mailed on August 7 in order to allow adequate time for delivery.

Bills can also be paid on a "by-statement" basis. With this plan processed invoices (approved for payment) are filed, *by supplier*, awaiting receipt of a statement of account. When the statement is received applicable invoices are pulled and

FIGURE 9.1 Credit Memo

CREDIT MEMO   NUMBER _1070_

From _ABC Restaurant_   To _Acme Poultry and Seafood_
1501 Anywhere Street   (supplier)
Anytown, USA   _1500 Smith Ave._
                                            Anytown, USA

Credit should be given on the following:

Invoice number _7107_   Invoice date _3/18/—_

Product	Unit	Number	Price/Unit	Total Price
36/42 Shrimp	pound	20	4.15	83.00

Total _$83.00_

Reason: _Product waste to be frozen but_
was thawed on surface.

J. Jones   _B. Joyce_
(delivery person)   (authorizing signature)

(prepare in duplicate)

processed for payment (see Section 9.5), and all invoices covered by the statement (less adjustments, if any, required by credit memos) are paid at one time.

9.5 Preparing the Invoice/Statement for Payment

Regardless of whether bills are paid "by-invoice" or "by-statement," similar procedures are necessary to prepare the documents for payment.

Invoices must be matched with applicable in-house purchasing documents and with the delivery invoices. All such forms must be compared; the same items that were ordered must be received.

Any credit memo problems which require changes to the delivery invoice must be noted and adjustments made.

All arithmetic extensions must be verified.

Delivery invoices which have been properly processed are noted "approved to pay" by the bookkeeper.

Invoices are then filed until time for payment.

9.6 The Payment Process

When invoices are to be paid (either singularly or as part of several covered by a statement) order and delivery forms should again be checked in a manner similar to the steps above (Section 9.5).

The bookkeeper should total all invoices to be paid with one check and should then prepare the check for signing. Each invoice which is paid should be marked to indicate date of payment, amount of payment, and check number. Marking should be done in such a way that it is possible to verify that payment has been made. It is important to minimize the possibility of an invoice being paid twice.

9.7 Security Aspects of Cash Disbursements*

It is important to design procedures for cash disbursements which minimize the possibility for employee theft at the time bills are paid. The impact of an effective purchasing system is blunted if its benefits are neutralized by monetary losses when purchasing documents are processed for actual payment.

---

*Section 9.7 is adapted from J. Ninemeier, Food and Beverage Security: A Systems Manual for Restaurants, Hotels, and Clubs (Boston, Mass.: CBI Publishing Co., 1982).

Specific cash disbursement procedures should include the following items.

Payments (except for minor petty cash expenses; see Section 7.6.2) are always made by check. Payments are never made out of daily sales income *before* it has been deposited in the bank.

Unless both tasks are performed by the manager the processing of invoices and statements for payments and subsequent check-writing should be performed by two separate employees.

Persons who process sales income and/or prepare deposits are *not* involved in cash disbursement procedures.

Check protectors (to mechanically imprint the amount of checks) are used.

The person who signs the checks also mails them (they are *not* returned for mailing to the individual processing invoices for check-writing).

More than one signature by a management official might be required on checks in excess of a specified amount. No officer, management official, or other authorized check writer should be able to sign a check made payable to himself or herself.

Invoices and vouchers are *clearly* marked "paid" when checks are written. Invoices are filed, along with purchase record, purchase order, or other authorizing documents, by supplier name, for future reference.

Blank checks (for "emergency" or other use) are *never* signed. Checks are signed only after they are prepared.

A system to control spoiled, voided, or other unused checks is used; there is no way that such checks can be fraudulently converted by dishonest employees; they are mutilated to avoid reuse.

All checks are imprinted with the name of the property or business identity and are marked: "Void after 60 days." All checks are prenumbered by the printer.

Supplies of blank checks are kept securely locked. When check signing machines are utilized, signature plates are securely controlled when not in use. Also, the counting device on the machine (which shows the number of checks signed) should agree with the number of checks processed.

Banks are notified of all personnel who are authorized to write checks; copies of their signatures are on file and all authorizing documents have been completed.

All checks which are written are made payable to a person or company; no checks are made payable to "cash" or "to bearer." Management personnel routinely examine lists of checks to learn or to inquire about new suppliers and one-time transactions.

Unless checks are signed by the owner/manager, other signatories should not have access to petty cash funds and should not be in a position to approve cash disbursements and to record cash receipts.

A system is in use which makes it impossible for an invoice to be submitted two or more times for payment.

Interbank fund transfers (such as to charge the account for bank credit card discounts or to transfer funds into a payroll account) are promptly recorded.

Outstanding checks which are not returned or cashed promptly are followed up on and controlled.

Checks that have been paid by the bank should not be returned for further processing to an employee performing deposit tasks (if a check were made payable to himself or a false company it could be removed and cash receipts to cover the checks could be deposited).

All cancelled checks should be placed in sequential order. No checks should be missing; no check numbers should be altered. Checks should be used in number sequence, with no skipping or jumping ahead.

The name of the payee must be the same on the check, the check record, and on the invoice or monthly statement.

9.8 The Accounting Department and Capital Purchases

Normally, in the purchase of standard food, beverage, and supply items, accounting personnel are not aware of the purchase until after it has been received and purchasing documents are sent to accounting for processing and payment. This procedure may be modified in some operations which require a copy of the purchase order to be sent to purchasing when the order is placed.

The process involved in purchase of capital (large-expense) items must be modified from routine practices so that purchasing is notified about top management's approval of capital purchases *before* those items are ordered. This is necessary to permit purchasing staff to encumber (set aside) monies for a large-dollar purchase. Financial personnel also need to confirm for purchasing staff that funds are available in the department's budget for the amount authorized for the capital purchase.

9.9 Relationship between Purchasing and Accounting Departments

This section has identified the need for purchasing and accounting department staff to work closely together. A system must be designed to require:

Accounting personnel to have access to all available and related purchasing documents when bills are processed for payment.

Purchasing to know that budget funds are available for all purchases which will be made.

Credits on affected delivery invoices to be noted; payments for these invoices to be for the adjusted amounts only.

All of these tasks require effective communication and coordination between purchasing and accounting staff. Perhaps some of this interaction can be assisted by formal interdepartmental meetings or budget development sessions; however, it is just as important to assure that all daily and informal contacts between the two departments are cordial and cooperative. This might best be done by involving representatives from both departments in the design of procedures that affect them.

10

The Make or Buy Decision

The question of whether to "make or buy" generally relates to the use of convenience foods: products that have all or some of the labor necessary to prepare them built into the product at the time of purchase. The subject often creates an emotionally charged debate between those who favor or oppose their use.

The concept of make or buy might also refer to decisions about services: should managers use either contracted services or the operation's employees to perform necessary tasks within the food and beverage operation. (This topic is reserved for special treatment in Section 16.) Thus, this section will focus specifically on the use of convenience foods and products by the foodservice operation.

10.1 Make/Buy Decisions Are Difficult

Decisions regarding the usage of convenience foods are important and hard to make for several reasons.

Except for a few "traditional" items (such as frozen french fries, fresh baked bread products, and some canned grocery items) a great deal of subjective emotion often clouds the convenience foods issue, and, in the minds of many food and beverage operators the definition of convenience foods is not clear. In actuality, since few food and beverage operations have their own farms and sources to grow needed fresh food items, all of the meats, produce, processed fruits and vegetables, seafood, etc., are purchased in some convenience foods form; the labor necessary to raise the products is *not* provided on-site. Canned, dried, and frozen (processed) fruits and vegetables, portioned meats and seafoods, bakery and dairy products, etc., are all *really* convenience foods; in these "convenient" forms, they are used by almost every food and beverage operation.

Much of the "problem" of convenience foods stems from the concept and impression of "TV dinners," bulk frozen entrees, and some of the really terrible ready-to-serve baked desserts. What is needed is, first, an understanding that not *all* convenience foods are bad; many operations are presently making good use of convenience food items. Second, the decision to use convenience foods must be made on an individual product basis by considering what's best for the individual food and beverage operation.

Make/buy decisions are time-consuming to make if all of the factors which affect the decision are considered. Some elements—such as the energy costs to bake desserts—aren't known and are difficult to calculate. Others—such as quality and perceived guest reaction—are subjective and hard to measure. Ideally, both economic and noneconomic factors which affect the make/buy decision must be considered. Unfortunately, such a process is rarely completed.

In its broadest sense, a make/buy analysis can be done for almost every product sold by the food and beverage operation. This is obviously not possible or practical. Additionally, many operations with famous specialty products, equipment, and space limitations, etc., have, in effect, no decision to make regarding convenience food usage as an alternative for some products. They either must, or cannot, prepare these items on-site.

Communication and coordination difficulties between all parties affected by the decision also can make the decision difficult. Top management, marketing personnel, and employees of production, service, and purchasing departments are all involved in the decision-making process. In addition, past management decisions have established current operating patterns. This has three implications:

A precedent is established (personnel know that either "we have always" or "we have never" used the products before; "why change?").

The facility and equipment location are designed for the use of certain products and to prepare or serve selected items. This may pose physical limitations to proposed changes.

Operating procedures are set; changes in product usage will require changes in these procedures.

10.2   Decisions Are Not "All or Nothing"

Decisions about the use of convenience foods are not of the "all-or-nothing" type.

Few operations use either "all or no" convenience food items. Even "fast food" operations may require head lettuce for sandwiches; in fact, there is a trend toward salad bars (which require on-site processing of varied produce items) in some fast food chains.

The many types of convenience food products permit foodservice operations to add a little or extensive amounts of on-site labor. Consider one item: loaf bread. It is available:

Sliced, ready to serve;

Unsliced, ready to serve;

Frozen, proofed, ready to bake;

Frozen, unproofed, ready to proof;

In the form of flour, salt, yeast, shortening, etc. (the product must be totally prepared on-site).

According to the needs of the individual operation, more or less labor can be added to loaf bread on-site. The decision to "make or buy" loaf bread is not that simple; it must be modified to consider "how many preparation tasks should be done on-site, or should we purchase it completely made?"

10.3   Is a Make or Buy Study Necessary?

The decision-making process is affected by many factors which must be analyzed by the individual food and beverage operation. These include:

New product usage. As menus are redesigned and new items are added, managers will need to consider "make or buy" implications of new products. This concept applies to beverage operations as well. For example, a new specialty drink is added; should a processed mix be used or should ingredients be prepared at the bar?

Extensive revision of current products. The example above regarding menu changes also highlights this situation.

Problems with supplier performance. If, for example, suppliers cannot deliver convenience food products or raw ingredients, this may suggest a need to reexamine the form in which the product is being purchased.

Quality problems. If, for any reason, there is a problem with the existing quality of prepared or purchased products, a make/buy study may be in order.

Other situations which might indicate the need for careful study include:

Increasing or decreasing sales of specific products.

Suppliers who have specialized knowledge that food and beverage management officials can use in a study.

When items must be purchased in very large or very small volume.

When the facility has limited space and/or inadequate funds for capital purchases.

When there is a change in the quality of work or level of experience of current or prospective employees.

When there is concern about retaining a continuous source of supply.

10.4   General Overview of a Make/Buy Analysis

It is important for food and beverage management personnel to understand that the concerns basic to the purchase of any product apply to the purchase of convenience food products. Specifically:

Quality is important. If the required quality cannot be purchased in a convenience food product, no analysis is necessary; the product must be prepared on-site. If an acceptable quality product is available, analysis of other factors in this section becomes necessary. It may well be that two producers make an acceptable quality item; analysis then must be between *both* products and the alternative of preparing the item on-site.

It is likewise important to assure that the proper quality product can be made by the food and beverage operation. There may be no alternative but to purchase the required item ready-made because specialized equipment or skill is not available.

Quantity is important. Perhaps so much or so little of a product is needed that the only practical possibility (assuming acceptable quality) is to purchase the item ready-made. On the other hand, perhaps such a small quantity is needed that no source is interested in supplying the item; then it must be made on-site.

Cost is important. When quality is comparable for two options, cost considerations are frequently the primary basis on which a "make/buy" decision is made. Unfortunately, reality is not so clear cut. The cost to buy an item is known; the seller sets a price which must be paid. However, when a product is first prepared on-site, costs must usually be estimated. This, at best, is time consuming and risky; the estimate might be wrong. Therefore, all factors equal, a known higher supply cost might be better than a lower, estimated on-site production cost. (Cost concerns are discussed/illustrated in Section 10.5.)

Service is important. All of the technical and followup assistance which suppliers can provide is important whether service applies to providing ready-to-serve products or ingredients for on-site production. There may, however, be a larger problem with convenience food usage; there are fewer suppliers for a specific convenience food product than for raw ingredients. Likewise, continuity of suppliers is of potentially greater concern when convenience foods are purchased.

Timing is important. If the convenience food product is to be delivered, it must be at the property when needed. Likewise, if the item is to be prepared on-site, it must be ready at the correct time.

10.4.1 Possible Advantages of On-Site Production

When a make/buy study is undertaken (see Section 10.5) several possible advantages to on-site production should be considered to determine if they apply to the situation. Here are some examples.

If only small quantities of the product are needed, the amounts might be integrated with existing personnel schedules and equipment.

Quality needs might be better assured through on-site production, supervision, and quality control.

There may be more assurance of continued supply.

If no suppliers for the needed product exist, it must be made on-site.

It may be less expensive.

On-site preparation may serve to better utilize available personnel and/or equipment.

There may be "emotional" reasons favoring on-site production; less employee resistance and resentment is one example.

House "specialty" items may need to be produced on-site for marketing reasons.

10.4.2 Possible Disadvantages of On-Site Production

Disadvantages are, in effect, the opposite of the benefits cited above; for example, on-site items may be more expensive or of lower quality; equipment and personnel expertise may not be available, etc. Other possible disadvantages to on-site production include:

There is less of a purchasing/receiving/storage control problem when, for example, one item (such as a ready-serve entree) must be purchased as opposed to the individual purchase of all the ingredients needed to produce the item.

Reliance on skilled cooks to show up daily for work may be more of a problem than reliance on manufacturers to make and suppliers to deliver required products. Some of this pressure is relieved when standard recipes are used. Still, *someone* must prepare the required items.

More and greater levels of on-site supervision are required when items are produced on-site. Locating and paying these personnel are, then, possible disadvantages to on-site production.

When facilities are designed and equipment is purchased for convenience food operations, it is frequently awkward or impossible to utilize on-site production methods.

10.4.3 Possible Advantages to Use of Convenience Food Products

There are selected advantages to use of convenience foods. The benefits to be evaluated as a make/buy analysis is undertaken include:

Limited space and equipment may require use of convenience foods; lower capital investments often result.

Lack of skilled personnel favors convenience foods use.

Productivity of production personnel may increase (*if* labor hours are reduced as convenience foods are used).

Menu variety can often be increased without offsetting operating and management control related problems.

The quality of convenience food products might be consistently better than the comparable quality of on-site produced items.

When *all* costs are considered convenience foods might be less expensive than on-site products.

Product waste might be reduced if portion control items are prepared as they are needed.

10.4.4 Possible Disadvantages of Convenience Food Products

Specific factors in an individual food and beverage operation may point to disadvantages in the use of convenience foods. They include:

Quality and cost considerations, noted above, may be negative factors in some analyses.

Obviously, as costs increase, profits decrease. These two factors must be considered simultaneously.

Reliance on out-of-house personnel (for production and supply) may be viewed as a disadvantage.

Public acceptance might be reduced. For example, "truth-in-menu" laws which require food and beverage operations to provide at least accurate descriptions of products (if not the origin of product!) may work against the property. This would occur, for example, if management believed business would be harmed if guests knew that selected products were made off-site.

Increased freezer storage space may be necessary for holding convenience food products.

Employee resentment (perhaps even fear of job loss) may result from the use of convenience foods.

Reduced employee needs may not be taken advantage of when personnel must be available for production of other on-site prepared items.

If only one supplier is available, there may be concern that price increases will need to be accepted; there will be no alternative sources of supply.

10.4.5 Conclusions

Managers should generally be aware that:

The food and beverage operation can best be improved when management officials have an open, "neutral" attitude toward convenience foods.

Convenience food products may or may not be best for the operation. The result depends on, first, the specific product and, second, the specific food and beverage operation.

Management personnel must, then, recognize the importance of careful analysis to determine whether products should be prepared on-site or purchased in a ready-to-serve form.

While it is time-consuming to consider details of analysis and comparison of products, the time and effort spent to quantify these details are well spent.

Specific procedures should be followed as an analysis of make/buy alternatives is undertaken. These are reviewed in Section 10.5.

10.5   Procedures for Make/Buy Analysis

It has been shown (Section 10.4) that there are advantages and disadvantages to use of both on-site and ready-to-serve foods. Factors that are important to an individual decision may well be unique. There are, however, basic procedures which are useful in performing any make/buy analysis. These are outlined in this section.

10.5.1   The Role of Purchasing Personnel

Specific activities to be performed by purchasing personnel include many services necessary to accurately consider the alternative of purchasing convenience foods. These are:

Identification of suppliers, along with information about their dependability, expertise, and service.

Identification of available products.

Assembling samples and general information materials.

Discovering *accurate* cost estimates for the purchase alternatives (costs are considered later in this section).

Generally providing other supportive information required of personnel who are in a staff, advisory role to line management officials. (As such, the advice of purchasing staff may be solicited; the ''final'' decision still rests with top management and user department officials.)

10.5.2   The Role of Production Personnel

Personnel in production units are required to meet the cost, profit, and quality expectations of top management. As such, working in close cooperation with top management, they must make the decision which essentially involves:

Gathering information about the "make" option in the analysis.

Assessing quality differences between purchased and on-site prepared items.

Making the final decision or, at least, a recommendation to top management.

Each of these tasks is outlined in detail later in this section. It is important that user department (production) personnel work closely with purchasing personnel as the decision-making process evolves.

Purchasing staff can provide much assistance (see Section 10.5.1).

The expertise of purchasing personnel can be helpful input as a decision is made.

Both departments are concerned about attaining organizational goals. The teamwork involved in doing this pertains to the make/buy analysis and to tasks involving procurement, budget development, etc.

10.5.3 Procedures in Make/Buy Analysis

The following procedures suggest general guidelines to be followed in an analysis of a make/buy decision.

10.5.3.1 Define the problem. Purchasing and production personnel must know:

What is prompting the analysis to be undertaken? Perhaps one or more of the factors noted in Section 10.3 indicates the need for analysis.

What will determine the "best" solution? Are quality, cost, service, customer acceptance, or other factors most important? How will analysis applicable to these and other factors be undertaken?

What will be the role of each department in analyzing the alternatives? What is the role of top management?

What are time restraints? How much time can be spent on the make/buy decision? When must a decision be made?

What other special things must be known "up-front?" (Examples include opinions or attitudes of key personnel, definite limitations imposed by space, existing equipment, available funds, and corporate level policies for multi-unit companies, etc.).

10.5.3.2 Consider quality first. The need to determine the desired level of quality is obvious.

If desired quality cannot be made, it must be purchased.

If desired quality cannot be purchased, it must be made.

Quality must be defined in terms of the customer's desires. What quality does the customer want? It is important that top management be aware if a decision is made to compromise on minimal quality standards in order to take advantage of convenience food products. Top management, then, should be involved in the process of defining required quality and in assuring that all products being considered (including those which can be made on-site) meet this minimum quality standard.

If more than one purchased product is available, the analysis will need to concern whether the product should be produced on-site or whether one (and which) of the alternate products is "best."

Quality is much more than an assurance that samples submitted during the analysis period attain minimal quality expectations. There is also a need to assure that *all* products will be of a *consistent* quality over the life of any resulting purchase decision.

10.5.3.3 Consider costs of all alternatives.   After quality analysis tells what the alternatives are, the costs of each must be carefully assessed.

Costs incurred in the purchase of convenience food alternatives are generally easier to assess than costs of their on-site produced counterparts. The direct product costs are normally developed from analyses performed by purchasing staff. Costs which should be determined for purchased products include:

The direct costs of buying must be converted to an edible portion (EP), per meal, or per serving cost. Purchase costs often include warehousing and delivery costs incurred by the supplier. If not, these must be added to the product costs.

There is a wide array of other overhead, direct, and indirect costs associated with provision of convenience foods. (These are reviewed in the discussion of costs applicable to on-site prepared foods: categories of these costs are applicable to both types of products.)

Production of items on-site involves assessment of several categories of other costs:

Purchase cost of raw ingredients. This cost (again converted to edible portion, per serving, or per meal) must be established. When standard recipes are used this task is somewhat easier since a definite quantity of raw ingredients is utilized each time a quantity of the product is prepared.

Indirect costs. These also must be estimated. The categories of costs are the same for both convenience foods and on-site prepared items. These indirect costs include purchasing, receiving, and inspection labor costs. These may be lower for convenience food products since a number of ingredients, otherwise handled separately, will need to be processed.

Direct labor costs. Costs of actual product preparation and service should be lower for convenience food products; this is, after all, one of the major reasons why they are used. However, labor costs are only reduced if total labor hours are cut back with the result that lower total salaries and wages are paid and benefit costs are reduced. If, on the other hand, labor hours are not reduced, product costs will be higher, labor costs will be identical, and the "bottom line" will be increased operating costs when convenience foods are utilized.

Management and supervision costs. It might be reasoned that these costs will be similar since supervisory talent must be available on-site for performance of many other tasks anyway. However, in large facilities where first-line supervisory personnel are involved in the control of food production workers, cost savings might be significant.

Allocated inventory and storage costs. A "fair share" of these costs might be assessed against alternative products being considered. It is possible that storage costs might be higher for convenience foods, especially when frozen storage space is required.

Direct energy costs. Utility costs incurred in the production of on-site items will often be higher than costs incurred in reconstituting convenience foods for service.

Capital costs. If new equipment is needed to produce or reconstitute on-site or convenience food products, these costs must be assessed. Likewise, there must be enough space for the equipment, and space costs (for heating, insurance, interest payments, and similar costs) must be prorated.

Training costs. While these costs might be considered a part of direct labor charges, it is important to recall, especially as existing systems are changed, that time (and expense) will be necessary to train employees in regard to new procedures and equipment.

10.5.3.4 Consider other factors. In addition to quality and costs, other factors are sometimes important:

Acceptance of product(s) by employees;

Suitability of convenience food packaging;

Expertise of suppliers in providing technical help for use of products;

Consistency of portion sizes (when applicable);

Compatability of product (either convenience food or on-site prepared) with the market, facility, and equipment.

10.5.3.5 Make comparisons. After cost and other factors

associated with products of acceptable quality have been developed, comparisons of the alternatives can be made.

> Purchasing staff input is advisory only; they do *not* make the final decision.

> Production personnel, working with top management personnel, should be responsible for arriving at the decision.

> Ideas and suggestions should be solicited from affected production department employees.

> It is generally a wise idea, when practical, to ask valued customers about their taste preferences for alternative products.

> Comparisons and decisions must be made on the basis of the factors initially identified in Section 10.5.3.1. Will the selection of the "best" product resolve the problems which prompted the make/buy analysis initially?

10.5.3.6 Implement the decision.
After the decision is made, it must be implemented. This involves:

> Developing purchase specifications; in the case of convenience foods this is most effectively done by specifying a brand designation (perhaps with an "or equal" statement if similar products are available).

> Purchasing the required products (in convenience food and/or raw ingredient form).

> Purchasing, locating, and installing any necessary equipment.

> Training affected staff in all required procedures.

> Closely monitoring employee and product performance during periods of initial use.

10.5.3.7 Evaluate the decision.
Even with careful analysis and implementation, it is necessary to evaluate customer acceptability of the decision and to assure that no problems with product handling have arisen since the implementation of the decision. Careful review of the current operations may suggest additional areas of study, factors which may affect the convenience food/ on-site preparation decision, etc. It can then be seen that the analysis process is cyclical; implementation leads to evaluation, which can lead to implementation of additional procedures.

10.5.4   Examples of Make/Buy Analysis

Two simple examples of a make/buy analysis follow. Food and beverage managers might review the process to better understand the basic procedures listed in Section 10.5.3.

Example A: Cleaning Options

A small food and beverage operation is considering an on-site laundry to clean the tablecloths and napkins used in the dining room. In the past, it has utilized a commercial laundry specializing in "industrial" cleaning and garment care. In this operation employees are expected to launder their own uniforms and aprons; the only need (except for occasional hot pads) is for cleaning these front-of-house items.

The first decision to be made is *not* economic; it is a quality concern:

> Can the food and beverage operation clean the needed items as well as the commercial cleaners or (at least) to the minimum quality requirements of the food and beverage operation?

> Assuming that the commercial laundry firm maintains and repairs the items, can the food and beverage operation also do this?

> If not, will the replacement rate increase?

> Are there special concerns (such as heavy starching of napkins to accommodate special napkin folds or the need to use "exotic" solvents to clean food, wine, and other stains) which cannot be met by the food and beverage operation?

If the food and beverage facility is convinced that minimum quality needs can be maintained by either on-site or off-site cleaning, an economic make/buy study can be undertaken.

First, the current costs of using the commercial firm can be assessed (studying recent invoices should make this task relatively easy):

Weekly napkin usage 850 napkins at .095	=	$ 80.75
Weekly tablecloth usage 270 units at .48	=	129.60
Total weekly costs for commercial laundry		$210.35

The above costs include laundry purchase, maintenance, repair, replacement, and delivery; there are no additional costs to the food and beverage operation.

Next, costs must be assessed for use of an on-site laundry. Assume that space is available for the equipment and that utilities (electric, water source, and drain) are available. Assume also that the charge for installing a dryer ventilation duct will be $350:

(a) *Equipment cost*

Washer at	$850
Dryer at	550
Ventilation	350
Total estimated equipment cost	$1,750

If useful life is 7 years, the annual cost is $250 ($1750 ÷ 7); the weekly cost is $4.80 ($250 ÷ 52).

Weekly cost of equipment = $4.80

(b) *Napkin purchase*
Assume a useful life of 125 launderings (uses), with 150 napkins needed daily
Annual needs = 150 each day × 312 days* = 46,800
Annual usage rate ÷ 125 average uses = 375 napkins needed yearly

375 ÷ 12 = 31 dozen at $18/dozen: $558 annually
Costs ÷ 52 weeks = $10.75 estimated weekly costs
Weekly cost of napkin purchase = $10.75

(c) *Tablecloth purchase*
Assume a useful life of 450 launderings (uses), with 45 cloths needed daily:
Purchase 45 tablecloths at $5 each = $225
45 × 312 days* = 14,040 annual usage rate
45 × 450 launderings = 20,250 estimated uses

$$\frac{20,250}{14,040} = 1.4 \text{ years use from initial purchase}$$

$$\frac{225.00}{1.4} = \$161.00 \text{ annual cost} \div 52 \text{ weeks} = \$3.10 \text{ estimated weekly costs.}$$

Weekly cost of tablecloth purchase = $3.10

(d) *Labor costs*
Assume 2 hours needed daily at $4.50 an hour (including fringe benefits) = $9 in daily labor costs
6 days per week × $9 per day Weekly labor cost of $54

(e) *Detergent/chemicals costs* Weekly supply cost of $7

(f) *Utility*
Estimate for water and electric/gas charges from
the utility company Weekly utility cost of $5.00
Total estimated weekly costs
for on-site laundry $84.65

The third step in the analysis is to compare estimates of commercial and on-site laundry costs.

Commercial laundry costs	$210.35
On-site laundry costs	− 84.65
Estimated savings per week with use of on-site laundry	$125.70

To the extend that the cost estimates are reasonably accurate, the analysis suggests that there is a definite cost advantage to an on-site laundry. Since quality

---

*The facility is open 6 days each week; annual days total 312 (52 weeks × 6 days weekly).

factors in the two alternatives were judged to be equivalent, the food and beverage officials should go ahead with plans to purchase and install equipment and otherwise prepare for the on-site laundry.

Example B: Drink Mixes

The foodservice operation is considering the quality and cost differences between purchasing a commercially prepared Bloody Mary Mix and preparing a product on-site.

A group comprised of the property's food and beverage directors, beverage manager, "head" bartender, and several cocktail waitresses sample prepared mixes and, almost unanimously, determine that one product is of extremely good, and, hence, acceptable quality. In fact, there will be no need to add any other ingredients on-site to yield a product to meet the quality/requirements of the officials and staff members. The selected mix costs $21 per case of 12-quart bottles. There is a 5 percent reduction when the product is purchased in 5-case lots. It is very acceptable to purchase in this quantity; thus the per quart cost is $1.66 [$21.00 − 5% ($1.05) ÷ 12 bottles].

The facility has been making its own product. Identified costs are:

(a) *Product costs.* The current costs of ingredients used in the standard recipe (which yields two gallons) is $10.45. The product cost per quart is, therefore, $1.30 ($10.45 for 2 gallons ÷ 8 quarts).

(b) *Labor costs.* A time study suggests that the bartender (who prepares the mix) spends approximately 15 minutes in assembling the 2 gallons of mix. First an issue requisition must be completed, approved, and carried to the storage area. The ingredients (tomato juice, lemon juice, Worcestershire sauce, etc.) must be assembled (while the bartender waits). The ingredients are then carried back to the bar area and combined according to the recipe. The utensils and the work area must be cleaned after the product is prepared.

The bartender is paid $4.25 per hour, with approximately 15 percent in fringe benefits. The actual hourly labor cost is, therefore, $6.38 ($4.25 + 15% of $4.25). The labor cost to prepare the 2 gallons of mix is $1.60 ($6.38 hourly rate for 15 minutes—¼ of an hour). Since 2 gallons of mix are prepared, the labor cost per quart is $.20 ($1.60 ÷ 8 quarts). The total estimated product and labor cost to prepare one quart of Bloody Mary Mix on-site is

Product cost	$1.30
Labor cost	+ .20
Total cost	$1.50

The final step in the make/buy analysis is to compare estimates of costs when the product is prepared on-site in convenience (prepared) form.

Cost of on-site production	$1.50 per quart
Cost of purchased product	− 1.30 per quart
Estimated savings per quart with use of prepared product	$ .20 per quart

The study suggests that $.20 per quart can be saved through purchase of the pre-prepared Bloody Mary Mix. While the unit (quart) savings may not seem significant, the savings of $.80 per gallon ($.20 per quart × 4 quarts) is equal to $1.60 daily (since 2 gallons are used). This is equal to a weekly savings of $9.60 ($1.60 per day × 6 days) or an annual savings of $499 (.60 per week × 52 weeks).

The two examples presented above illustrate the principle that analyzing alternatives in a way which reasonably identifies the major costs of each can help the food and beverage operation to minimize expenses without sacrificing quality standards.

10.6 Miscellaneous Comments: Make/Buy

Several concluding general comments about the make/buy decision appear in order.

10.6.1 Decisions Aren't "Right" Forever

Situations change in the operation. Just because a careful analysis or study is made does not mean that the decision, "right" when made, will be "right" forever. Costs, customer acceptance, required quantities, etc., may change in a way which affects the decision. Likewise, decisions dealing with the short run may not resolve long-run problems.

Food and beverage managers must remain alert to changing conditions which then require altering, or at least reconsidering, current operating procedures.

10.6.2 Decisions Must Be Made

It is important not to ignore make/buy analysis. It is not proper to think that "the way we have always done things will always be right." Conversely, to change "because everyone else does" is not a correct philosophy. Management personnel must be alert to factors which suggest the need to do a make/buy analysis as outlined in this section.

10.6.3 Accuracy Is Important

Obviously, incomplete and inaccurate analyses affect the decision-making process. If the analysis is too sloppy, the wrong decision will very possibly be made; therefore, it is important to allocate an adequate amount of time and to carefully consider all economic and noneconomic factors. If sufficient time is not available, the time which is spent might be wasted and costly. Since time spent on analysis does correlate with the resulting accuracy which is expected, the advice is clear: allow sufficient time to do an accurate, thorough analysis.

10.6.4 Other Concerns

Several concluding concerns can be noted:

Top management must be involved in the process. They must, first, justify and allocate time to be spent on the analysis task; and, second, should provide technical input to the decision as it is made.

Costs are not the only factors to be considered. An emphasis about quality concerns and other factors has been provided in Sections 10.5.3.2 and 10.5.3.4.

Production concerns are very important to develop as analysis is undertaken. It must, however, be recalled that they also are but one of many factors which must be considered in a comprehensive make/buy analysis.

11

SECURITY CONCERNS IN PURCHASING

There are security concerns within each component of the management process used to control food and beverage operations. This section highlights these concerns and presents procedures that can be used to maintain security precautions during purchasing, receiving, and storage.*

11.1 Need for a Security Control System

Security concerns involve much more than employees who steal sales income or food and beverage products from the storeroom. Significant monetary losses can occur even before products are received, stored, produced, and served. A variety of conditions affect each food and beverage operation.

In small properties where owner-managers purchase the products themselves there is less concern about theft at time of purchase.

Absentee owners who hire managers may want security systems to control the operation.

In small properties concerns might focus on developing an assurance that value (price relative to quality) is received; theft can occur when low-quality products are substituted for high-quality products when "high quality prices" are charged.

Even when owner-managers purchase products other personnel are often involved in receiving and storage activities; security control procedures are necessary for these tasks.

As a food and beverage operation gets larger more personnel become involved in more purchasing-related tasks; the dollars at stake also grow larger. More detailed control procedures are important.

Owner-managers of all sizes of food and beverage operations should, then, understand that internal security begins at the time of purchase. Basic, common sense precautions can reduce the possibility of losses because of dishonest suppliers or employees.

11.2 Types of Theft at Time of Purchase

There are several common methods of theft at the time of product purchase.

---

*Material in this chapter is adapted from J. Ninemeier, Food and Beverage Security: A Systems Manual for Restaurants, Hotels, and Clubs. (Boston, Mass.: CBI Publishing Co., 1982).

11.2.1 Kickbacks

There are several types of kickbacks. Each involves the purchaser working in collusion with someone from the supplier's company. In one kickback scheme, food and beverage products are purchased at higher than necessary prices; the two thieves split the difference between the real and inflated price. The "payment" can be in money or gifts; either way the food and beverage operation is the loser. This type of theft is best controlled by the owner-manager reviewing the invoices on a routine basis (for example, why are so many products purchased from the same supplier?) and by soliciting price quotations on a random basis to assure that the prices being paid are the "best" for the required quality product.

Another kickback procedure involves "padding" the invoice (adding items that were not received and/or increasing the invoice by adding unreasonable "handling" or other charges). This scheme works well when the employee who purchases also does the receiving. This should prompt the manager to design a system which separates the purchasing and receiving tasks.

11.2.2 Fictitious Companies

Personnel who purchase can steal by setting up a "dummy" company which submits invoices for products that were, of course, never received. Managers should periodically review the names of payees on company checks. Unless the manager is specifically familiar with a supplier, checks should *never* be sent to companies with a Post Office Box address (unless another address is provided on invoices).

11.2.3 Processing Thefts

Suppliers may send an invoice through twice if the operation does not have an internal system to verify which invoices have not been paid and to cancel invoices that have been paid. Proper processing of purchasing documents is discussed later in this section and also in Section 9.

11.2.4 Credit Memo Problems

Theft can occur when products are not delivered or rejected and when no credit memo is issued to reduce the original delivery invoice by the value of the nondelivered items. Managers and receivers should never accept a "we'll deliver it later and not charge you" comment from the truck driver. A credit memo should be made immediately and should be attached to the delivery invoice. The manager should also call the supplier to assure that proper processing of the credit to the operation's account has been undertaken by the supplier. (Credit memos are discussed at length in Section 9.3.)

11.2.5 Delivery Invoice "Errors"

Intentional arithmetic errors, short weight/counts, quality problems, and similar "mistakes" can cost the operation money. It is important for management and bookkeeping personnel to check the arithmetic on invoices and for proper receiving practices (reviewed in Section 11.3) to be undertaken to catch these "mistakes." Regardless of whether these are "innocent" errors or intentional frauds, the "bottom line" is the same; the property is going to lose money.

11.2.6 Quality Substitutions

Downgrading a product with the hope that it won't be noticed is another type of theft. Paying more for a lower quality product can be prevented by proper receiving practices (see Section 11.3). Brand label substitutions can also become frequent problems if receiving personnel are not familiar with products which the facility orders.

11.2.7 Other Possible Problems

A wide variety of other theft practices can be used by "creative" purchasers. Examples include purchasing for one's own benefit, purchase of products "wholesale" for selected employees, etc. Each can be controlled through use of an effective purchasing system such as that discussed in this handbook.

Personnel with purchasing duties may be offered gifts, free meals, attendance at holiday parties, etc. All of these activities are, in large part, designed to increase the supplier's business. Basic purchasing ethics suggest that buyers must put the company first and make decisions on the basis of what is best for the company rather than on the basis of what is best for the buyer.

11.3 Theft at Time of Receiving

There are many opportunities for employee and supplier theft to occur when food and beverage products are received. Managers must guard against these problems.

11.3.1 Examples of Common Problems

Possible receiving problems include:

Receiving wrong items (such as inexpensive foreign wines instead of higher quality wines, or 70 percent fat content ground beef instead of 80 percent fat content beef) and paying a high price for a lower quality product.

Short weight or count: The food and beverage operation pays for more product than was received.

Receiving, for example, thawed product which is represented as fresh and for which a higher price is charged.

Grinding ice into ground meat products, adding fillers (such as soy products or nonfat dry milk extenders) in applicable products, selling meat with excess trim, etc.

Including the weight of ice and/or packaging in the amount of product for which a price is charged.

"Slack out" seafood: Thawing frozen fish, packing it in ice, and selling it as fresh.

Combining expensive steaks and inexpensive meat items into one container, weighing the entire container and billing the operation for a greater poundage of expensive steaks and a lesser poundage of inexpensive meats.

Including one empty liquor bottle in a case of, for example, twelve bottles.

The list of possible ways that suppliers can steal from the property by overcharging for amount or quality of product received may be endless. Problems can occur with almost any product which is ordered.

11.3.2 Precautions in Receiving

To guard against theft at the time products are delivered basic principles should be followed to control product receiving.

Receiving tasks should *not* be done by the same person who purchases (unless, of course, the owner-manager performs both duties). Someone *must* be trained to receive; receiving is important and should not be left to the dishwasher or whomever else is handy.

Whenever possible, product deliveries should be made at non-busy times so that receiving personnel (who may have other duties) will have time to correctly receive the products.

Deliveries should be made to a specified area of the facility. Receiving scales and other equipment (a clipboard with purchase records, a thermometer to check the temperature of refrigerated products, carts, etc.) should be available in the area.

After receipt, products should be removed immediately to storage. Chances for employee theft increase as products remain unattended.

Salesmen, delivery/route persons, etc., should *not* be permitted in storage areas. It is not proper for these personnel to have access to back-of-house production and storage areas. The receiving area should be located close to an outside exit and should be under view of management personnel.

Since the outside door should be locked an audio signal can be installed to permit delivery personnel to signal when they have arrived. With this plan, delivery men are under visual supervision by receiving personnel during the entire time that they are present.

Specific receiving procedures involving the verification of products delivered require the receiving personnel to:

Check all incoming goods against the purchase record or purchase order (to determine that the correct amount and type of foods which were ordered were received and that the agreed upon price is charged).

Check all incoming goods against the delivery invoice to assure that the type and amount of items that will be charged for were received.

Mark the delivery date and price information on containers at the time they are received and placed in inventory. This facilitates taking inventory and helps to assure that stock is rotated properly.

Weigh and count all products. If, for example, fresh chicken is received, it should be removed from its case and ice to determine the correct weight. It is also possible to weigh cases of liquor to assure that all bottles, full, are present. Naturally, any beverage cases which are wet (or show signs of having been wet) should be opened; each bottle should be checked.

Detailed procedures for product receiving are outlined in Section 20.

11.4   Theft During Storage

Security concerns at time of storage involve:

Knowing how much product *should* be available at all times.

Knowing how much product *is* actually available (to determine if any product is missing).

Preventing physical access by persons who do not need to be present in the storage area.

The first two concerns above are met when an effective inventory control record keeping system is utilized. The third concern involves keeping storage areas secure.

11.4.1   Keep Storage Areas Secure

It is critical to assure that the storage areas are kept physically secure. This means that:

There should be limited access. It is generally unwise to let just anybody into the storage area; only authorized personnel should enter storage areas. This policy is best policed by locking storage areas except during times of product issue.

Storage areas should be secure. It should be possible, for example, to lock the freezer (whether walk-in or reach-in), and the dry storage and liquor storeroom. In addition, a locking shelving unit in a walk-in refrigerator can protect wines and other expensive items. One or more compartments of a reach-in refrigerator should be lockable; expensive fresh meats, seafoods, etc., would be kept in these units.

Inventory control practices should be used. Items that are expensive and "theft prone" should be controlled through use of a perpetual inventory system (see Section 11.4.2). Items that are in work stations, broken cases, or other storage areas in small operations may not be under perpetual inventory (in which case this may be where theft occurs).

Items in work stations are put back under central inventory control at the end of each shift.

If items which are kept in locked storage are needed during the shift, a management official with access to storage area keys should retrieve the product.

The physical storage area must be designed with security in mind. While no property can be made completely safe against a professional burglary, it can more easily be made secure from ever constant employee access. Locking up the area is the first place to start. Naturally doors must extend to the ceiling, and lock clasps, door hinges, etc., must be reasonably secure. Check the ceiling also (to assure that employees cannot enter through the ceiling from another room). There should be no windows.

Some food and beverage operations keep "precious" items under separate, locked storage within storage areas. Examples of these valuable items include liquor, sterling silver or other serving ware, etc.

Adequate lighting in storage areas "robs" thieves of a place to hide. Closed circuit television systems can be used to keep an eye on receiving and storage areas and building exits.

In many instances basic common sense coupled with the question "How would I steal from my storage areas?" will provide sound, inexpensive ideas and methods to make food and beverage products physically secure from employee theft during storage.

11.4.2 Utilize an Inventory Control System

A procedure is necessary to get accurate information on quantities of products available in inventory.

Small properties might utilize a simple physical count system. With this plan, when the cost of food-sold calculations are made (for accounting records) or when quantities of goods to be purchased must be determined a physical count is made of items in storage areas. This counting process identifies the quantities of each item which are available in storage.

A perpetual inventory system is a more effective control procedure. With this plan there is a continuous update of product quantities in inventory. As items are received inventory balances are increased; as items are issued, balances are decreased accordingly.

Even small operations can make use of a perpetual inventory system for liquors, wines, expensive meat, seafood, and other food items. With this plan a running balance is kept at all times of the amount of products in inventory. A perpetual inventory form can be used to log in and out all items which are judged valuable enough to keep under this tight control system. It is then possible to know the amount of each product in storage at any point in time.

If, for example, the perpetual inventory record indicates that 35# (7-5# boxes) of a certain size of frozen shrimp should be in the freezer, an actual, physical count should reveal this quantity. If there is a variance and if no arithmetic errors have been made and if it can be determined that no products were withdrawn from inventory without a reduction in the perpetual inventory record, it can be assumed that a theft has occurred. When theft can be quantified it helps the manager determine when additional controls are needed (in this case tighter security on frozen shrimp is in order).

Detailed procedures for implementation of an effective inventory control system are presented in Section 21.

11.5 Theft During the Payment Process

Proper processing of purchasing documents can help eliminate "sloppy" operations which promote theft when bills are paid. The following procedures should be integrated into the existing purchasing system.

A record should be kept of all products ordered, along with the quantity and price. In small operations a formal purchase order is not necessary; a simple purchase record form will work very well (see Section 22.21). The form is for internal use only; it will "remind" the owner-manager of the important facts about each purchase he or she makes.

When the products are received, the delivery invoice should be compared with the purchase record to assure that type, amount, and price of delivered products are consistent with the agreement made at the time of purchase.

The delivery invoice should be attached to the purchase record and sent to the secretary, bookkeeper, or other official who will process the invoice for payment. When the invoice is to be paid (either alone or along with other invoices as part of the monthly statement from the supplier) the two forms (purchase record and delivery invoice) should again be compared. At this time all arithmetic (extensions, column additions, etc.) should be checked.

When the invoice or statement is paid it should be clearly marked "paid" along with information about (1) the date of payment; (2) the check number; and (3) the amount of the check.

The invoice or statement should be filed with the attached purchase record for future inquiry or other use.

Since timely payments will be made, no invoices, older than thirty days (or other billing period) are expected. If older invoices appear a check should be made to assure that payment has not already been made. An attached purchase record should serve to verify that the products were, in fact, received.

A credit memo system is necessary to handle variations between purchase records and delivery invoices. When items are short, missing, or below quality level (and, hence, refused) the delivery driver should sign the invoice noting the problem(s). A management official should reduce the invoice by the applicable amount. When the product(s) is received it should be accompanied by a new invoice. The new invoice (or credit memo issued by the supplier) should be included with the original purchase record and the first invoice to be processed together. Under no condition should a verbal agreement be made that "we'll deliver it next time without charging for it." Proper documentation of all products delivered (and not delivered) should always be available.

Cash payments should be avoided; pay by check whenever possible. The cancelled check does become, on return by the bank, a receipt for payment. Purchasing personnel should not pay bills unless they are the owner-manager. Verification of invoices, comparison with purchase records, and other procedures for payment processing should be done by the manager in a small property and probably within the accounting department in larger operations.

Detailed procedures for processing bills for payment are discussed in Section 9.

11.6 Theft During Withdrawal from Storage

Food and beverage products must be made secure during the issuing process (during which time food and beverages are withdrawn from the storage areas and transferred to kitchen and bar areas). Products can, of course, be stolen during this phase of the security system; therefore, practical steps should be taken to reduce this possibility.

11.6.1 Food Theft

In many small operations the withdrawal of food from storage is simply a matter of walking back to the storage area and removing what is needed. Obviously, with "open door" storage practices theft can occur in at least two ways:

Anyone can go into an unattended storage area at any time to steal products.

The employee who is removing products for preparation can remove an additional amount for personal use. This fact, coupled with the common practice of not removing only the quantity needed as noted on standard recipes (and, often, not even in terms of anticipated sales forecasts!), means that more products can be easily stolen.

The above common methods of storage and issuing can be tightened up immensely by use of the following procedures:

Storage areas should be kept locked. Management personnel should unlock storage areas at specified times and supervise the withdrawal of food products.

Sales forecasts of quantities of food products needed should be made; standard recipes should be used. These two procedures will place a control standard on the amount of each food product which would normally be expected to be removed from storage.

If a perpetual inventory system is used, a simple listing of the type of and amount of expensive products removed from inventory is necessary in order to update perpetual inventory records. This can be done through use of a simple issue requisition (Section 22.5). At an appropriate time management personnel can transfer information from the issue requisition to the perpetual inventory record. Random checks of quantity on hand after issue (from the adjusted perpetual inventory record) should be compared to the actual amount of product available (from physical count).

If a management official supervises food product issue and if specific quantities only are withdrawn from inventory, security control during the issuing process can be effective.

For expensive entree items (such as steak) a system can be used which involves issuing inventory to a work station with subsequent control based upon the number of items sold and remaining.

11.6.2 Beverage Theft

Beverages should always be issued to replace empty bottles. In other words, if two bottles of the house whiskey are emptied during a shift, they should be replaced at the end of the shift by two full bottles of house whiskey.

Security control principles to minimize theft of liquor include:

Issues, to replenish bar par-levels, should be made at the end of each shift, or, at least, once daily.

Empty liquor bottles should be collected and the beverage issue requisitions (Section 22.9) should be completed. The proper number of full bottles of liquor should be issued to replenish the bar par. *No bottles should be issued without the return of an empty bottle.*

Empty bottles which are returned should be disposed of by breaking (or by compliance with any applicable local or other law) in order to prevent reuse.

Before issuing, full bottles should be marked with a hard-to-duplicate stamp, adhesive tag, or other symbol to certify that the beverage was purchased for and issued from the operation's beverage department. This is done to make it unlikely that the bartender will bring in a bottle to pour from, then keep the sales income collected on that bottle.

A management official should check the beverage issue requisition by comparing it to the number of empty bottles. In small operations supervision of issuing and (perhaps) the transport of full bottles to the bar area may be a management duty.

Information from the beverage issue requisition should be used to update the perpetual inventory record which is kept for each liquor product.

12

ETHICAL CONCERNS IN PURCHASING

Many ethical concerns must be identified as the purchaser performs required work. The purchaser has obligations to the employer, to the supplier, and to himself or herself. This section will identify many of these factors and will suggest ways to form proper working relationships with all of the partners in the purchasing task.

12.1 Introduction

Ethics, stated simply, concerns decisions about "what is right and wrong." Obviously, this decision can vary both by the individual and by the situation as the individual perceives it. Each person is a "product" of his or her experience, education, and "common sense." Each of these factors, really the entire background of an individual, influences one's belief about what is "right and wrong." Since this is the case it is important for food and beverage officials to consider the need, if any, for company policies to guide purchasers in so-called gray areas where, otherwise, they would be left on their own to decide "right from wrong."

12.2 The Importance of Ethical Relationships

There are several reasons why establishing and maintaining good, ethical relationships with purchasing "partners" is important:

The good of the food and beverage operation is best served when the operation is fair in its dealings with suppliers and purchasing personnel.

Purchasing staff represent the food and beverage operation to the suppliers. There is a need for consistency in all interaction with suppliers.

The food and beverage operation will suffer if, for example, a purchaser makes a decision based upon "what is best for me" rather than on the basis of "what is best for the company."

If there are ethical standards established for the purchasing task this attitude of "doing what's right" can spread throughout the entire food and beverage operation.

12.3 Goals of Ethical Policies

There are several objectives to the establishment of policies which define, for the food and beverage operation, what is "right" in selected situations:

First, policies can help assure that the interests of the organization are considered *first* as alternatives are evaluated.

Second, purchasers will better attempt to seek maximum value for each dollar they spend.

Third, honesty and fairness standards will be established for the food and beverage operation. Few would disagree that, over the long run, these concerns are equated with an increased possibility for attaining organizational goals.

12.4 Obligations of Purchasers

As they perform their jobs, purchasers have obligations to fulfill. These obligations relate to several parties.

12.4.1 To the Food and Beverage Operation

These obligations include:

To understand objectives and policies of the food and beverage operation.

To perform in a way that maximizes attaining goals and in a manner consistent with the policies.

To obtain maximum value for dollars spent.

To protect the legal rights of the food and beverage operation.

To refuse any gift, gratuity, or other supplier concession designed to influence the purchase decision.

Never to disagree with food and beverage operation policies in public.

Not to divulge company "secrets" to the public.

To act without prejudice toward all eligible suppliers and to be receptive to all proposals, ideas, and suggestions offered for company benefit.

To ensure that the food and beverage operation has a reputation for fair dealing in its interaction with all suppliers.

12.4.2 To Suppliers

Purchaser obligations to suppliers include:

To maintain effective, professional relationships with all suppliers. (The topic of supplier relations is discussed in Section 12.5.)

Not to disclose unique suggestions and ideas provided by a supplier to other suppliers.

To treat all eligible suppliers fairly and decently.

To consider the supplier as a "partner" in the purchasing task; in the long run the relationship which is established must be mutually satisfactory to both the company and the suppliers.

12.4.3   To the Profession

The purchaser in the food and beverage operation is a professional. As a member of a profession of concerned hospitality industry officials, several obligations can be noted.

The profession can only be improved through contributions by its members and by examples set by its members.

The purchaser has social responsibilities which reflect "professionalism." Recent examples include concerns to conserve energy, control pollution, hire handicapped employees, improve working conditions for employees, etc.

To adhere to a professional code of ethics for purchasing (see Section 12.6).

Participation as an active member in allied professional associations (such as National Restaurant Association, American Hotel and Motel Association, and Club Managers Association of America) can also be considered an obligation of food and beverage purchasers.

12.4.4   To Oneself

The purchaser does have personal obligations. The following can be listed:

To perform in ways which do not violate high standards of ethics, such as those included in a professional code of ethics (see Section 12.6).

To remain unprejudiced in all relationships.

To plan for and advance toward personal and professional career goals.

To consider ways in which organizational and personal goals can be closely meshed; when this occurs, "what is good for the company is good for me."

12.5   Effective Supplier Relations

Many ethical concerns relate to the relationship between the purchaser and suppliers. Perhaps a "Golden Rule" of vendor relations can be established: "Treat the supplier the same way you would like to be treated." Basic common sense, courtesy, and professional and personal human concern for the supplier "as a person" can be a guide to establishing effective policies concerning supplier relations.

12.5.1 A Close Look at the Relationship

The best description of the relationship between buyer and seller is that of a partnership.

The seller helps the buyer by providing at a fair price the products and services needed by the buyer.

The buyer purchases products which helps the seller remain in business.

A cooperative relationship helps both (for example, the buyer "understands" seller problems which occasionally affect delivery timing; the seller "helps out" with occasional "emergency," rush order deliveries).

Given the cooperative, partnership influences of the buyer-seller relationship the basic approach to outlining requirements of an effective relationship becomes easy.

12.5.2 What Buyers Expect from Sellers*

In their relationships with suppliers, buyers want the following:

The same service and price which suppliers give to favored customers.

Help in controlling inventory.

Information about new products.

Prompt correction of all problems.

Suppliers' representatives should tell their vendors about the desires and needs of the food and beverage operation.

Delivery of emergency, "rush" orders.

Help in finding suppliers for hard-to-locate items.

Advance warning about price changes.

The same degree of loyalty that the supplier receives from the buyer.

12.5.3 What Sellers Expect from Buyers

In their relationships with buyers, sellers want the following:

Buyers to be open and receptive to the supplier's sales messages.

Buyers should not request a return visit when there is no possibility for the order.

Buyers should not request special or emergency orders unless there is a real need for them.

Buyers should be fair and honest at all times.

Buyers should not employ unethical practices to obtain lower prices.

---

*Information in Sections 12.5.2 and 12.5.3 is adapted from H. Hodges, Procurement: The Modern Science of Purchasing (New York: Harper & Brothers, 1961), p. 240–242.

12.5.4 Basic Procedures for Effective Supplier Relations*

Food and beverage purchasers should attempt to follow selected practices when interacting with supplier representatives. A partial listing includes:

Suppliers are told about applicable purchasing policies.

Suppliers are informed about potential volumes of product purchases required by the food and beverage operation; estimates are reasonable.

Suppliers are given suitable time to prepare responses to requests for price quotations.

Suppliers are informed about preferred visiting or calling times.

Suppliers are thanked when advice is given.

Suppliers' advice is solicited.

Sales managers are informed when salespersons provide extra service and assistance.

Salespersons are given a courteous reception; their time is not unduly wasted.

Salespersons are promptly told if there is no time for a visit; if there will be a wait they are told how long it will be.

Suppliers are interviewed in turn, without favoritism.

Appointments with salespersons are promptly kept whenever possible.

Supplier ideas for changes in purchase specifications are considered.

All suppliers are notified when there are changes in purchase specifications.

All eligible suppliers are invited to quote prices.

Suppliers who unsuccessfully quote prices are told why they did not obtain the order.

Rush and emergency orders are kept to a minimum.

Some tolerance is allowed when extenuating circumstances occasionally affect the supplier's ability to comply with all requirements of an order.

Vendors are given suggestions about how their products can more closely meet specification requirements.

Complete honesty is an integral part of all relationships with all suppliers.

All procedures enhance the operation's reputation for fairness.

Vendors are not taken advantage of even in times when it is legally possible to do so.

It is recognized that vendors have a right to a fair profit.

All agreements with all suppliers are honored.

---

*Adapted from J. Bedford, "How to Improve Vendor Relations." Purchasing (February, 1953), p. 81.

The above points have been developed into a checklist for effective supplier relations in Section 22.20. Instructions for use of the checklist are also included in that section.

12.6   A Code of Purchasing Ethics for the Hospitality Industry

A guide which incorporates basic ethical considerations can be used as the foundation for developing necessary policies. The Code of Purchasing Ethics for the Hospitality Industry which follows* can serve as a review of important concerns as the hospitality industry purchaser goes about his or her job.

Code of Purchasing Ethics for the Hospitality Industry

As a professional purchaser in the Hospitality Industry I accept the following obligations as I go about my work:

1. To give primary concern to the best interests of my company.
2. To try to obtain maximum value for each dollar that I spend.
3. To be active in professional groups which help improve my profession.
4. To desire and accept as necessary advice from colleagues, top management, and suppliers.
5. To be fair and honest in all my dealings with management, fellow employees, and supplier representatives.
6. To practice effective, ethical procedures which enhance relations with suppliers.
7. To learn as much as possible about all products and services which are needed and purchased.
8. To honor all my obligations and to be sure that all commitments are consistent with good business practice.

These obligations should become the foundation on which decisions about what is right or wrong should be made. It is obviously not possible to read and refer to the code as daily decisions are made; rather, the code should be accepted by top management as a formal statement of basic ethical beliefs. It can then be used as the basis for establishing policies which are consistent with management's intent.

---

*Codes of the National Association of Purchasing Management and National Association of Educational Buyers were utilized as the basis for formulating this code.

12.7 Purchasing Policies: Ethical Resolutions to Possible Problems

Top management must determine that high standards of ethical conduct are required by purchasers within the food and beverage operation. After study and, perhaps, modification of its basic feelings (expressed in the purchasing code), policies should be developed to translate management concern into ethical practice.

12.7.1 Definition of Policy

A policy is a statement of procedures required by management. When a certain situation occurs the policy spells out a definite course of action that must be taken.

The policy, then, is used to guide purchasers; it indicates what management wants purchasers to do when they are confronted with a specified situation.

12.7.2 Need for Policy

When they are followed, policies help provide consistency in management action. *Each* time a situation occurs it will be handled in the same way regardless of which employee is involved in the matter. A policy is used to implement desired management action to handle a routine, recurring problem. Policies are desirable for several reasons:

As noted above, they help provide consistency; a problem is always resolved the same way.

Problems will be resolved in the way that management wants them handled (in this case, in a way which helps implement the food and beverage operation's code of purchasing ethics).

Personnel don't have to guess about management's position; it is clearly stated within the policies.

12.7.3 Purchasing Policies

It is important for top management, after seeking advice from purchasing personnel, to develop policies which concern matters of importance to management. In this manner a policy indicates what management thinks is the right way to handle a situation; management does not need to rely on individual employees with differing backgrounds and experience to determine for themselves what is right and wrong.

The following list describes practices or situations which top management may wish to express concern about through a policy statement. If management believes that problems can occur because of the stated problem, a policy might be helpful. A suggested management position on the topic is also given; to the extent that the position accurately reflects management's attitude it can, of course, be adopted. After policy statements are defined they must be reviewed with affected staff; purchasing personnel cannot be expected to comply with policies with which they are unfamiliar. A meeting might be held to explain, defend, and justify management policy statements which, from the time of the meeting, become the way things are to be done.

12.7.3.1 Accepting gifts.
No employee of the company shall accept any commission, fee, or other monetary benefit from anyone having any business relationship with the company. Further, no gift, meal, or other gratuity having a value in excess of $10 shall be accepted for any reason (see Section 12.7.3.17).

12.7.3.2 Supplier favoritism.
All eligible suppliers will be encouraged to do business with the company. No supplier will be accorded favoritism for any reason. All purchase decisions will be made on the basis of receiving maximum value for company dollars expended (see also Sections 12.7.3.5 and 12.7.3.6).

12.7.3.3 Personal purchases.
Purchasing employees will not use their position within the company to purchase products at a special price or to otherwise receive preferential treatment; no personal purchases are to be made through the company's purchasing system. Reimbursing the company at cost for purchases made through the company will likewise not be permitted. Only products and services needed by the company will be purchased by purchasing staff.

12.7.3.4 Purchases for others.
Purchasing personnel are not permitted to purchase any item for any employee, friend, relative, or any other person under any condition.

12.7.3.5 Reciprocal purchases.
Only top management may authorize and approve reciprocal purchases. In the absence of this approval, all purchases are to be made without favoritism to any supplier.

12.7.3.6 Using local suppliers.
Only top management may authorize and approve purchases from local suppliers. In the absence of this authorization all purchase decisions are to be made without favoritism to any supplier.

12.7.3.7 Conflict of interest.
A supplier is not eligible to do business with the company if any management official, purchasing, user department, accounting, or other employee involved in purchase decisions owns more than 5 percent of the stock in a supplier's company. Likewise, this policy

equally applies when a relative of a staff member with involvement in the purchase decision owns more than 5 percent of the stock in a supplier's company.

12.7.3.8 Competitive bids. Specific management approval is required when there is only one price quotation for a product order. Otherwise, the order is to be awarded to the supplier quoting the lowest price for the product or service required by the purchase specification.

12.7.3.9 Speculative purchasing. Only top management personnel may authorize a purchase made on the basis of estimates of future price increases or decreases. In the absence of this authorization the quantity of product to be ordered is that required by existing purchasing and inventory management procedures.

12.7.3.10 Back-door selling. A supplier's representative should not attempt to influence user department personnel in their product consideration task without prior approval of the purchasing department. In the event that this occurs that supplier will be withdrawn from the list of eligible suppliers for a period of two (2) years.

12.7.3.11 Purchasing for "company's best interests." There is no other approved reason to purchase than when it is in the company's best interests. In each case, without exception, this consideration will be the single most important determinant in awarding an order.

12.7.3.12 Cash and other discounts. Purchasing staff should consult with accounting staff in an attempt to assure that cash and other discounts are taken whenever possible. This policy, however, does not include authorization to borrow funds in order to receive discounts for early payment.

12.7.3.13 Trial orders. Whenever an order is placed with a new supplier or for a new product from an existing supplier a trial order shall be placed. A trial order is one in a quantity not to exceed three (3) days' supply of product ordered.

12.7.3.14 Payment by cash. Without prior approval of top management no purchase in excess of $5 shall be paid in cash. When authorized, cash payments shall be made according to acceptable procedures required for use of the petty cash fund (see Section 7.6.2). All routine cash payments required by law or through common practice with specific suppliers will be processed according to procedures developed by management.

12.7.3.15 Vendor relations. All procedures and practices used in interactions with all suppliers will be those which build an effective, professional relationship between the company and suppliers. These practices are outlined in Section 12.5.

12.7.3.16 Samples.
Samples of all new products will be required before they are purchased. They will be purchased at current market prices from suppliers; they will not be accepted on a "free of charge" basis.

12.7.3.17 Free meals/entertainment.
No employee of the company will accept any free meals, drinks, entertainment, or other favor from anyone having a business relationship with the company if the value of such quantity is in excess of $10 in any one month.

13

LEGAL ASPECTS OF PURCHASING

Many of the responsibilities and obligations of purchasing personnel have roots prescribed in the law. Even though a purchaser's primary responsibility is to purchase necessary products, this is frequently done through the creation of legally binding commitments. Part of the job of the purchaser, then, is to use knowledge of the law in a way which avoids the need for possibly expensive, time-consuming, and destructive litigation.

13.1   The Best Legal Advice is from an Attorney

The information provided in this handbook is for general, background information only. It should not and cannot be used in place of competent legal counsel. Laws vary between states; laws change (so current discussions in this handbook may become outdated). Handbook users are therefore urged to consult their lawyers when specific information is required regarding problem situations.

While it seems hard to believe, it is true that a purchaser must understand enough about the law to know when it is necessary to contact a lawyer. The provision of some basic information about legal aspects of the purchasing task is the objective of this section.

13.2   Purchaser as Agent*

Except when he or she is the owner of the food and beverage operation, the purchaser acts on behalf of someone else. This "someone else" (called a principal) may be the owner or the stockholders in the company. Even when the principal hires a manager, who then hires a purchaser, the buyer still acts on behalf of ownership, *not* management. This relationship between the purchaser and principal is called "agency"; the purchaser acts as an agent for the principal.

13.2.1   Agent Relationship and Authority

The agent (purchaser) represents owners and uses authority delegated by them in dealing with suppliers. In this capacity the purchaser-agent has the power to obligate (commit) the food and beverage operation. Thus, for example, if it is within the authority of the purchaser to make agreements with suppliers regarding purchasing products, the food and beverage operation becomes legally responsible to abide by the terms of agreements which the purchaser makes with suppliers. It is just as if the owner or stockholders agreed to terms of the purchase

---

*Information in this section is based upon data presented in G. Aljian, Purchasing Handbook; 3rd ed. (New York, N.Y.: McGraw-Hill, 1973), pp. 4–4 to 4–10.

agreement. Generally, there is no specific requirement that the purchaser's authority be given "in writing." While there may be a written statement of the purchasing agent's power, there may only be verbal agreement. Even in the absence of a specific verbal statement, the authority may be implied (as occurs when a food and beverage operation hires a purchaser "to do the purchasing").

In any event, the purchaser is an agent for and can legally obligate the food and beverage operation if the purchaser:

Is formally told to represent the company and to make purchase agreements.

Has been allowed to act as though he or she is performing on behalf of the food and beverage operation. In other words, the purchaser makes agreements and no one (for example, top management) says that this is not proper.

As a matter of interest, a salesperson is *not* generally considered an agent of the supplier he or she represents; rather, the salesperson's role is to generate business for the supplier. This is different from being authorized to obligate the supplier. This task of making a "binding" agreement is generally reserved for the sales manager or another management official representing the supplier. It is, therefore, important that the purchaser understand what the supplier's representative can and cannot do. If, for example, the salesperson quotes a price lower than the authorized one, this price may not be honored by the supplier. A purchaser must know both the limitations of salespersons and who has the authority within the supplier's company to negotiate prices and other agreement terms.

13.2.2 Legal Duties of the Purchaser

Specific legal duties of a purchaser, acting as an agent for ownership, include:

To represent the best interests of the owner/stockholders whom he or she represents; there should be no conflicts between the purchaser's best interests and those of the food and beverage operation.

The purchaser must keep confidential any secret information of the company; this duty continues even if the purchaser is no longer employed with the food and beverage operation.

The purchaser must follow instructions which are within the law.

The purchaser's expressed or implied authority should not be exceeded.

13.2.3 Legal Liability of Agent

The purchasing agent is normally not personally liable for decisions made within limitations of his or her authority. There are times, however, when the purchasing agent is legally liable:

When the purchaser makes a contract without having the proper authority to do so.

When the agent agrees to be personally responsible for performance.

When the purchasing agent has received money from the supplier which is due to the food and beverage operation.

When the purchasing agent has received money from the food and beverage operation which is due to the supplier.

13.3 The Purchase Contract

A contract is a statement of promises (terms) that is made between two or more parties. When it is agreed to, each party to the contract becomes obligated to follow its terms. Thus, for example, a purchaser might agree to buy a quantity of products at a specified price. Other terms such as delivery date, when payment is due, etc., are also included in the agreement. The supplier agrees to provide the products to the buyer according to those terms. Both parties (the supplier and the purchaser) become obligated to do what they have agreed to do.

The law provides for redress (remedies) when contractual obligations are not met. Contracts can be written, made orally, or can be created when the acts of the purchaser and supplier indicate an intent to enter into a contract.

13.3.1 Parts of a Contract

There are four essential elements to a contract. All are required in order for a contract to be binding.

Parties involved in the contract must be capable of entering into the contract.

Parties must voluntarily and mutually agree to enter into the contract. There must, then, be both an offer and an acceptance.

The objective of the contract must be within the law.

There must be a reason to enter into a contract; this involves an obligation to do (or not to do) something.

The contract becomes the foundation of the agreement between the purchaser and the supplier. Any subsequent events will be judged according to the contract. For example, if there is a later question about the proper price, the contract will be the basis for the final price. So it is very important that the purchaser understand all agreements before entering into them. If, for example, an oral contract is made (an order is placed over the telephone) the purchaser should still make a written note of basic information (product, quantity, price, delivery date).

13.3.2 Fraud and Deceit

There are several conditions which must exist before a food and beverage operation can take legal action against a supplier because of allegations regarding fraud and deceit.*

The supplier must have made a significant misrepresentation of the truth.

The misrepresentation must have been untruthful at the time it was made.

The supplier must have known that the misrepresentation was false (or the supplier must have misrepresented without knowledge that it was, in fact, true).

The misrepresentation must have been made to encourage the purchaser to buy.

The purchaser must have acted because of the misrepresentation and suffered damage and/or injury because of the act.

In each case the false statement must have been made before the contract was signed or an agreement was reached.

13.3.3 Special Legal Considerations

Many special conditions can cause legal problems between buyer and seller. As they become important in specific situations, the terms of applicable purchase contracts should include statements of agreement about them. Some of the most important considerations are reviewed in this section.

13.3.3.1 Inspection. Unless the contract states otherwise, a buyer is not obligated to pay for an order until after the supplier has delivered the products or provided the services. The purchaser must have a reasonable opportunity to inspect the product or services provided to assure that they are in compliance with the contract.

13.3.3.2 Acceptance/rejection. There is no formal requirement as to how a buyer notifies the seller that he or she will accept goods. Clearly, signing the delivery invoice is a sign of acceptance. Likewise, placing items in storage areas signifies acceptance. Any sign or act on the part of the buyer which indicates acceptance can be taken as such by the seller, even if the products or services do not meet the expressed requirements of the contract.

Products or services can be rejected if they do not meet contract terms; however, since the buyer wants the goods and since legal action is uncertain, time consuming, and expensive, it is frequently more beneficial to both parties to make adjustments whenever possible. If there is no serious contract violation, a simple

---

*From H. Hodges, Procurement: The Modern Science of Purchasing *(New York, N.Y.: Harper & Brothers, 1961), p. 339.*

warning may be sufficient. Price adjustments may be possible in instances where products are marginally usable. In other instances products are rejected and returned to the supplier at the latter's expense. While in this last situation a legal action is avoided, there should be review of need to continue doing business with the supplier. This is especially true as rejection for problems of this nature becomes more frequent.

13.3.3.3 Warranties.

A warranty is a statement or understanding about a product; for example, a manufacturer may make certain quality claims about a product for sale. There are two types of warranties:

Express warranties—These statements or promises are specifically indicated in an agreement. They can arise from negotiations, statements in catalogs, advertising literature, on labels, in letters, conversations, etc.

Implied warranties—In the absence of specific, express warranties, a product or service must still generally be usable in the way that it is ordinarily and conventionally used. For example, food products must be wholesome (fit for consumption). An oven, by implication, must be able to heat. Obviously, an offer to sell implies that the seller has the right to sell and can give good title to the buyer for products purchased.

While the legal language of warranties is cumbersome to the average food and beverage purchaser, practical implications—really "common sense"—include:

The purchaser must know what is needed.

If the supplier is informed about the purpose for which a product is to be used and expressly agrees that the product will perform in an acceptable manner when put to that use, the supplier must stand behind the product.

If the supplier knows the requirements for product use and will not expressly agree that the product will perform, the purchaser must make a decision based upon his or her judgment only; there is no supplier obligation.

It is implied that all products supplied to the food and beverage operation will be fit for the customary purposes for which the products are normally used.

13.3.3.4 Order cancellation.

After the purchaser and supplier agree to the terms of a contract, it is expected that they will both abide by it. Sometimes, however, one party wishes to cancel the contract.

It is hoped that the "partner" relationship referred to throughout this handbook will prevail; if both parties attempt to understand each other's problems, they can often work out a reasonable resolution of them.

Generally, when an order is changed by the purchaser, the seller has no obligation to meet the agreed-upon delivery date.

Likewise, if the supplier does not meet delivery date requirements, the purchaser can cancel the order at that time.

If the seller desires to cancel the order (or fails to deliver it on a timely basis) a breach of contract results. While there may be a legal remedy, the purchaser wants and needs the product, not court action. In this instance, the purchaser often must work with the supplier to obtain the order (then to reconsider the supplier's eligibility for future orders).

If the buyer desires to cancel the order, a breach of contract also results. Again, from the supplier's perspective an attempt to negotiate to recover, at least, the supplier's incurred costs may be a better option than going to court.

13.3.3.5 Breach of contract. A breach of contract is a failure to abide by terms of the contract. When this occurs the innocent party may be entitled to damages *if* the matter is referred to the courts.

As noted above, it is generally best for the parties to attempt to work out problems to avoid the time and expense involved in court action.

When agreement is not possible the innocent party is generally entitled to be compensated for "damages" only. This is the value of the bargain lost because of the contract breach. For example, the difference between the price agreed with the seller and the actual price paid to another supplier might be the starting point for calculating damages. Attorney, court, and related costs may also be paid by the party who violated the contract.

Punitive damages in excess of normal compensation might also be awarded to the innocent party when misrepresentation (fraud and deceit) have occurred.

Money damages will normally be paid. Seldom will a supplier be required to perform (deliver products) according to the original contract.

Most purchasers and suppliers want to avoid court action; therefore, provisions may be made at the time of contract negotiations to refer disputes to an arbitrator with an agreement to accept the resulting decision.

13.3.3.6 "Honest" mistakes. Conditions unique to each specific situation determine "what happens" when an honest mistake is made.

A mistake made by one party does not make a contract void unless the other party:

Is aware of the mistake.

Should be aware of the mistake (for example, a purchasing agent *should* know that an error has been made when a price quotation for $100 has been received for a walk-in refrigerated unit valued at approximately $10,000).

Accepts an offer without knowledge of the error, and it is not a significant mistake (so that the purchaser is not or cannot be aware of the error); the contract is then considered valid.

13.3.3.7 Patent laws.*

A patent holder is protected by law; he or she has an exclusive right to produce, sell, and use the potential product for a specific time period.

If a patented product is produced, sold, or used during this period, a patent infringement has occurred; the patent holder can sue for damages.

The food and beverage purchaser generally has no way of knowing whether suppliers are legally selling patented materials. Buyers would, however, be guilty of patent infringement if such items were purchased and used.

Concerned purchasers can include a statement in purchase agreements which indicates that the supplier will "hold harmless" the food and beverage operation from any resulting infringement allegation.

13.3.3.8 Restraint-of-trade laws.

There are federal laws designed to prevent price discrimination in interstate (between state) commerce. Thus, for example,

A supplier cannot offer the same quantity of a product to different food and beverage operations at different prices unless (1) it can be shown that costs incurred are lower when a product is offered to one purchaser than to another; or (2) a low price is offered to compete against a price quotation of another supplier.

Additional state laws may deal with trade restraints on intrastate (within state borders) shipments.

Purchasers must be aware of specific federal and state laws applicable to trade restraints. A buyer violates the law when he or she knowingly attempts to receive or accepts a discriminatory price.

13.3.3.9 Unpriced orders.

It is always best to agree on a firm price before a contract is made. Sometimes this is not possible, for example, when an agreement is made for the purchase of a computerized data machine that isn't available yet. In this instance:

The purchaser should protect the food and beverage operation by inserting an estimated and a maximum price in the agreement.

Section 13.3.3.7 is adapted from L. Lee, Purchasing and Materials Management: Text and Cases (N.Y.: McGraw-Hill, 1965), p. 521.

In other instances where repeat orders are placed for products without price quotations, it is *assumed* that the purchaser expects to pay the same amount charged for earlier orders. While the supplier has an obligation to inform the purchaser about price increases, this may not always happen. It is, therefore, always best to include price agreements in each separate order.

13.3.3.10 Legal signatures.   There is a common misconception that for a document to be "legal" a personal signature is required. While this may be preferable from an internal control perspective, it has no legal status. Thus, written contracts are binding when "signed" by any one of a series of symbols:

personal signature	rubber stamp
typewritten name	fingerprints
teletyped name	hand-printed name
engraved name	photographed name

In fact, since oral contracts are acceptable, it might even be said that "verbal" signatures are legally binding.

13.3.3.11 Purchase order clauses.   In many food and beverage operations the purchase order becomes the formal agreement between the purchaser and the seller. As such, *all* terms and conditions of the sale agreement should be included in the purchase order. Topics of clauses which might be important to individual food and beverage operations are listed in Section 22.6. Purchasers and/or top management officials should contact their attorney for advice on the need, if any, for these clauses and for the specific wording which is required to provide adequate protection to the food and beverage operation.

13.4   Title Considerations

When does a product become the property of the food and beverage operation? There are several possibilities and the wording of purchase contracts often determines the answer to this question. Normally, title (ownership) is determined by the way in which the purchase agreement is developed. There are several common possibilities.

13.4.1   FOB Purchaser's Location

With this plan legal title is assumed by the buyer when products are delivered to the food and beverage operation. The supplier is, then, responsible for freight, insurance, and similar costs. This is probably the most common arrangement used for the purchase of most routine products and supplies used by the food and beverage operation.

13.4.2 FOB Supplier's Location

When this procedure is used, the purchaser takes title when a carrier accepts the product for shipment at the supplier's or manufacturer's location. This may occur when, for example, the food and beverage operation purchases a major equipment item directly from the manufacturer. When this plan is used, the purchaser must pay costs of shipment, insurance, etc., and must also frequently select the carrier to be utilized.

13.4.3 FOB Supplier's Location: Freight Paid For Purchaser

This plan is similar to 13.4.2 with the exception that the seller pays for the incurred freight charges, *not* the buyer.

13.4.4 COD Shipments

In some instances, especially for one-time orders, a COD (collect on delivery) system is used. When the product is received, it is paid for by check or through the petty cash fund. Passage of title is not affected by when or how payment is made. Agreements about title consideration, then, must be made at the time the purchase agreement is made.

13.4.5 Conditional Sale

A conditional sale is used to help assure the supplier that he or she will receive payment for products delivered. With this plan the purchaser must make specified payments at specified times before receiving title to the products. When this arrangement is used, the supplier retains ownership until the payment(s) has been made. This plan is the same as installment-purchase arrangements which are often used for purchase of autos and other "big ticket" items.

13.4.6 Liens or Chattel Mortgages

A lien is a retained interest on real or personal property which is held by a supplier or institution with a financial interest in the property. The lien is held until the title passes from seller to buyer.

A lien may exist against an item of food production equipment. The lien holder (such as a bank) must be paid before the equipment is sold or else receives proceeds from the sale. This is necessary to obtain "clear title," which is required in order for the equipment to be sold at some time.

A mechanic's lien may be placed when labor and materials are used in constructing, remodeling, repairing, etc., the business property. This legal action provides the supplier with an interest in the property that must be satisfied before the property can be sold.

A chattel mortgage arises when a buyer obtains title to equipment or other property which has not entirely been paid for. With this plan the purchaser gives the supplier a mortgage on the equipment for the amount yet due. If the purchaser defaults on payments, the seller can claim and sell assets other than the original equipment item in order to receive the balance due on the chattel debt.

13.5   Lease Contracts*

The concept of leasing is considered in great detail in Section 18; however, legal aspects of leasing contracts and the leasing relationship are highlighted in this section. This is done in order to present, in one section, the basic background knowledge of the law which is important to the food and beverage purchaser.

13.5.1   The Concept of Bailment

A lease is a special type of contract known as bailment. A bailment occurs when the following commitments are met:

Property is delivered by one party to another.

The property is intended for a specific purpose.

There is a contract (expressed or implied) that outlines the specific obligations of the parties.

The property is returned or accounted for when the specific purpose is completed (or it is retained until claimed by the owner).

Under the terms of a lease contract (bailment) ownership of the property does not change. Use and control of the equipment does change, however.

13.5.2   Types of Lease Contracts

While many leasing arrangements are developed for a specific situation, there are several general types of lease contracts. These include:

Finance lease—The equipment owner provides the equipment and is responsible for dispensing of it at the end of the contract. The equip-

---

*Section 13.5 is adapted from D. Metz, Leasing: Standards and Procedures (Kaukauna, Wisc.: Thomas Publications, 1968), pp. 1K-7K.

ment user is responsible for all maintenance, taxes, insurance, and other costs involved with use of the equipment. A special aspect of the finance lease requires the equipment user to reimburse the equipment owner at the end of the lease for any difference between the disposal price and the balance which is still owed by the owner. If, on the other hand, the disposal price is greater than the amount owed by the owner, this difference is refunded to the equipment user. With this plan the equipment owner is assured that the entire capitalized cost of the equipment will be paid by the equipment user. If, for example, the user defaults, the equipment is sold and the difference must still be paid by the user. This plan provides the least risk to the owner and the most risk to the user.

Net lease—This arrangement is similar to the finance lease except that the equipment owner, *not* the user, is responsible for any loss which occurs when the equipment is sold or disposed of. Conversely, the owner receives the benefit of any surplus funds received at the end of lease.

Maintenance lease—With this plan the equipment owner (*not* the user) is responsible for necessary maintenance over the lease term. The user's responsibility is generally limited to paying a fixed leasing amount and to using "reasonable" care when the equipment is operated. This plan places most of the financial responsibility on the equipment owner.

13.5.3   Basic Lease Contract Considerations

Each of the basic types of leases discussed above presents obvious differences in financial implications. Purchasers know that as the amount of risk or cost increases for the equipment owner, the amount charged to or paid by the equipment user will also increase.

After the basic type of lease contract is determined, a lease specific to the situation must be developed. The lease contract shares basic similarities with any other type of contract.

The contract has two purposes: (1) to indicate the obligations of each party to the lease; and (2) to serve as a guide for how the contract should operate.

The contract must identify parties to the contract.

It must not be based upon any misrepresentations.

It must *clearly* indicate the obligations which each party assumes as the lease is agreed upon.

The term of the lease must be indicated.

The amount of and payment schedule for lease payments must be identified.

Warranties, if any, on the equipment must be considered and explained in detail.

There should be a default clause which enables the equipment owner to repossess (with right of access to the food and beverage operation's property).

The lease must contain clauses necessary to make the agreement specifically applicable to the situation.

14

EVALUATION OF PURCHASING

The process of purchasing must be evaluated in order to determine (1) the extent to which purchasing goals are attained, and (2) how the purchasing process can be improved so that future goals can be attained even more effectively.

The evaluation process is frequently overlooked. Purchasing staff and top management officials who might perform aspects of the evaluation get caught up in the routine involved in running the day-to-day operation. Nonroutine tasks, especially those that may not generate immediate improvements, are not given a high priority; time, then, seldom becomes available to spend on the evaluation process. This is very unfortunate; study of this section of the handbook will place a proper perspective on the evaluation process.

14.1 Introduction

If purchasing begins with planning, the process ends (or really begins again) with the task of evaluating. In effect, the management of purchasing is an ongoing, cyclical process. Plans are developed and implemented. Evaluation is later undertaken to determine the extent to which the goals which were outlined in the plans were attained. Evaluation suggests changes that modify plans, and this analysis continues through the process again.

The actual evaluation process can be explained as follows:

Standards, expressed in the form of goals, are developed. (Stated another way, goals are expressed in measurable terms so that it becomes possible to assess objectively whether or not they are attained.)

Standards must then be explained to and be understood by all personnel involved in achieving the goals.

The task of purchasing is undertaken; "actual" results of the purchasing are measured.

The standard, expected performance is compared with the actual performance.

Corrective action is taken when the comparison suggests that the standards were not met.

Evaluation again becomes necessary to assure that the corrective action (1) did resolve observed problems, and (2) did not create new problems.

The process of purchasing evaluation can compare actual purchasing performance with:

Standard performance. For example, how many "rush" orders did we *expect* to have? Did we have?

Past performance. For example, how many rush orders did we have in the previous period? In this period?

Financial statement standards. Economic aspects of purchasing can be evaluated by comparing, for example, budgeted performance with actual performance on financial statements (especially the income—profit-and-loss statements for previous and present periods).

It can be seen, then, that there are ways to evaluate purchasing. It becomes most important to determine first what we want to evaluate and, second, the best way to carry out the evaluation process.

14.2   Reasons to Evaluate Purchasing

Several important reasons stress the need to evaluate purchasing:

Management needs to know the extent to which purchasing goals are attained. The first function of management is to establish goals and to plan how they are to be met. It is critical to evaluate this process in order for purchasing (and all other management tasks) to be improved.

The result of evaluation is an awareness of how purchasing can be done more effectively.

The purchasing department, containing only one or a *very* few personnel, generally spends well over 50 percent of all of the sales income generated by the food and beverage operation; almost any cost-control program must begin with purchasing. It is imperative that purchasing dollars be wisely spent. Purchasing should be at the center of an effort to coordinate company cost objectives in order to minimize expenses.

More profit results from improving purchasing than will result from the same effort in any other area of the operation; if more profit is desired (and what commercial food and beverage operation doesn't want more profit?) an increase can most easily come from improving the purchasing process.

Study of the purchasing evaluation process helps to establish the basis for evaluating purchasing department personnel. This evaluation of individual employees is an important part of the personnel administration process.

Purchasing evaluation can help determine the need, if any, for internal reorganization and reassignment of functions, duties, and responsibilities among departments within the food and beverage operation.

14.3   Who Evaluates Purchasing

The process of evaluating purchasing can be done by personnel within and outside of the food and beverage operation.

14.3.1   Internal Organization Review

Using employees of the operation to evaluate purchasing staff is the most common technique. It can be done by:

Top management personnel. Food and beverage management officials are generally most concerned about the economics of purchasing. How much are we spending? How much can we save? Quality concerns are also important, but they are more difficult to consider objectively. Management, in one sense, constantly reviews purchasing as various financial statements are studied. The problem is, of course, that if costs are high it is difficult to determine reasons for the high costs. For example, did purchasing staff pay too much? Did storage personnel have high spoilage rates or theft? Did production personnel have recipe, portion control, or other problems? Was sales income stolen by service employees? It becomes very difficult to look at the numbers to determine individual departments' responsibilities for higher-than-anticipated costs. Therefore, the operation needs a special process to identify the specific role of the purchasing department and the cost for which it alone is responsible.

Purchasing department personnel. The staff members can evaluate their own effectiveness. This type of self-evaluation generally concerns the extent to which policies, budgets, plans, etc., are adhered. This type of evaluation can often be effective when management has worked with purchasing staff to establish goals, when methods to measure goal attainment are available, and when management sits down with purchasing staff on a formal, scheduled basis to see what happened. This self-analysis can be used to develop plans for organizational improvement.

There are advantages to internal evaluation. Among these are:

It can be time effective. Since internal operations staff know the process time and money are not wasted learning the procedures before the staff can be evaluated.

It is less expensive than hiring outside organizational personnel to do the evaluation.

It can be an effective way to evaluate; problems can be discussed *if* the disadvantages reviewed below can be overcome.

The knowledge, ability, and experience of internal reviewers are known since they are employees. This is not usually the case when outside personnel are brought in; even with the best screening, consultants may not have the ability to identify and resolve problems.

There are also disadvantages to internal evaluation. Consider the following:

Existing purchasing staff may want to "cover up" problems traceable to them; this may be done because of concern for losing jobs or loss of esteem from colleagues, because of theft or fraud practices, fear of discipline, etc.

There can be a case made for the thought that, if purchasing staff knew what to do, they would do it; any existing problem, therefore, is due to their lack of knowledge about what needs to be done.

As noted above, if evaluation is to be done by internal personnel it simply may never be done; higher priority concerns will be met first. Evaluation does not often receive its necessary high priority.

14.3.2 External Organization Review

It is rare for a food and beverage operation to hire external consultants to specifically evaluate the purchasing process; rather, as large problems are noted and consultants are retained, purchasing becomes one of many processes which are examined.

Advantages to use of external consultants include the fresh look that is given to purchasing and the lack of a need to hide anything. The high cost associated with external consultants is the largest disadvantage to be cited.

14.3.3 The "Best" Approach

Before an outside consultant is retained food and beverage management personnel are best advised to perform internal evaluation by following procedures in this section. (A simple plan of evaluation which can be followed is given below.) Only after this approach has been tried and proven ineffective should external consultants be employed. In this case, food and beverage officials will no doubt discover that internal problems extend beyond the purchasing department through the entire operation. (The improvement of non-purchasing tasks is, of course, beyond the scope of this handbook.)

14.4 The Evaluation Process

How should purchasing evaluation be done? This section presents a simple approach which can be used.

14.4.1 State Goals in Measurable Ways

Since purchasing evaluation indicates how well goals are attained the evaluation process really begins when goals are defined. Food and beverage operation managers must, of course, perform this task specifically for the property; the following "sample" goals are presented to suggest how the process is done.

Goal #1: Purchasing will be done at the "right" price.

1. Total cost of purchased goods will be no more than 10 percent above last year's costs. (Note however, the concern in Section 14.3.1; the gross purchasing cost is influenced by the quantity needed; if there is waste and theft in other departments a larger quantity will need to be purchased. These problems are not controllable by the purchasing department.)

2. Per unit costs of expensive and large-volume products will increase by no more than 10 percent above last year's per unit costs of the same items. (While purchasing personnel obviously cannot control market costs, if there are several eligible suppliers they can constantly assure that buyers are receiving the "best" price. For example, purchasers can retain supplier price quotation sheets or other evidence which indicates that the most suitable market price of products was paid.)

Goal #2: The "right" quantities are purchased.

Examples of measurable goals which concern this point include:

1. There will be no more than a total of ten stockouts for all items this year.

2. Items in inventory in excess of the maximum limit will be controlled so that this does not occur more than ten times during the year.

3. Not more than $100 worth of perishable items will need to be discarded. (This assumes that a check of dated products indicates that proper stock rotation is practiced; the purchasing department cannot control waste when storage personnel don't use the oldest products first.)

Goal #3: The "right" suppliers will be used.   Possible
goals include:

1. There will be no more than five complaints of any kind against any supplier within the coming year. (The supplier evaluation process reviewed in Section 8.11.1 will be the basis for this analysis.)

2. Accounting department staff will have no more than two problems during the coming year with a supplier concerning bill processing and payment.

3. There will be no cases of "back door" selling by a supplier this year.

Goal #4: The "right" product quality will be purchased.

Examples of goal statements are:

1. Items will be rejected and price adjustments will be made no more than five times this year because of quality problems.

2. Items accepted from a supplier will not later be noticed to be of inferior quality more than one time this year.
3. Suppliers will be asked to provide suggestions about quality requirements at least two times this year.

Goal #5: Products will be received at the "right" time. Consider the following:

1. There will be no more than ten rush orders this year.
2. A supplier will not deliver on a later day than agreed upon more than eight times this year.
3. Suppliers will *never* deliver more than one week early.

Miscellaneous goals might include:

1. Purchasing staff will perform six make/buy analyses this year.
2. Purchasing staff will develop twelve purchase specifications this year.
3. Purchasing staff will conduct six equipment purchase studies this year.

14.4.2   Measure Actual Performance

Records must be kept to assess actual performance. Most of these have already been described. For example:

Request for price quotation sheets (Section 22.23) and actual invoices are available to record prices paid for products. These records can be compared to applicable documents from previous periods.

Supplier performance rating sheets (Section 22.4) can be used to keep a running record and to periodically review supplier performance against stated goals.

Credit memos and other correspondence kept by accounting personnel will indicate any payment processing problems with suppliers.

Purchase records (Section 22.21) and receiving clerk's daily reports (Section 22.7) list delivery problems. Data from these forms can be entered on the supplier performance rating sheets to assemble a complete record of performance for each supplier.

Perpetual inventory forms (Section 22.18) will indicate stockouts and times when inventory volumes violated minimum-maximum inventory requirements.

Purchasing department "work logs"—actually diaries—can be kept to assess the number of make-buy, purchase specification development, and equipment purchase studies which were completed.

14.4.3　Compare Actual Performance with Anticipated Goals

If goals are expressed in a measurable way (examples were given in Section 14.4.1) and if records are kept which review actual performance it becomes possible to compare standard, planned performance (goals) with actual performance.

This technique is at the heart of the evaluation performance task. To the extent that goals have not been attained, purchasing improvements are in order. Only through evaluation can problems be noted and subsequent plans be made.

A formal comparison might be made twice yearly. Goals are expressed in terms of anticipated results over a six-month period; operating results are collected and the evaluation process is performed.

When comparisons are made some variance may be allowed. For example, if no more than ten rush orders are anticipated a 10 percent variance (one rush order) might be permitted. If there are more than eleven rush orders their causes must be investigated. Clearly, regardless of the variance limit, problems become more significant as they occur more frequently. Since this is the case, problems that occur more often than anticipated must be analyzed first. This is especially so when problems can be converted into lost dollars or customer dissatisfaction.

When comparisons are made special attention must be given to assuring that:

Records which review performance are accurate.

Goals which state planned performance are reasonable.

Activities being evaluated are within control of the purchasing department.

Purchasing staff—as well as top management—are involved in the comparison process.

If comparisons are made between records kept in differing time periods it is necessary to assure that the information was collected in the same manner (and that it means the same thing).

14.4.4　Take Corrective Action

When comparison indicates that planned and actual performance is not within allowable variances, corrective action becomes necessary.

The most significant observed problems (they occur most frequently or are of largest economic concern) should be corrected first.

The approach to corrective action involves:

Defining *exactly* what the problem is.

Deciding what alternatives might be used to resolve it.

Ideas suggested in this handbook and from conversation with suppliers, user department personnel, purchasing employees, and others might be most effective in generating ideas about resolving problems.

Considering each alternative in terms of how well it might resolve the problem.

Implementing the best alternative solution to the problem.

Purchasing staff should be allowed to interpret and explain the results of the comparison. This can be of great assistance in redefining basic, standard procedures to better apply them to the specific situation. Since purchasing staff work with the problem daily their suggestions should be helpful in resolving problems.

Persons affected by corrective action changes must be informed of new procedures and trained to utilize them.

Some time may be necessary after changes are made for minor problems to work themselves out. A problem may not be resolved by a workable alternative the first time it is implemented.

14.4.5 Evaluate New Procedures

New procedures that are implemented to resolve problems noted when standard and actual performance are compared must be evaluated. This is done (1) to assure that problems are resolved; and (2) to assure that new "spinoff" problems haven't been created.

Evaluation should be done according to the same procedures initially used to determine that a problem existed. For example, standard plans may allow for no more than one rush order per month. It is clear that this standard will need to be met in order for the procedure implemented in the corrective phase to be judged beneficial. Likewise several months may need to lapse in order to assure that no more than one rush order monthly occurs with use of the newly implemented procedure(s).

All personnel involved in the process being studied should be involved in its evaluation. Ideas regarding further improvements, additional potential problems, and time or costs associated with newly incorporated procedures can all be contributed by different persons viewing the purchasing process from a variety of perspectives.

If this process indicates that observed problems have been corrected the evaluation has helped to improve the purchasing task. If, however, evaluation indicates that the problem continues or that additional problems have been created the reviewers must return to the corrective action phase (Section 14.4.4) and reconsider and implement other alternatives.

14.5   Others Aspects of Purchasing Evaluation

The sections above have stressed the need to evaluate purchasing in terms of the extent to which goals have been attained. Other aspects of the evaluation process include study of:

The actual organization of the purchasing department. Is it effective? Are all positions cost-justified? Are there clear channels of coordination and communication?

Are purchasing policies reasonable? Are there additional "gray areas" which need to be considered for policy statements?

Are the purchasing reports and records which are sent to top management adequate?

"Qualitative" aspects of purchasing can also be reviewed:

Does management support purchasing?

Are purchasing policies written and are they understood and consistently followed by staff personnel?

Are purchasing activities centralized within the food and beverage operation?

Are there (or should there be) any non-buying functions in the control of purchasing personnel?

Are purchasing staff qualified for and capable of performing in their positions?

Do purchasing staff participate in company activities?

What is the relationship between purchasing and other departments?

What is the relationship between purchasing and suppliers?

How do purchasing staff select the best suppliers?

Are purchasing staff providing appropriate assistance to user departments in developing purchase specifications, in performing make/buy analyses, etc?

Have purchasing staff obtained a reasonable amount of usable suggestions from suppliers?

Is the layout of the purchasing department adequate?

14.6 An Aid to Purchasing Evaluation

The need to involve all affected personnel in the purchasing task has been noted throughout this section. One way to do this formally includes use of a purchasing evaluation guide. A blank copy of this form along with instructions for its use are found in Section 22.10.

The purchasing evaluation guide enables staff members (from the purchasing, accounting, food and beverage departments), management officials, and others to consider the purchasing activities in which improvements are needed. As more staff members indicate that the same activity needs improvement this trend should suggest that a real (not an imagined or isolated) problem exists. The identification and ranking of activities in which improvements are necessary can be an aid to establishment of purchasing goals to resolve the identified problems. It can also be useful to identify areas in which purchasing staff can focus improvement concerns in the absence of a formal evaluation process.

15

PURCHASE OF FOODS AND BEVERAGES

The buyer must be aware of a good deal of information as food and beverage products are purchased. This information is critical both at the time purchase specifications are developed and during the task of receiving when an inspection is necessary to assure that quality requirements have been met.

In a handbook of this type it is not possible to provide all of the information to indicate quality considerations in the perhaps hundreds of products purchased by many food and beverage operations. Instead, an attempt is made to provide information about general purchase concerns applicable to categories of products. This information can be supplemented with additional information from references provided in this section.

15.1   Quality Foods and Beverages are Important

It is important to purchase products of the "right" quality. Section 5.1.1 indicated that "right" refers to an item being suitable for its intended use; therefore, required quality is not the same as highest quality. U.S. Fancy Tomatoes (the highest quality) may not be necessary when the product is to be chopped for a casserole product. A lower quality (and lower priced) U.S. No. #1 grade is probably adequate.

Quality concerns are important because:

Food and beverage production personnel can not prepare and serve the "right" quality items unless they have the proper quality products with which to work.

We have already seen that a product of higher than required quality increases costs; this is obviously not desirable.

At its most basic level quality affects the cleanliness and freedom from unhealthy substances that relate to one's health and well-being. Food and beverage products must be wholesome when they are purchased.

15.2   Concerns When Writing Purchase Specifications

Section 5 provided details which must be considered as purchase specifications are written. It is important to recall that a buyer must know what quality product he or she desires and must then be able to describe it so that suppliers know what is needed.

The role of suppliers in writing purchase specifications is important. The following procedures apply to the purchase of any food or beverage product and can be helpful in determining necessary quality.

Select a sample (for example, rib eye roll steaks or green pepper) currently in inventory which user department personnel and purchasing staff agree is of acceptable quality.

If a new product is being added to the menu give a general description of need verbally to suppliers; samples provided can then be used to confirm what an acceptable quality product is like.

Ask the supplier providing the acceptable product to describe it (size, grade, general condition, etc).

Use the description to write a purchase specification.

Ask other suppliers to comment on it to assure that the specification represents a product which (1) is of the correct quality, and (2) can be supplied by more than one vendor.

Make any necessary modifications in the purchase specification which arise because of ideas from other suppliers.

Utilize this final purchase specification by sending it to suppliers with the request that prices be quoted for products that meet the quality indicated by the purchase specification.

15.3 Purchase of Meats

Meats are the highest-priced category of food purchase expense in most food and beverage operations. One expert* indicates that meats may represent between 30 percent (for an institution) to 70 percent of total food costs (for a commercial steak house). This can convert to as much as 20 percent (for institutional foodservice) to 40 percent of all operating expenses (for commercial foodservice). Regardless of the number, all food and beverage purchasers know that significant dollars can be spent and saved in the purchase of meat items.

15.3.1 Specific Purchase Concerns

Food and beverage purchasers must, as a minimum, incorporate the following concerns into the development of purchase specifications for meats.

Inspection.   Meats shipped in interstate commerce (products which move between states) must be federally inspected to assure wholesomeness. This means that the meat product is free of disease and has been safely processed in a sanitary meat plant. If products are shipped in intrastate commerce (products move only within a state) inspection is still generally required. A wise buyer uses only federally inspected products *or* assures that state and/or local inspection

---

*R. Peddersen, Specifications: The Comprehensive Foodservice Purchasing and Specification Manual (Boston, Mass.: CBI Publishing Co., 1977), p. 69.

programs are acceptable substitutes for federal inspection. Likewise, the buyer must assume that local and state requirements are enforced.

Grading. Grading of meat products refers to a voluntary service that indicates quality. Grades show the extent to which a specific product meets a standard established for the product. There are two types of federal grades:

Quality grading—Measures the product against factors which suggest how the meat will taste.

Yield grading—Tells the purchaser about the amount of yield (the percentage of boneless, trimmed retail cuts which will come from a carcass).

Grading is influenced by class of animal (for example, steer, heifer, and bull classifications for beef). Buyers wishing to use the optional federal grading requirements as part of the specification should include the class they desire (specific information about grading is found in Section 22.11).

IMPS and MBG descriptions. The U.S. Department of Agriculture's Institutional Meat Purchase Specifications (IMPS) and National Association of Meat Purveyors' Meat Buyers Guide (MBG) contain descriptions of available meat products that serve as invaluable aids when writing purchase specifications for meat. The MBG contains illustrations of standard meat cuts and portion cut products. These photos, along with written descriptions, enable the food buyer to accurately determine the product which is desired. The IMPS or MBG identification number can become an integral part of the purchase specification for meat products. When they are listed in the specification meat suppliers should not have difficulty understanding what product is needed; most suppliers are familiar with the IMPS and MBG numbers and product description.

Acceptable weight or thickness limitations. When standard meat cuts are ordered the weight should be specified in pounds. When portion-control products are ordered weight should be stated in ounces, or, as an alternate, thickness of portion-cut products can be stated. In either case a tare allowance (the range above or below the desired weight that the product may weigh) should also be included.

Fat limitations. Except when yield grades are specified for beef and lamb products, the allowable thickness of surface fat may be stated.

State of refrigeration. Food buyers should specify whether a chilled (refrigerated) or frozen product is desired.

Miscellaneous information regarding meat specifications. Several other information items are included in meat specifications:

When tying is required this should be stated.
Procedures for boning can be listed.

Packaging closures and instructions should be outlined.

Requirements regarding sealing and marking of containers are useful.

15.3.2 Additional Information

A listing of information to be included in purchase specifications for meat is included in Section 22.15. Buyers desiring excellent source material on meat buying are referred to:

Pedderson, R. *Specifications: The Comprehensive Foodservice Purchasing and Specification Manual*, 1977. (Available from : CBI Publishing Co., 51 Sleeper St., Boston, Mass. 02210.)

National Association of Meat Purveyors. *Meat Buyers Guide*, 1976. (Available from: National Association of Meat Purveyors, 252 West INA Road, Tucson, Arizona 85704.)

15.4   Purchase of Seafoods

Fish and shellfish are found on the menus of many commercial food and beverage operations. These products are gaining in popularity as nutritious alternatives to often more expensive meat products.

15.4.1 Specific Purchase Concerns

Seafood buyers should be aware of the following specific purchase concerns:

Types.   There are two basic types of seafoods:

1. Fin fish, which are scaly fish with backbones and fins.
2. Shellfish, which are mollusks—shell without segmented bodies—such as clams, oysters, and scallops. Crustaceans—shell with segmented bodies—include lobster, shrimp, and crayfish.

Fin Fish can be purchased several ways:

Whole—From the sea

Drawn—Eviscerated

Dressed—Eviscerated without head, tail, fins

Fillets—Lengthwise half of the fish cut from the backbone

Sticks—Fillets cut into pieces

Steaks—Cross-sections of dressed fish without skin

Shellfish can be purchased several ways:

Alive (such as lobster and crab)
Whole, in the shell (such as cooked lobster and crab)
Shucked, with the shell removed (such as oyster and scallop)
Headless (such as shrimp)
Cooked meat (picked from cooked shellfish, such as crab and shrimp)

Availability— With modern transportation systems fresh fish are essentially available anywhere in season (although transportation costs for "nonlocal" fish can be high and quality can rapidly deteriorate). Frozen seafood products are usually available almost everywhere year-round.

Quality— Quality of fresh fish is evidenced by:

Flesh that is firm and elastic: it should not be separating from the bone; it should not have loose scales; the flesh should rebound when pressed with the finger.
No odor.
Eyes that are bright and clear, bulging from the head.
Gills that are reddish-pink, with no slime.
Skin that is shiny without faded color.

The quality of frozen seafood is evidenced by:

Flesh that is frozen solid; there should be no discoloration (such as brownish freezer burn).
No odor.
Wrapping of acceptable freezer quality material.

Grading and inspection—Inspection for wholesomeness is voluntary, *not* required; however, the U.S. Public Health Service must approve shellfish beds from which these products are harvested. Federal quality grades have been developed for many common forms of frozen fish by the U.S. Bureau of Commercial Fisheries.

The U.S. Department of Commerce has developed grades for some fresh fish. Flavor, texture, and odor characteristics are used to establish Grades A, B, and C products. In order for fish to be graded they must first be inspected which, as noted above, is a voluntary procedure.

Processing—Fresh and frozen seafood products are commonly used in commercial food and beverage operations. It is also possible to purchase products in canned, dried, and smoked condition. Portion-controlled patties, sticks, and similar products are also commonly used.

15.4.2   Additional Information

A listing of information to be included in purchase specifications for seafood is included in Section 22.15. Buyers desiring excellent source material for seafood are referred to:

Kotschevar, L. *Quality Food Purchasing*, 2nd ed, 1975 (Available from : John Wiley and Sons, 605 Third Avenue, New York, New York 10016).

15.5   Purchase of Poultry

Purchasing poultry products is not difficult if basic purchasing practices are followed. Since poultry is a relatively inexpensive protein source it may serve a vital purpose for attracting the price-conscious diner.

15.5.1   Specific Purchase Concerns

Poultry buyers should be aware of the following specific purchase concerns.

Kind and class of poultry.   Kind of poultry refers to species; class refers to age and sex characteristics of poultry of the same kind. Details are included in Section 22.12.

Inspection and grading.   USDA inspection is required for all poultry products moving in interstate commerce. Grading is voluntary and is based upon factors noted in Section 22.12. Grades of A (highest quality), B, and C (lowest quality) result.

Style.   Orders should require a style of poultry for delivery. Examples are:

Whole, ready to eat	Thighs
Breasts	Wings
Breasts with ribs	Halves
Drumsticks	Quarters

Size.   Weight limitations for the required style of poultry should be specified.

State of refrigeration.   Products are commonly purchased fresh or frozen. Other syles (such as canned) are also available.

Breed.   Yield and flavor of poultry meat are affected by breed; for example, broilers frequently come from a cross between a Rock Cornish Game Hen and a white Plymouth Rock.*

15.5.2   Additional Information

A review of factors to include in purchase specifications for poultry is listed in Section 22.12. Buyers desiring excellent source material for poultry are referred to:

Kotschevar, L. *Quantity Food Purchasing,* 2nd ed., 1975. (Available from: John Wiley and Sons, 605 Third Avenue, New York, New York 10016.)

15.6   Purchase of Eggs and Egg Products

Information concerning procedures used to purchase eggs are included in this section.

15.6.1   Specific Purchase Concerns

Purchase specifications for eggs should consider a number of factors.

Inspection.   All eggs and egg products should be inspected for wholesomeness.

Grading.   Quality grading is voluntary and considers the following factors (cracked, dirty, and broken eggs do not receive a grade even if the egg itself is of high quality):

Shell—Cleanliness, shape, texture, and cracks are considered.

Amount of air cell present.

White—Thickness and color are considered.

Yolk—Location and height are important.

U.S. Grades for shell eggs are:

1. U.S. Grade AA—Egg covers small area; white is thick; yolk is firm and stands high (good for frying and poaching).

Peddersen, Specifications: The Comprehensive Foodservice Purchasing and Specification Manual, ibid., *pp. 387–389.*

2. U.S. Grade A—Egg covers a moderate area; white is reasonably thick; yolk is firm and stands high (good for frying and poaching).
3. U.S. Grade B—Egg spreads; white is thin; yolk is flat (best used in cooking and baking).

Purchasers should specify that eggs be delivered within 2 to 3 days of grading at a temperature of approximately 40°F.

Size.   Shell eggs: egg sizes and weights per dozen are:

1. Jumbo   30 oz.
2. Extra large   27 oz.
3. Large   24 oz.
4. Medium   21 oz.
5. Small   18 oz.
6. Peewee   15 oz.

Size/type of pack.   Shell eggs are normally packed in cases of 30 dozen each; 1/2 cases are frequently available. Processed egg products are available in many sizes of packages. Most common are 30# and 10# cans, 10# plastic bags (frozen), and 1# and 5# cartons (dried eggs).

Fresh or processed.   In addition to shell eggs, processed eggs are available. Common forms are:

Whole, frozen   Egg yolk, frozen
Egg whites, frozen   Egg yolk, with sugar, frozen
Egg roll, frozen   Eggs, dried

Egg Condition.   Shell eggs are classified as "fresh" if they are under twenty-nine days old and "storage" if they are more than twenty-nine days old. Another classification, "processed storage," applies when the egg shells have been oiled before storage.

15.6.2 Additional Information

A review of specific factors to include in purchase specifications for eggs is listed in Section 22.15. Buyers desiring excellent source material for eggs are referred to:

Peddersen, R. *Specifications: The Comprehensive Foodservice Purchasing and Specification Manual,* 1977. (Available from: CBI Publishing Co., 51 Sleeper St., Boston, Mass. 02210.)

15.7 Purchase of Dairy Products

Milk, butter, and cheese are the principal dairy products. They are reviewed in this section.

15.7.1 Milk and Ice Cream

Good quality milk is usually assured through rigid adherence to regulations recommended by the U.S. Public Health Service. Quality milk has a low bacterial count, good flavor and appearance, and high nutritional value. Commonly purchased milk is Grade A, which indicates a high quality milk product.

There is a variety of types of milk.

Pasteurized milk. Milk is heated to a specified temperature for a specified time in order to kill organisms that might cause disease.

Homogenized milk. Milk is mechanically treated in order to break up and dispense fat throughout the product. This prevents separation of the cream.

Kind of milk. Many kinds of milk are available to the food and beverage buyer. A description of several of the most common include:

Fresh whole fluid milk—Contains at least 3.25 percent butterfat and 8.25 percent nonfat milk solids.

Fresh skim fluid milk—Contains less butterfat than whole milk, usually 0.10 percent.

Two percent fluid milk—contains 2.0 percent butterfat.

Buttermilk—A milk product which is cultured with a specific bacteria and incubated until a specific acid content has been reached.

Chocolate milk—Whole fluid milk flavored with a chocolate syrup or powder.

Half and half—A mixture of milk and cream which contains between 10.5 and 18.0 percent butterfat.

Light cream—Cream which contains between 18 and 30 percent butterfat.

Heavy cream—Cream which contains at least 36 percent butterfat.

Size/type of container. Milk and milk products are available in many types and sizes of packaging units. Requirements should be specified.

Additives. Vitamins A and D may be combined with milk and milk products in approved quantities. Other ingredients may be added such as flavorings and certain "carriers" for vitamins.

Ice cream. Ice cream is frequently purchased in plain (vanilla) or flavored varieties. Plain ice cream contains a minimum of 10 percent butterfat, a minimum of 20 percent milk solids, and must, as a minimum, weigh 4.5 pounds per gallon. Flavored ice creams contain a minimum of 8 percent butterfat and 16 percent milk solids, and must also weigh 4.5 pounds per gallon.

It is not usually necessary to develop detailed purchase specifications for milk products. Normally a specific supplier is selected for a time period and his or her brands are used.

15.7.2 Cheese

There are literally hundreds of varieties of cheeses available. Two basic kinds used in food and beverage operations are natural (made from animal milk) and processed (made by combining natural cheeses).

Another classification of cheese considers type of ripening:

Nonripened—Examples are cottage, cream, and ricotta.

Mold-ripened—Blue and roquefort are examples.

Bacteria-ripened—Parmesan, American, Swiss, and cheddar are included in this type.

Other important information applicable to the purchase of cheese includes:

Federal standards of identity exist for many American cheeses.

Inspection of cheese is voluntary.

Federal grades exist for some varieties of American-made cheese; the highest grade is U.S. Grade AA.

Cheeses purchased in quantity by commercial food and beverage buyers are often purchased in 1#, 5#, or 10# package sizes. Common cheeses used in food and beverage operations are:

American Cheese	Cottage Cheese
Blue Cheese	Cream Cheese
Buck Cheese	Swiss Cheese
Cheddar Cheese	Parmesan Cheese

Processed cheese foods (which contain less butterfat, more milk solids, and additional moisture) may also be used.

15.7.3 Butter

Butter is a common product made with milk and/or cream. It may have salt or additional coloring and must contain at least 80 percent butterfat.

Grades of butter include:

U.S. Grade AA (93 score)—Highest quality

U.S. Grade A (92 score)

U.S. Grade B (90 score)

U.S. Grade C (89 score)—Lowest quality that is given a grade.

Grades note characteristics of selected flavors, body, color, and taste sensations of salt. Aroma is also a factor.

Market forms. Butter is commonly purchased:

In pound cubes (64# or 50#/case)
In prints (30 - 1# prints/case)
In pats (72 or 90 pats/# in 5# box)

Classification of butter. The types include:

Sweet cream butter—Made of sweet cream kept sweet until processing.
Creamery—Factory made from milk from many herds.
Sweet butter—No salt; made from sweet or sour cream.
Salted butter—Butter with added salt.
Farm/dairy butter—Generally unpasteurized butter made on the farm
    from a single herd.
Sour cream butter—Most common butter; made from cream that has
    naturally soured.

Other concerns. Good butter:

Shows rough, irregular shape when it is forceably broken;
"Stands up" at normal kitchen temperatures; it shows no visible moisture.
Has a clear, even color with no visible streaks.

15.7.4 Additional Information

A review of factors to include in purchase specifications for dairy products is listed in Section 22.15. Buyers desiring excellent source material for dairy products are referred to:

Peddersen, R. *Specifications: The Comprehensive Foodservice Purchasing and Specification Manual*, 1977. (Available from: CBI Publishing Co., 51 Sleeper St., Boston, Mass. 02210.)

15.8   Purchase of Cereal Products

Wheat, rice, corn, oats, and other cereal products are utilized by many commercial food and beverage operations.

15.8.1   Specific Purchase Concerns

When developing purchase specifications for cereal products, consider the following information:

Processed cereal grains are turned into flour, starch, oil, syrups, and other
    commonly used products.
Specifications for grain products can include:
    Grain to be of sound/high quality.
    Must come from latest crop.

To be fully matured before processing.

Bright color.

Dry, clean, and free from imperfections and adulteration.

When possible, the cereal should be vitamin fortified.

Grades for wheat are U.S. No. 1 (highest quality), U.S. No. 2, U.S. No.3, U.S. No.4, and U.S. No.5 (lowest quality). Another grade, "U.S. Sample," exists for products not meeting higher grades.

Wheat is classified by protein content (gluten). Types include:

Hard wheat—High in protein; bread flour and macaroni are common products.

Soft wheat—Lower in protein; cakes, cookies, pastry, and crackers are common products.

Pasta/macaroni products are actually "alimentary" pastes (shaped and dried doughs). Egg whites, salt, vegetables (onions and celery), bay leaves, and water are often added to the flour product. High-quality products are yellow in color, brittle, and break clean with an audible snap. There is a slight shine at break surface, and a pleasing flavor and odor are present.

Good white flours have no gray colorations, taste fresh, and are relatively odorless. They will be free of lumps and foreign materials. Generally, flours are purchased by brand.

Rice is often classified by grain length:

Long grain—Used for salads, stews, chicken, and meat dishes. When cooked, long-grain rice separates and becomes light and fluffy.

Medium/short grain—Used for croquettes and puddings. When cooked shorter grain rice becomes more moist and tends to stick together.

Brown rice has only an outer layer of hull and a small amount of bran removed; white rice has additional layers of bran removed.

Precooked rice is cooked after milling. Moisture is then removed; parboiled rice is steamed under pressure before being milled.

Federal grades for rice exist: U.S. Nos. 1,2,3,4,5 and U.S. Sample grade. The last is not available for brown rice; grades 1 or 2 usually represent the quality desired by food and beverage purchasers. Grades are affected by:

1. Cleanliness, wholesomeness of product.
2. Quality of milling.
3. Color.
4. Absence of foreign matter.
5. Mixture and varieties of rice in processing batch.

Wild rice is not a "real" rice in a botanical sense; it is a type of grass seed.

Miscellaneous cereal products include:

Corn—Hominy, grits (the latter are a smaller grind), and corn meal are common examples.

Barley—Used in soups and in malt (used for "malted" milks and, of course, for beers).

Oats—Cooked breakfast cereals; also baked items.

Package sizes for many cereals and flour products include 1# (packed 24 per case), 2#, 5#, 25#, 50# and 100#.

Larger lots are also available, up to and including railroad car sizes (100,000 pounds).

15.8.2 Additional Information

Buyers desiring additional information about the purchase of cereal products are referred to:

Kotschevar, L. *Quantity Food Purchasing,* 2nd ed., 1975. (Available from: John Wiley and Sons, 605 Third Avenue, New York, New York 10016.)

15.9 Purchase of Fresh Fruits and Vegetables

Modern technology and transportation systems enable the food and beverage purchaser in almost any area of the country to obtain a wide variety of high quality fresh fruits and vegetables.

15.9.1 Specific Purchase Concerns

Buyers should consider the following aspects of fresh fruits and vegetables.

Fresh products are harvested and shipped in the fresh state; they are often free of soil and insects. Temperature is controlled in an attempt to provide a quality of product at the point of purchase which is similar to quality levels when the products are harvested and shipped.

It is often wise to purchase fresh produce when it is in season: quality is higher and more consistent. Attempting to obtain high-quality products when they are not in season (or at the beginning or end of the season) may not be possible and, if it is, will certainly be expensive.

Food and beverage purchasers often find the purchase of fresh produce to be somewhat difficult:

When grades are specified there is no assurance that the condition of the product will be maintained during transportation and storage; the product may deteriorate, so *careful* inspection on receipt is required.

Not all products (even commonly used ones) are available all the time; certainly not all grades are available all the time.

Prices can fluctuate daily.

Buyers in less urban areas may have difficulty finding a supplier who can provide needed quality.

There are many types of many varieties of products available; how do we determine the type of apple, onion, or lettuce we desire?

Food and beverage purchasers should insist upon "freshness" when they order fresh products. Color, crispness, weight/size, shape, and absence of decay are good indicators.

Grading and inspection of fresh produce are often voluntary. There is an effort under way to standardize the grade names which currently differ for various products. Grades* are used to describe quality characteristics such as:

Size, appearance, uniformity of size, maturity, color, cleanliness, shape, freedom from specified injury or damage, interior structure of the product, absence of seedstems, etc. Grades set up tolerances of permissible variations since it is not possible to pack produce which meet all specifications to the required quality limit.

Generally, U.S. No. 1 grade represents a good product quality; Grades 1 and 2 are those most commonly used by food and beverage operations.

Specifications for fresh fruit and vegetables should indicate the following, as applicable:

Grade—Specifying a grade has a definite meaning which indicates important details that otherwise would need to be included in the specifications.

Additional quality requirements, if any.

Variety (not as important in the purchase of vegetables).

Size.

Quantity.

Brand (if desirable).

Growing area (less important in purchase of vegetables).

Information about fresh produce grading and requirements for specifications are from R. Peddersen, Specifications: The Comprehensive Foodservice Purchasing and Specification Manual *(Boston, Mass.: CBI Publishing Co. 1977), pp. 475–477.*

Type of pack (cardboard or plastic cases without staples might be specified; bags, bushels, etc., are also frequently specified).

Count per container.

15.9.2   Additional Information

Buyers desiring additional information about the purchase of fresh produce are referred to Section 22.15 for a specific listing of factors to include in purchase specifications. Detailed supplementary information is found in:

Moyer, W. *The Buying Guide for Fresh Fruits, Vegetables, Herbs, and Nuts*, 1976. (Available from: Blue Goose, Inc., Post Office Box 46, Fullerton, California 92632.)

Peddersen, R. *Specifications: The Comprehensive Foodservice Purchasing and Specification Manual*, 1977. (Available from: CBI Publishing Co., 51 Sleeper St., Boston, Mass 02210.)

15.10   Purchase of Processed Fruits and Vegetables

Food and beverage buyers use canned, frozen, and dried fruit and vegetable products. Information concerning their purchase is presented in this section.

15.10.1   Specific Purchase Concerns

There are a number of items of special interest in the purchase of processed fruits and vegetables.

Canned fruit and vegetable products have long been popular. Purchase specifications should consider:

Grades. They indicate the quality characteristics of products and tell whether a canned good meets a generally recognized standard. Grading standards consider quality factors such as color, uniform size and shape, absence of defects, texture, aroma, tenderness, flavor, consistency, finish, size, syrup (including clearness), maturity, texture, wholesomeness, and cut. General requirements also consider fill, drained weight, and syrup density (amount of sugar in the packing medium). Purchasers desiring more specific descriptions of required quality can also indicate a point score (used as the basis to establish broad grade ranges below which products must not fall).

Drained weight. Indicates the minimum amount of food to be included in a can.

Packing medium. Canned fruits are packed in water or in juice containing varying amounts of sugar.

Other information. Where applicable, purchase specifications can also indicate product style, count (actually sieve size), packaging requirements, source, variety, and miscellaneous other information designed to specifically identify the product desired.

Can size. Size of can should be included in the purchase specifications. Sizes of commonly used cans are in Table 15.1.

Table 15.1 Common Can Sizes

Name of Can	Volume in oz.	Approx. Cups	# of Cans in Case
No. 303	15.6 oz.	2	12/24/36
No. 303 cylinder	19.0 oz.	2 1/3	12/24/36
No. 2 1/2	28.5 oz.	3 1/2	12/24
No. 10	103.7 oz.	12 3/4	6
No. 1, picnic	10.5 oz.	1 1/4	24/48

Frozen fruit and vegetable products are also popular. Generally, concerns for the purchase of frozen products are very similar to those for the purchase of canned items.

Flavor. Frozen products generally have a fresher flavor since they have not been cooked during processing: Likewise, they are frozen soon after harvesting (when, supposedly, they are at peak flavor).

Sizes. Package sizes for frozen products provide a great variety of alternates:

For frozen fruits: packs include 10 oz., 12 oz., 16 oz., 6#, 6 1/2#, 20#, 25#, and 30# containers.

For frozen vegetables: packs include 10 oz., 12 oz., 16 oz., 2#, 2 1/2#, 3#, and 5# containers.

In the case of both fruits and vegetables, the number of packages per purchase container may vary.

Dried products. Some limited use is made of low-moisture products. Dried potatoes and fruit products are the most commonly used. Buyers might do well to sample the products available from local suppliers, then to purchase these items on a by-brand basis.

15.10.2 Additional Information

Types of factors to include in purchase specifications for canned and frozen fruits and vegetables are found in Section 22.15. More specific information regarding the purchase of these products is available in:

Kotschevar, L. *Quantity Food Purchasing*, 2nd ed., 1975. (Available from: John Wiley and Sons, 605 Third Avenue, New York, New York 10016.)

15.11 Purchase of Alcoholic Beverages

Operations which sell alcoholic beverages have special concerns as selection decisions regarding these items are made. Brands to be purchased are determined by considering the market (clientele) to be served. The major elements of brand selection are very similar to those which are important for planning food menus. The guest must be considered, and there must be an attempt to select beverage brands based on judgment about the guest's expectations and how they can be met.

15.11.1 Selection of House Brands (Liquor)

House-brand selection is closely related to the marketing decision. Attitudes of management range from "don't use anything you wouldn't be proud to display on the back bar" to "use the least expensive; let people pay extra for a premium brand." In practice, a middle-ground compromise is frequently used; neither the least expensive nor the most expensive brand is generally desirable for house liquor use. Quality and value, relative to the price charged the customer, are major factors in determining house brands. Many other factors which should be considered as house brands are purchased are reviewed in Section 22.14.

The quality of house brands, in some cases, can be traced back to the distilling company. Some manufacturers bottle a "call brand" product and also produce beverages under different, perhaps lesser known, labels. These products are generally of high quality and might provide very acceptable house brands for many facilities. Purchasing staff should talk with their suppliers about the availability of these products.

15.11.2 Selection of Call Brands (Liquor)

Call-brand selection is also related to the marketing decision; however, it cannot be a goal of the beverage operation to have available every possible "call" liquor which might be ordered. Not everyone can be pleased all the time. A better approach is to have available those call brands most frequently ordered by customers within the market. If a call brand is not available many guests will order another brand. If a liquor is frequently asked for or desired by regular customers it should, obviously, be available and should be added to the list of beverage products routinely purchased. The reverse is also true; many operations carry call brands which have lost popularity (perhaps they were a "fad" at one time or a regular customer who has since moved from the locality had a favorite). These should be "run out" and then removed from the purchase list.

Beverage product issue records should be reviewed occasionally; items which do not move should not, of course, be reordered.

15.11.3   Selection of Wine and Beer

The "marketing" concerns noted to be important in selecting brands of house and call liquors are also important when determining wines and beers to carry. Each food and beverage operation must consider what its clientele desires; these products should, of course, be offered. A large, high-check average property will probably need a more extensive offering than its small, low-check average counterpart.

A simple wine list might be constructed as follows:

An expensive and less expensive sparkling wine ("champagne").

An expensive and less expensive dry white wine.

An expensive and less expensive fruity white wine.

An expensive and less expensive hearty red wine.

An expensive and less expensive lighter red wine.

A moderately priced dry and fruity dessert wine.

Appetizer wine(s) as appropriate.

Many commercial food and beverage operations offer wines by the glass or carafe. As this is done, "house" wines, perhaps purchased in "jugs" (3 liter, 4 liter, and/or gallon sizes) are in order.

Beers are selected on the basis of customers' preferences. Many facilities will offer one or more "premium" products to complement less expensive, standard products. Depending upon the atmosphere desired draft beer may also be available.

15.11.4   Additional Information

An excellent source book of detailed information about alcoholic beverages is:

Grossman, H. *Grossman's Guide to Wines, Beers and Spirits.* 6th rev. ed., 1977. (Available from: Charles Scribner's, 597 Fifth Avenue, New York, New York 10017.)

16

PURCHASE OF CONTRACTED SERVICES

Most food and beverage operations "purchase" services that might otherwise be performed by employees of the facility.* Decisions about the use of contracted services are similar in many ways to "make/buy" decisions which concern the need, if any, to buy ready-to-serve, convenience foods or to make products (see Section 10).

16.1 Similarities to Product Purchases

Some ways in which the purchase of services is similar to the purchase of products include:

While it is not always best to accept the lowest price it is wise to contact all of the known suppliers of the desired services. To the extent that food and beverage purchasers and management personnel can explain needs and assess a supplier's abilities to provide needed services at required quality levels, interacting with all eligible suppliers is helpful.

It is a good practice to look at alternatives. Food and beverage management may purchase services or they may determine that it is best for employees of the food and beverage operation to perform required work.

Purchase of some unnecessary services can be delayed if cash flow or other management or financial related problems arise.

If a decision is made to contract with an outside firm alternatives are still available (who should be hired?).

The process of determining need for service, *quality* and *quantity* (perhaps measured by frequency of need), *price* concerns, and *timing* (when a service must be performed) is the same.

Value concerns (price relative to service quality) are present.

A study of all factors—economic and noneconomic—is important as decisions are made.

16.2 Differences from Product Purchases

Differences in the purchase of contracted services also must be considered:

Services are more intangible (less "physical") than products; how do we know when we "receive" them in the proper "quality"?

---

*This section is loosely based on G. Aljian, Purchasing Handbook, 3rd ed. (New York, N.Y.: McGraw-Hill, 1973, Section 18).

Many contracts involve large costs and very high risks.

The food and beverage operation is exposed to many potential legal liabilities.

Many contractors perform locally only; they often operate with minimum finances and do not have an extensive track record that can be evaluated.

It is often difficult to determine when a service has or has not been provided. Often problems stemming from provision of a contracted service cannot be resolved; it may be "too late" (as when an outside consultant service, after study, makes a "bad" suggestion that the food and beverage operation expand in another location).

Work to be performed is often difficult to completely define; for example, there are not quality "grades" available for bookkeeping services such as there are for many food products.

There are few standards—even proven "guidelines"—for contract formats or even for required general conditions of service contracts.

16.3   Types of Services

Contracted services can generally be broken down into three broad types:

1. Professional services—Legal, accounting, financial, consulting, etc.
2. Facilities and equipment related services—Such as janitorial, landscaping, equipment maintenance, etc. (This is the largest category of contracted services for most food and beverage operations.)
3. Personnel/employee related—Uniform, vending machine, and similar "personal" services are included here.

Special concerns are required as each type of service is purchased. These are reviewed in the next section.

16.4   Concerns in Purchase of Services

The following basic concerns should be addressed in the purchase of services.

16.4.1   Professional/Consulting Services

When the purchaser is attempting to contract for professional consulting services several basic problems may need to be dealt with.

When possible, it is best to define the *exact* service(s) to be provided in terms which make measurement or compliance possible.

Time schedules for completion of the required work are important ("as soon as possible" is no longer sufficient!).

A third major concern relates to determining *who* is best qualified to perform the required work within the allotted time intervals.

It is necessary to do several things in order to deal with these problems:

First, be sure that no one within the food and beverage operation can perform the required services. If they can, a decision regarding "staying inside" or "going outside" the food and beverage operation is necessary.

Describe exactly what is to be accomplished.

State objectives for hiring a contracted service.

List, in as detailed a fashion as possible, exactly what is to be done in order to accomplish stated objectives.

State any limitations on the required services.

List questions to be answered as a result of the service being provided.

Provide a detailed time schedule which includes starting date, a schedule for interim reports, if any, and a completion date requirement.

Food and beverage management should require that a consultant's proposal to do required work list the following:

Qualifications.

Experience (check references).

A description of techniques to be used.

A statement of problems and plans to resolve problem(s) which illustrates that the proposed resource person does, in fact, understand what must be done.

If subcontractors will be used, they should be identified and their qualifications should be indicated.

Total, *firm* price which includes travel and other related expenses and a description of payment, terms, and conditions.

It is important to have verbal discussions to ensure that both food and beverage management officials and consultants understand the other's needs and requirements.

16.4.2 Facilities/Equipment Services

Most food and beverage operations employ several types of equipment services. This is also an area in which serious analysis is needed to determine whether contracted service or in-house personnel are needed.

16.4.2.1 Examples of services.   Possible services which can be contracted out to non-food and beverage personnel include the following; depending on results of analysis, each might also be performed by food and beverage employees.

>Laundry (napkins, table cloths, *etc.*) cleaning
>Security protection
>Janitorial
>Grounds maintenance/grooming
>Routine foodservice equipment maintenance
>Pest control services
>Window/wall/carpet cleaning
>Snow removal
>Public and employee restroom cleaning
>Knife sharpening

Other types of services generally need to be contracted out because of specialized skills and/or equipment required. Examples are:

>Office equipment maintenance and repair
>Electronic register/data machine maintenance and repair
>Fire protection equipment maintenance
>Time clock service
>Water conditioning equipment service
>Landscape services
>Exhaust/ventilation hood steam cleaning
>Outdoor sign maintenance and repair
>Exterior building maintenance and repair

16.4.2.2 Important concerns in contract development.   Several important concerns to be identified and agreed upon as food and beverage personnel enter into agreements for facilities/equipment services include:

>*Exact* definition of the work to be performed.
>Economic terms (payment amounts and schedules, *etc.*).
>Times of access to food and beverage operation.
>Limits of authority under contract.
>Company obligations for bonding its employees.
>Supplies, equipment, *etc.*, to be provided by the service company.
>Conditions under which contracts can be terminated for alleged non- or
>>unsatisfactory performance.
>Quality of products and equipment to be utilized in providing the service.
>Time limitations of the contract.

Other aspects of contracts discussed in Section 13 also apply to the development of service contracts.

16.5   Types of Contracts

Two basic types of service contracts are commonly used.

1. *Cost-reimbursable contracts.* These are based either on time and material or labor and machine time. These types of contracts are not desirable since it is difficult to determine allowable costs and because there is less incentive to keep incurred costs low. There is, then, some difficulty determining "up-front" what the cost implications of the contract are.

2. *Fixed-price contracts.* Those contracts—in which there is a better assurance/knowledge that costs/charges will be reasonable—are preferred. With this plan the food and beverage management-purchasing team knows the definite cost of the contract.

General rules for selecting the basic type of contract to use include:

If the tasks to be performed under the contract cannot be accurately defined and/or satisfactory performance cannot be measured, a cost reimbursable contract may be best.

If the tasks to be performed under the contract can be defined and if performance can be measured, a fixed-price contract may be best.

16.6   Contract Terms and Conditions

Many terms and conditions applicable to any contract are necessary in service contracts. While it is important that a trained attorney draw up or, at least review, proposed contracts of this nature, some important service contract terms and conditions may include obligations relating to the following:

The service contractor must include a "hold harmless" clause to protect the food and beverage operation from liabilities which may arise because of acts (or failure to act) by the contractor.

Adequate insurance coverage must be provided for.

Description or limitations of the service agreement should be specified.

Period of service.

Contract termination date.
All matters relating to payment.
Taxes (payment responsibilities).
Inspection rights and procedures before payment.
Changes in required work after the contract is implemented.
Assignment/subcontracting by service company.
Affirmative action obligations.
Liens to be released.
Required safety and health protection.
Permits.

17

PURCHASE OF CAPITAL EQUIPMENT ITEMS

Food and beverage management and purchasing personnel must occasionally make capital equipment purchases. These "big ticket" purchases demand special attention. Procedures for managing the purchase of these items are presented in this section.

17.1 Definition of Capital Equipment

The term "capital equipment" describes items that have a long life, are expensive, and are carried on the food and beverage operation's balance sheet. As such, they are depreciated over time based on the extent to which their useful life is judged to be expended in the generation of income for the applicable fiscal period. For example, a deep fryer or oven would be a capital equipment item. Each is expensive, is included as a long-term (fixed) asset on the balance sheet, and is depreciated. If the oven cost $1,000 and has a useful life of ten years, $100 would be included as an expense on the income (profit and loss) statement annually.

17.2 How Capital Equipment Purchases are Different

There are several important differences in the purchase of capital equipment which set this process apart from the routine, recurring purchase of products and supplies. Examples of the differences include:

Capital items are purchased infrequently; routine procedures are often not established for their purchase as would be the case when products are purchased often.

Such purchases represent a long-term investment. Since the equipment item has a long life, the food and beverage operation may have to live with the item for many years.

Capital purchases will affect the production of the food and beverage operation; thus, an oven which is not "right" for the operation may affect meal production in the entire kitchen.

Generally, a requisition from the user department does not authorize purchase of the equipment item; rather, a special budget appropriation is necessary to allocate funds for purchase or to begin negotiations with lending institutions, the equipment supplier, or leasing companies as necessary.

Greater lead time is needed for the purchase; few suppliers have a large variety of items available for immediate delivery. Items must be ordered and shipped from manufacturers in many instances.

The amount of investment is much greater; as more food and beverage funds are being obligated, there is a greater need to take special care with the purchasing process.

The extent of negotiation with suppliers is greater. Seldom do food and beverage purchasers accept a first-price quotation on a major item without making an attempt to reduce the price or to increase supplier services.

Procedures for negotiation are reviewed in Section 7.4. More members of the food and beverage operation are likely to be involved in the purchase decision in this situation. When products and supplies are being purchased perhaps only user department and storage and purchasing staff are involved. When capital equipment is purchased, top management and, perhaps, accounting staff are also included in the decision-making process.

Detailed records regarding both the identity and use of capital equipment are required for accounting, security, and maintenance and repair purposes.

Capital equipment may less likely be affected by frequent price fluctuations. While the prices of these items obviously follow inflationary spirals, their costs do not fluctuate daily or weekly (as would be the case, for example, with fresh produce).

17.3   Overview of Capital Equipment Purchase Procedures

A general review of procedures used to purchase capital equipment items is included in this section.

17.3.1   Recognition of Need

Most often personnel in the food and beverage department recognize the need for equipment purchase. This recognition generally involves the recurrence of a problem which they believe can be resolved by purchase of equipment. Often the need to purchase a particular equipment item is not absolute or immediate; frequently alternative equipment items can be considered. There are many instances when the purchase can be delayed until management determines that an appropriate time has arrived.

Management confronts a special problem when trying to determine whether an existing equipment item should be repaired or replaced. Consider the following:

"Problems" with existing equipment may be caused by the demand for the equipment to do work it was not designed to do. For example, a deep fryer may be required to work at a greater capacity than its rated output; its purchase was either a "bad" decision in the first place or production requirements have increased since its purchase. To repair a defective fryer in this instance may be unwise; the purchase of a unit with greater capacity may be in order.

Equipment of low quality (again the result of a poor purchase decision) may not be "worth" the repair. Some consideration must be given in the decision as to whether the equipment can perform in a manner which makes it effective; that is, it must be able to adequately perform required tasks.

If defective equipment can be replaced with new equipment that creates labor savings which at least partially pay for new equipment, this creates justification for replacement rather than for equipment repair.

When maintenance and repair of older equipment approaches the monthly purchase costs of new equipment, a purchase decision can often easily be made.

When technological advances have created new equipment items that can perform the work older units cannot do, their existence also points to replacement rather than repair. An example might be new data machines that outperform the older cash registers used by many food and beverage operations.

17.3.2 Budget Indications

The large expenses involved in capital equipment purchases require careful study of the operating budget before any purchases can be authorized. If the item is in the budget the purchase process may go forward; a commitment can be made. If not, preliminary work will probably be needed to determine the specific equipment needed, its costs, and other considerations. When funds are allocated for capital equipment purchase, it is often helpful for accounting personnel to encumber (set aside) monies so that they will be available for equipment purchase.

To review, it is frequently necessary first to obtain management authorization to purchase an equipment item and, second, to allocate funds in the operating budget for its purchase.

17.3.3 Role of the Purchasing Department

As capital equipment is purchased, the role of purchasing personnel, serving in a staff, advisory role may include these jobs:

Obtaining general information from equipment suppliers about items which may be useful to resolve user department problems (this help can come from collecting equipment brochures and fact sheets and from verbal interviews with suppliers and equipment users in other facilities).

Providing help with cost-benefit studies.

Developing final purchase specifications.

Requesting price quotations from suppliers.

Comparing quotations.

Undertaking supplier negotiations.

Advising the user departments about the decision it must make.

Making purchase obligations and following through on delivery, payment, and any necessary warranty coverage concerns.

In general, the role of purchasing department staff in the process of equipment purchase *after* an obligation has been made is very similar to its role in the purchase of other items. Unfortunately, there may not be a great number of suppliers who can provide the necessary equipment. On the one hand this makes the purchase task easier; on the other hand it makes it very important.

17.3.4 Role of the User Department

It has already been noted (Section 17.3.1) that generally personnel in the user (food and beverage) departments first recognize the need for an equipment item. Other tasks of these personnel include:

To determine specifically what type of equipment is necessary (such as an oven).

To explain, defend, and justify this need to top management.

To work with purchasing personnel and suppliers to determine the specific equipment needs (such as a convection oven with specified capacities and capabilities).

To analyze information presented by the purchasing staff.

To help develop, based upon this information, a cost-benefit or other type of economic analysis to help determine what, if any, item should be purchased.

To help determine purchase specifications.

To work with the supplier who is awarded the order in regard to equipment installation, training, and other tasks.

To promptly notify purchasing and top management if problems occur that require supplier or manufacturer assistance.

17.3.5 Top Management

Top management officials have a clear role to play in the purchase of capital equipment.

They must confirm that a need exists and authorize a study or analysis.

They must determine, as the basis of priorities, that items should be purchased.

They must make budget allowances for the purchase.

They must formally approve the equipment purchase.

They may indicate what specific item to purchase after studying the information and analysis done by the purchasing and user department staffs.

17.4   Selecting the Supplier

The process of selecting the supplier may be easy or difficult. It is best to determine the specific brand or model of desired equipment first, *then* to select the supplier from among those who carry the desired brand. However, if there is an exclusive territory agreement between a manufacturer and supplier (so that only one supplier can—or desires to—carry a particular brand of equipment), the supplier selection decision may have been made when the brand of equipment to purchase was determined. If a specific brand is desired perhaps only one (and certainly just a *very* few) suppliers can be used.

To review, then, when possible a supplier should be selected after the equipment decision is made. In this manner operating and engineering differences between the equipment alternatives have already been considered. Likewise, by this time economic analyses will have been performed to verify that the equipment will be beneficial.

The selection among suppliers who are carrying the required equipment should be based upon a number of factors:

Reputation—Past experience with suppliers is a very important consideration in the selection decision. While past *personal* experience is best, the comments of friendly competitors are also helpful. It is very important that the selected supplier stand behind the product; he or she must be available when needed. Suppliers who don't pay bills don't get equipment shipments from manufacturers; they might also be out of business before the equipment arrives (or afterward, when assistance is needed). An honest, credible supplier with a track record of honest business practices should be chosen.

The services which a supplier provides are also an important concern. For example, there are at least three areas to review:

Pre-purchase assistance.—Some suppliers are more helpful than others during the preliminary investigation stage needed to generate ideas and to find out alternates for resolving problems. Some suppliers are genuinely helpful; many might give useful suggestions which do not directly benefit them. This type of action is a clue that the supplier is concerned about potential customers.

Payment terms, price, and credit arrangements—these are, of course, important aspects of the decision. It is not reasonable to use low price as the only determinant for supplier selection, but it is surely an important one.

After-purchase assistance—Suppliers may include in their price quote charges for delivery, installation, on-site testing, demonstration and training, and initial maintenance. Others might extend factory warranty coverage or provide reduced cost repair coverage. These kinds of details must be decided upon so that the "real" price charges for the equipment can be determined.

17.5 Equipment Purchase Contracts

Purchase of capital equipment often requires the use of a formal contract which states the obligations of the buyer and seller. Even when this is *not* judged necessary, it is important that both parties understand:

All matters pertaining to payment.

What the price includes. (For example, is price FOB supplier's warehouse? Will equipment be delivered to the food and beverage operation? Will it be uncrated? Set in place? Installed? Is training provided? Are there supplemental installation/"hook up" parts included? etc.). Each of these and similar factors should be specifically identified and agreed upon in the contract.

Any written information (such as buyer's proposal, seller's quotation, catalog stated price/warranty, etc.,) helps to assure that no "communication" problems will arise at a later date.

Any inspection procedures that will be used to confirm that the equipment performs according to advertising and verbal "understandings" with the supplier.

Since the equipment purchase contract is basically a contract with identical legal implications of other contracts, the discussion about contracts noted in Section 13.3 of this handbook can be reviewed.

17.6 Other Factors in Equipment Purchases

Equipment must be suitable for its intended use. It must also be a good value to the food and beverage operation relative to its cost. This concept of value is an important first step in determining the "worth" of an equipment item to the operation. Many components of "quality" must be considered as equipment selection concerns are identified and analyzed. Management, purchasing, and user staff should answer these questions:

Will the equipment satisfy our exact needs?

Does its price, relative to quality, represent a value investment?

Is the anticipated delivery time acceptable?

Is it compatible with existing equipment?

Is it appropriate for existing utility sources at the proposed location?

Are there space, location, or physical problems which must be overcome?

Do staff who must work with the equipment desire it? Understand its need? Agree with its purchase? Have they been involved in the decision-making process in order to assure that the equipment will be effectively and properly used?

Does the equipment provide some flexibility? (Single purpose items and those with no other use except in a specific, *exact* situation may not be desirable.)

Are all safety concerns satisfied?

Are warranty coverages adequate?

Can repair parts be secured quickly?

Is reliable, effective service available locally?

Is the equipment easy to operate?

Is routine maintenance practical? (Is there need for special expertise and tools, or is excessive time required for the tasks?)

Is the equipment durable? Will it last?

Does it provide for productive use of employee labor?

Is it energy efficient?

Is it easy to clean?

Is the machine cost-effective? (This might be expressed in terms of a payback period.)

Are specialized supplies needed for its use?

This partial listing of factors which must be considered in the purchase of equipment indicates how broad and far-reaching this type of decision is. However, study of answers to these and related questions are often necessary to assure, first, that the equipment is needed and, second, that the "best" equipment item available is selected.

17.7 Financing Capital Equipment Purchases

Since the purchase of capital equipment involves a major cost, financing the purchase may be necessary.

Adequate funds may not be available without creating cash flow problems to pay for capital equipment purchases up front.

Consideration of the leasing alternative (Section 18) may suggest that this approach is not warranted.

Procedures for financing of the equipment purchase must, then, be studied. Alternatives include several different approaches.

17.7.1   Financing by the Supplier

Sometimes the supplier will finance the purchase. In fact, willingness to do so may be a consideration in the supplier selection decision.

Frequently "earnest" money in some amount is given to the supplier at the time equipment is ordered. This protects the supplier against costs incurred if the order is cancelled before delivery.

Another payment is made at the time of delivery—usually after the equipment is determined to be in acceptable, workable order.

The remaining balance is financed—often with less than going rate interest charges—by the supplier. Conditional sales or chattel mortgage agreements (Sections 13.4.5 and 13.4.6) may be involved in this arrangement.

Food and beverage management and purchasing staff should discuss the possibilities for these and similar agreements at the time of negotiation. It may be possible to arrange no-interest financing arrangements with suppliers eager for the business. This may be very attractive to the food and beverage operation even if arrangements for cash payments could otherwise be made (the principle of working with "another's money" is well known).

Food and beverage managers should also be aware that suppliers may assign their notes to third parties (for example, when this commercial paper is used for collateral on a loan). In this case installment payments may need to be made to the third party.

17.7.2   Financing by Banks and Other Lending Organizations

When large amounts of capital must be financed or when suppliers will not finance the purchase, it may be necessary to secure funds from other sources.

The bank which is used for the operation's general checking account, and perhaps payroll account (and which may carry the note(s) for building purchase, remodeling, or other start-up costs) is an obvious first place to start. The process of applying for an equipment loan is fairly straightforward.

A bank may desire some information to suggest the purchase has been thought through; that is, that the purchase is necessary (the need for this "loan defense" probably correlates with the bank's perception of the operation's financial position and its ability to repay the loan).

Recall that chattel mortgage or other contractual obligations likely will provide the lending agency with title and perhaps other rights to protect its equity until the loan has been retired.

Recall also the need to include loan initiation, processing, and interest fees and any other associated costs in the analyses used to justify the cost of the equipment.

In today's high "money cost" market it is important that management consider alternative means to obtain funds to purchase needed equipment. If careful thought is not given to this matter, the "wise" decision to purchase equipment may turn into a "bad" one.

17.8 Disposal of Surplus or Obsolete Equipment

Generally, the responsibility for disposing of surplus or obsolete equipment (such as what is being replaced by the purchase of a new equipment item) rests with the owner-manager of a small facility and with the purchasing department in a larger operation. There are possible outlets for this equipment:

It may be most practical to negotiate a trade-in value when new equipment is purchased. This is especially likely when equipment is purchased from a supplier who does a large business in the sale of used equipment.

Used equipment dealers may purchase and haul away the item.

Food and beverage operators in the area may have needs; advertising in the local paper might alert interested officials. Also, in some states restaurant associations provide announcement services in newsletters and magazines.

It is also possible to ask food and beverage salespersons (who call on many different properties) to keep alert to competitors in need of specific used equipment items.

While it is, of course, desirable to obtain as much as possible from the sale of surplus or obsolete equipment, there is often a more pressing need to remove it from the facility in order to free necessary space. When negotiating the sale of used equipment, be sure to seek an understanding regarding a warranty, if any, and costs for removal and relocation of the equipment item(s).

17.9 Purchase of Used Equipment

Food and beverage purchasers are aware that new equipment can be purchased when there is a need for it. Section 18 suggests that equipment can also be leased. A third alternative is to buy used equipment. There are times when this is a most reasonable option. Wise purchasers are, at least, very familiar with this possible alternative.

17.9.1 Reasons to Consider Used Equipment

There are several very attractive possible advantages to the purchase of used foodservice equipment items. Among these are:

Price. The cost of used equipment is, of course, much less than the price of new equipment.

Delivery timing. Frequently, used equipment is available immediately; there is not the long lead time which is often required when new equipment must be ordered.

Satisfy user needs. There may be situations when limited need suggests that the purchaser cannot "get his money's worth" from a new equipment purchase. An inexpensive, used item may be very satisfactory for the required purpose.

Duplicate design of older equipment. Used equipment may be more compatible with older, existing equipment.

Long equipment life is not needed. When a long service life of new equipment is not needed, a used equipment item might be very acceptable. Purchasers considering used equipment must carefully match the advantages to this alternative with the disadvantages noted in the next section. It is important to make a decision based on the specific needs of the food and beverage operation.

17.9.2 Potential Disadvantages

Foodservice purchasers are aware of potential disadvantages to the purchase of used equipment. Examples include:

There is generally no warranty; the equipment is purchased "as is."

Used equipment is often sold on a "cash only" basis.

Responsibilities for equipment relocating, installing, etc., are frequently borne by the purchaser.

Usable life expectancy is frequently shorter for used equipment.

Used equipment may not have newer, preferred design qualities and features.

There may be a need for more maintenance.

There is generally difficulty in evaluating competitive bids.

It may be difficult to match required specifications with available used equipment.

It is hard to determine the severity of previous use.

The purchaser may need to have business dealings with an unfamiliar source.

There may be difficulty in securing required service or parts.

17.9.3   Sources of Used Equipment

Purchasers of used equipment may be able to locate desired items from several sources.

Dealer "trade-ins." Talking with suppliers of new equipment may uncover used equipment which they have in their inventories.

Sales or auctions of discontinued businesses are a good source.

Government agencies may have "surplus" items for sale.

Surplus equipment from other food and beverage operations could be available. Checking newspaper ads, talking with competitors at association and trade meetings, etc., may help to locate these sources.

Used equipment dealers may have reconditioned, rebuilt, or other equipment available.

Leasing companies may have equipment that remains from expired leases or from terminated lease contracts.

18

THE LEASING DECISION

When acquisition of capital equipment is necessary, purchasing (new or used) items is not the only alternative. Equipment can also be leased. This section explores this relatively new management option in detail.

18.1　Definition of Leasing

Leasing provides foodservice officials with equipment that is legally owned by someone else. This is done with a contract which regulates the use and possession of the property. The lease is for a specified time, and definite payment amounts are required. Large cash outlays at the time of purchase (or shortly thereafter) are replaced with monthly payments spread out over the useful life of the equipment. Depending on the type of lease, ownership of the equipment may or may not revert to the food and beverage operation at the conclusion of the lease. Often when this does occur a payment reflecting "current market value" must be made before title to the equipment is transferred.

18.2　Advantages of Leasing

There are several reasons why equipment leasing may be advantageous to the food and beverage operation. These include:

Funds are free for other uses.

Equipment can be purchased even when there may be cash flow or other problems that would otherwise make purchasing difficult.

Debt is lower; this may increase the operation's ability to borrow funds for other purposes.

Leasing leaves normal bank "lines of credit" unused.

Leasing provides for long-term financing without diluting capital funds.

Management can pay for equipment (through monthly lease payments) out of before-tax earnings rather than after-tax profits. Food and beverage officials should know that principal payments on loans are not an "expense of doing business." While interest payments are an expense—and are used to reduce taxable income—payments on loan principals are not; they are paid for "out of profits."

Stated another way, then, leasing permits food and beverage officials to pay for the use of equipment out of present earnings rather than out of past profits.

Leasing hedges against inflation. Since the dollar has decreasing value, paying for today's equipment with tomorrow's dollars is an advantage to the lessee (the party who receives leased equipment).

The risk of obsolescence is minimized. If equipment is continually being up-
dated (such as electronic registers and automated beverage equipment) the lessee does not need to buy and use equipment that may
soon be outdated and need to be replaced.

Time and effort needed to acquire equipment are reduced. Many of the
procedures noted in Section 17 dealing with acquiring equipment
would be handled by the leasing company rather than by food and
beverage purchasing officials.

Under some types of leasing arrangements costs for the maintenance and
repair of leased equipment are the responsibility of the leasing company.

The cost of leasing may be lower than the purchase/ownership alternative.
This is discussed more fully in Section 18.4.

Leasing offers the convenience of making only one monthly lease payment
rather than several payments for loan repayments, insurance, property taxes, etc.

Leasing contracts can often be tailored more to the needs of the food and
beverage operation than financing agreements from lending institutions are.

If there is a question about the suitability of equipment it might be leased,
with decisions about subsequent ownership made on the basis of
experience during the leasing period.

18.3 Disadvantages of Leasing

Leasing may create disadvantages for the food and beverage operation. Consider the following:

A frequently noted disadvantage is the often higher costs associated with
leasing; that is, the sum of the monthly payments and other charges
at both "ends" of the lease may be more than the costs associated
with ownership.

The leasing company retains legal control of the equipment during the
leasing period.

Some leasing agreements give any remaining value of the equipment to
the leasing company at the end of the lease.

Leasing may reduce or eliminate the flexibility to dispose of unsuitable
equipment before the end of the leasing agreement.

It can eliminate "prestige" or "pride of ownership" factors.

Equipment may be repossessed if payments are missed during periods of
cash-flow difficulty.

18.4   Factors to Consider in the Leasing Decision

Obviously advantages and disadvantages must be considered as the leasing alternative is considered for the individual food and beverage operation. Leasing is also not an "all or nothing" decision; that is, not all new equipment should be either leased or purchased. The situation must be carefully considered each time that a new equipment item is judged necessary. Food and beverage purchasers may then find individual occasions when purchase is attractive and other times when the lease alternative is best.

Since costs and services will be critical determining factors in the leasing decision it is necessary to contact several reputable leasing companies. This is just as important as it is to consider several suppliers when products are to be purchased.

Specific procedures involved in the leasing decision include:

It is obvious that, if little cash is available for purchase, the leasing alternative is the likely option if new equipment is to be acquired. (Used equipment available for much fewer purchase dollars may still be an option.)

Food and beverage management officials should list all of the advantages (the list cited in Section 18.2 provides many examples) applicable to the situation. They should consider the costs and savings in dollar terms whenever possible. When this is not possible (for example, "pride of ownership" is difficult to place a dollar value on), a subjective decision becomes necessary.

List all disadvantages (see Section 18.3) and again try to emphasize the dollar impact of the specific factor.

Determine the *net* dollar savings or loss from the proposed leasing alternative.

Then consider the subjective advantages and disadvantages to determine whether a decision based on economics alone should be adjusted. For example, a study might indicate that leasing is *not* advantageous when all costs and savings are considered; however, since food and beverage management is not certain that the equipment is exactly what they desire, a short-term lease will:

give them access to use of the equipment;

allow them to review its suitability (which will influence a later purchase decision);

let them use equipment while technology "works" to improve the item; at the time of later purchase a more advanced model may better suit the needs of the individual operation.

Another approach is to consider the answers to the following questions when making a decision about lease or purchase.*

---

*Adapted from D. Metz, Leasing: Standards and Procedures (Kaukauna, Wisc.: Thomas Publications, 1968), pp. 4D–15D.

Are all costs of ownership taken into consideration? "Hidden" costs which are not considered may make purchase a more attractive alternative than it really is.

How often must equipment be replaced? As the useful life of an equipment item decreases the advantages to leasing may increase; the term of most leases is adjusted to the useful life of the capital equipment.

Is there a salvage value of the equipment at the end of the lease? If there is, if it is high, and if it reverts to the leasing company these factors weigh in favor of equipment purchase.

Is working capital (current assets less current liabilities) released by leasing? If there is an excess of working capital, equipment purchase may be in order.

Are there advantages realized by leasing equipment now rather than purchasing it later (when cash may be available)? If there are, leasing may be best.

What are the down-payment requirements when equipment is purchased? If they are greater than available funds, purchase may not be possible. (High "up-front" payments to the leasing company must also be considered.)

If loans are necessary for equipment purchase does this affect any minimum cash balance which the food and beverage operation must carry in the lender's banks? If there is, this becomes a leasing advantage (since funds need not be borrowed).

Are lines of credit (amounts which can be borrowed) affected by leasing? As funds are borrowed for equipment purchases less is available in lines of credit. This affects future financing alternatives and suggests another advantage to leasing.

Are there tax advantages to leasing? Generally, this question must be answered by the food and beverage operation's accountant.

What type of lease is being considered? (The types of leases are discussed in Section 13.5.)

What is the actual difference in cost between leasing and purchasing equipment? *All* costs associated with both options should be considered; total costs are a very important determinant in the purchase or lease decision.

19

PURCHASE OF CONSTRUCTION

Neither food and beverage purchasers nor top management personnel can be experts in everything. Construction is expensive, whether it is a new building, extensive remodeling of an existing facility, or even "minor" work such as roof repair or parking lot repaving. These "one-time" purchases must be made as effectively as possible. Information provided in this section will supply a foundation of information that will help personnel who "purchase" construction.

19.1   Introduction

Construction projects for food and beverage operations are often handled by a contractor independent of the operation. He or she is responsible for the work performed, and to see that work is done in accordance with blueprints, drawings, and detailed specifications.

The contractor may perform the work of a general contractor. In this instance the contractor assumes responsibility for all aspects of a given project. He or she either performs all of the work or hires and supervises subcontractors to do specialty parts of the work (such as plumbing, electrical, heating-ventilating, air conditioning, etc.).

In some instances management officials hire a construction manager who, while not performing the work with his or her own labor force, subcontracts work which is to be done. When this approach is used the construction manager does planning, coordinating, supervising, and administering tasks for the food and beverage operation.

In some large, fast-growing operations a construction manager may be a top management staff member who is hired by the food and beverage operation on a permanent basis to do work associated with the construction of ongoing expansion programs.

19.2   Types of Construction Services to be Purchased*

Purchasers of construction normally purchase one of the following classes or types of services. Specific contracts are based on the food and beverage operation's exact needs.

Engineering services. In some instances engineering aspects of construction are purchased separately; for example, mechanical or electrical engineers may be hired to develop detailed plans that will be incorporated into construction plans by others. The equipment and layout

---

*Section 19.2 is adapted from a general discussion provided by G. Aljian, Purchasing Handbook, 3rd ed. (New York: McGraw-Hill, 1973).

design consultant may be considered an "engineer." He or she develops detailed drawings and specifications that indicate type, amount, and placement of foodservice equipment in food production and service areas.

Purchase and construction services. In this procedure food and beverage officials hire a contractor, who in turn purchases materials and construction of all or part of the project. This may involve utilization of engineering specifications and requirements purchased under a separate contract, such as noted above.

Engineering, purchasing, and construction services. In this instance food and beverage officials hire a contractor who performs or who in turn hires others to perform all tasks necessary for the construction project. This approach is sometimes referred to as the turnkey method.

Construction services. With this system the food and beverage officials provide, or hire the services of, personnel to develop engineering requirements and to purchase construction materials. Specialty contractors are then hired to take delivery of materials on the job and to erect, install, and otherwise provide the services required of the contract with the food and beverage operation.

19.3 Important Concerns in Selection of Required Services

Many important factors must be considered as food and beverage officials determine the types of construction services they will require. Among these are:

Anticipated profits from the new, expanded or remodeled facility. It is obvious that the construction is being planned to increase or preserve profits. Very careful analysis must first be undertaken to determine that the project is justifiable. Then, depending upon required construction time, food and beverage officials may find it advantageous to "contract out" more of the work as construction urgency increases. This is an especially useful idea if increased profits will result from an earlier completion date for the project.

Available technical skill of the staff of the food and beverage operation. Few food and beverage operations employ persons who are skilled in detailed planning and supervision of construction projects. In the absence of skilled staff assistance, food and beverage managers are well advised to select a competent general contractor who, by contract, will assume specific responsibilities for construction and for supervision of construction. While this does not, of course, relieve food and beverage management personnel of the need to assure that the contract obligations are met, it does relieve them of much intermediate planning and supervision.

248   *Purchasing, Receiving, and Storage*

Selection of required construction materials. While food and beverage purchasers are generally skilled in the purchase of specialized food and beverage equipment few will be competent to select the construction materials needed for a project. This also is best left with the chosen contractor or architect who develops the specifications used as the basis for bidding. The input of food and beverage officials is, of course, desirable and necessary but, within limitations based upon their collective experience, some of the decision-making regarding purchase of materials must be left to construction experts.

Time requirements of food and beverage staff. Few food and beverage operations will have management officials who have the free time needed to provide extensive supervisory and planning help to the construction team. The absence of this required time also serves to justify the employment of a contractor.

Project size. As the size of a construction project increases so does the potential need for outside assistance. It is recognized that much specialized assistance may be very critical for even "small" projects, but "large" projects almost always require considerable outside technical assistance.

Number of construction projects planned. If a one-unit food and beverage operation plans a one-time construction project there is little need to hire a staff construction specialist. As a growing multi-unit company involves itself with a continuous expansion program the need for such a staff specialist obviously increases.

19.4   Types of Construction Contracts

Each of the legal concerns about contracts noted in Section 13 applies to construction contracts; however, these contracts are often classified by the type of payment plan required by the contract.

19.4.1   Lump-sum (Fixed Price) Contracts

As implied by its name this type of construction contract requires that the food and beverage operation pay a definite amount to the contractor. The actual amount may be set either by competitive bidding or by negotiation with one or more contractors selected by food and beverage officials to submit prices.

From the perspective of the food and beverage operation, one advantage of this type of contract is that obligated costs are known "up front" of the project. A possible disadvantage is that there may be a tendency to substitute lower quality materials or to otherwise compromise on construction quality as the contractor approaches his cost ceiling. It is obviously very important that specifications and other project plans be as detailed as possible so that there will be no "surprises" about what is expected from the contractor or being purchased by the food and beverage operation.

19.4.2   Cost-plus-Fee Contracts

This type of contract involves paying the contractor for actual incurred costs with an additional fee (such as a percentage markup on costs or an agreed-upon, fixed amount). The food and beverage operation is protected against substitution of low quality products since there is no incentive for the contractor to reduce costs. Likewise, there is no need for the contractor to "protect" himself against price increases by quoting a higher than actual material price at the time a bid is developed.

On the other hand, the food and beverage operation does not know the actual cost of the project up front; the contractor's estimate will need to be the basis of budget calculations. Likewise, there is need to assure that costs cited by the contractor (and which must both be reimbursed and are the basis for setting the fee) must be verified by the food and beverage operation.

19.4.3   Guaranteed Maximum-Price Contracts

This type of contract places a maximum price limit, which is not to be exceeded, on the construction project. This may be used with a "shared savings" plan which, essentially, involves the contractor and the food and beverage operation sharing in savings (the difference between maximum price and actual price).

19.4.4   Other Types of Contracts

It is, of course, possible to negotiate contracts with a selected contractor. These can be designed to specifically meet the needs of the individual situation. They can be negotiated on almost any basis such as a combination of any of the above methods; they can also incorporate labor, unit pricing, or other variables.

An informal contract can be a verbal agreement over the phone or a handshake after a conversation. The obvious lack of legal protection provided by an "informal" agreement speaks against its use. It is far better to carefully consider the situation as a contractor is selected. Points to consider in contractor selection are noted in the following section.

19.5   Selection of Contractor

As with the purchase of capital equipment, the selection of the contractor is very important. Consider the following points when reviewing each contractor who should be invited to submit a bid on a construction project:

Past experience with contractors used for other projects. Often when an operation has had a good relationship with a contractor on an earlier project an effective approach is to negotiate a price with that contractor. However, there is still merit in determining the prices and services offered by other contractors.

Experiences of the "friendly" competition.

Check references with the Better Business Bureau and similar groups.

Look for membership in professional trade associations.

Check work in progress being done by the contractor.

Obtain/check the contractor's banking references.

Review financial statements.

Obtain an independent financial report (such as that provided by Dun and Bradstreet).

Check with owners of completed projects; was work done correctly and on schedule? Were there extra charges? This is especially important when previous work has included food and beverage operations. Interviews with owners of these facilities can be very helpful.

Size and capabilities of the contractor become increasingly important as the size of the project increases. Present amount of work being done, amount of available equipment, number of employees, and similar factors can help food and beverage officials to judge the current capabilities of the contractor to perform required work.

Price to be charged is obviously an initial factor. All contractors should quote a price on the same type of contract (Section 19.4). If contractors are being screened for selection their estimate of price is important; likewise, if they are being questioned to assess their eligibility to submit a construction bid this estimate would still be useful information.

The process described above is used to select a general contractor who will develop detailed specifications and other information for the job. The same concerns are important to review when contractors are invited to submit a bid (price quotation) when a formal purchasing procedure is used.

19.6 The Process of Purchasing Construction

The several steps involved in the process of purchasing construction include:

The food and beverage management must first recognize and state its needs. It must then develop general project plans and obtain funding. Top management must be convinced that economic and other justifications of the project warrant its undertaking. Funds must be available from an internal or external source to finance the project.

If consulting engineers or other experts are retained to develop detailed specifications and drawings these are done now so that they can accompany the request for bids.

A common approach used by food and beverage operations is to hire an architect first. He or she prepares preliminary plans which incorporate the facility's needs given cost limitations for the project. Architects can help in development of required engineering specifications in at least two ways:

Large architectural firms often employ electrical, HVAC, mechanical, and other engineers who can incorporate specialized requirements into the project plans. Smaller architectural firms often can help food and beverage operations to locate qualified engineers or, alternatively, may retain their services on an ad-hoc basis, billing the food and beverage project for professional fees paid for engineering services.

Architects work with engineers as plans are being developed and revised to help assure that limited project funds are used wisely.

Construction contractors may also employ engineering specialists. Therefore, if the food and beverage operation goes to such a contractor and, after a price estimate is given based upon a preliminary project plan drawing, the contractor's engineering staff may develop the necessary construction details for the project. Note that a contractor must first be selected; the contractor awarded the job will do (or subcontract for) necessary work.

Recall the types of construction services which can be purchased: the operation must either hire an architect and engineering specialists to develop plans which are the basis for bids which will be used to select a contractor, *or*, the architect and contractor are selected who will *then* perform engineering, purchasing, and/or construction activities.

It is also possible for a contractor to provide detailed specifications which are then used to request price quotes from other contractors. This is often done with an agreement that there is no charge for the special help if that contractor is later awarded the job; a fee is charged to the food and beverage operation if the contractor is not awarded the job.

Possible contractors to perform required construction are now contacted. This can be done formally with an invitation to bid (often used when detailed plans are already developed) or more informally through the process described in Section 19.5. Specifications, detailed drawings, minimum insurance requirements, and all other information necessary to explain exactly the job to be performed must be provided at this time.

Often by the time bid invitations are sent out there are changes in specifications, drawings, and other information upon which bids are to be based. These changes are formally made by sending an addendum to all bidders; it is important that construction planners receive and acknowledge receipt of this revised information.

Price (bids) quotations are sent by the required time to the food and beverage officials or their construction representatives. In formal arrangements these bids are used as the basis to select the contractor to perform work.

A contract must be developed and signed; food and beverage officials need legal counsel for this task.

19.7   The Contract for Construction

General information about legal aspects of contracts is provided in Section 13.3. A formal contract is desirable for most, if not all, construction activities planned by the food and beverage operation. Specific information applicable to construction contracts includes:

Food and beverage officials should be represented by an attorney as the contract is developed.

Construction contracts generally contain a "general conditions" section which indicates often routine but very important aspects of the agreement between the contractor and the food and beverage operation. This generally explains the requirements and obligations of the contractor and the food and beverage operation. Examples of general conditions include:

Licensing, insurance, and bonding requirements of the contractor(s).

Importance of and procedures for dealing with specifications and drawings.

The process of handling change orders after the contract is signed.

Guarantees about the quality of materials and project workmanship.

Policies regarding delays and time extensions.

Subcontracts, liens, payments, and similar operational aspects of the contract.

Standard clauses are often inserted into contracts to address these points of concern for the individual project.

Normally specifications, drawings, and any other documents and addenda used in the bidding process are attached to or considered part of the construction contract.

Terms of and conditions for payment must be specified. For example, if the price is based on a lump-sum payment schedule should be developed (by dates or by completion of certain project activities).

Procedures for work/change orders should be specified.

A schedule of project completion and/or intermediate activity deadlines should be listed.

If there are any special conditions which are not included in the reference specifications or in the contract itself these, of course, need to be included.

The contract should state that the contract document represents the only agreement between the contractor and the food and beverage operation.

If the contract is of the cost-plus-fixed-fee or percentage type the contract must clearly identify and define items of cost.

20

RECEIVING PRACTICES

20

RECEIVING
PRACTICES

This handbook has indicated the importance of effective purchasing in the initial control of food and beverage costs. Detailed procedures have been presented for a system to control these costs. Special cautions are also in order as purchased products are brought into the hotel, restaurant, or club. It is not reasonable to develop tight control procedures during purchase and use and to ignore the intermediate stages of receiving and storage (Section 21). The components of an effective and practical receiving system are presented in this section.

20.1 Overview of the Receiving Process

A typical receiving practice in many commercial foodservice operations involves permitting whoever is around when a delivery is made to sign the sheet and, at some point, to place the delivered items in storage. This observation may be oversimplified and may leave out some techniques practiced by some operators (liquor receiving, for example, often involves detailed verification of beverages received). Unfortunately, it is an all too accurate review of the receiving practices of many foodservice properties.

What is needed at the time of product receiving is a system which helps ensure that what is received (and will be paid for) is what has been ordered. What has been "ordered" is:

1. A certain product
2. At a specific price
3. Of predetermined quality
4. In a set quantity
5. At a specified time

The receiving process must be designed to recognize each of these factors and, additionally, must assure that problems noted at the time of delivery are resolved to the satisfaction of both the foodservice operator and the supplier.

20.2 Requirements for Effective Receiving

Three important factors influence the success or failure of a receiving system. These are reviewed in this section.

20.2.1 Knowledgeable Personnel

In order to receive ordered products properly employees must be trained to perform required tasks. It is not possible, as noted above, to "let whoever is closest and not busy" receive the incoming merchandise. Employees with receiving duties must:

Know the quality specifications for each product

Be able to recognize the required quality

Understand the process by which products are received by the foodservice operation

Know what to do if there is a problem with an incoming shipment

Have the time to perform receiving tasks (which is not always possible when there are conflicting priorities for an employee's time)

Know how to complete required internal receiving records

It can easily be seen that these tasks require some specialized skills and knowledge which must be learned through training. It does not seem practical to train all employees; the investment in time would be too great. Rather, in small operations the manager (who may also do the purchasing) and, perhaps, the chef, beverage manager, and/or other *responsible* personnel should be trained in, and subsequently perform, receiving tasks. Several concerns involving personnel with receiving duties include:

When possible, it is desirable to split the duties of purchasing and receiving; they should not be done by the same employee. The reason involves increased security concerns when one employee (such as a head bartender) is permitted both to order and receive products. In small operations this division may not be possible; it would then be wise for the owner/manager to assume the responsibility for both tasks.

In larger operations duties may be split. The manager, for example, may order products and the chef, head steward, or other employee may receive them. It is customary in many large hotels for the purchasing department to order items; receiving and, perhaps, storage duties are under the control of the accounting department.

As noted above, receiving personnel must be trained to do their job correctly. Most receiving tasks can be explained and easily demonstrated through an on-job-training process; however, learning company specifications and how to recognize them is often a difficult, time-consuming chore. It must involve the purchaser working with the receiving trainee and *physically* showing and teaching the quality expectations of the foodservice operation. Often one can learn what the purchaser *does* want by seeing what is *not* desired (an inferior quality product).

Employees must be told about the importance of product receiving. If the task has not been emphasized in the past, a change in approach may be met with resistance. It will therefore be necessary for management to explain, defend, and justify the need for a revised receiving system.

Employees with receiving duties must be allowed time to perform them. They should not perform receiving tasks "when they have time." Large facilities with full-time receiving personnel may have less disruptive pressure on their operations. Small facilities which need to combine receiving with cooking, steward, or other duties have more difficulty. Some foodservice managers resolve this problem by limiting delivery times to those in which receiving personnel are likely to have sufficient time or, at least, can give priority to receiving tasks.

20.2.2 Sufficient Space

Space and equipment are necessary in order to perform receiving tasks properly. In small operations a wide spot in the hallway may be sufficient while, as delivery volume increases, additional space becomes important. Special concerns include:

The receiving area should normally be located near the delivery door for at least two reasons: (1) union contracts of delivery persons may require "inside-door" delivery only; and (2) security concerns arise when non-employees are allowed access to back-of-house areas (as would be necessary, for example, when they had to transport products to a remote receiving area).

The amount of space allocated for use during receiving should be ample to allow all products in a delivery to be inspected at one time. They would then be removed to storage *after* the delivery person had left. This is a much better arrangement than to "check in" some products, "remember what they are," and place them in storage to make room for additional incoming items.

Some space is necessary for receiving equipment. The most space-consuming item may be the receiving scale. Other equipment items may also be used and, if so, space must be allowed for them (see Section 20.2.3).

20.2.3 Receiving Equipment

Proper equipment is needed in order to receive products. This includes:

Receiving scale. An accurate working scale is needed to verify the weight of products ordered, delivered, and paid for on the basis of poundage. The scale may be portable if receiving space is utilized for other purposes during non-delivery times. It is very easy to cost-justify expenses involved in maintaining and testing a scale for accuracy. This should, then, be done on a scheduled basis by competent technicians.

Dolly, mobile truck, or other transport equipment. If products, after delivery, must be transported to a remote storage area, equipment to ease this task may be in order. Heavy-duty utility carts may also be used and small operations might well appreciate this multi-purpose equipment item for other uses as well.

Calculator. If arithmetic extensions are to be verified as part of the receiving task (Section 20.5.3) or if a receiving clerk's daily report (Section 20.3.5) is to be completed, a calculator of some type is necessary.

Desk, chair, and file cabinet. In large operations office-style equipment is necessary to store the in-house documents referred to in Section 20.3. Sometimes equipment can be shared by receiving and storage personnel, especially when areas used for these purposes are located close together. (Receiving areas, however, should *not* be in the storeroom.)

Thermometer and other small equipment. If specifications require some products to be delivered at frozen and/or chilled temperatures, a thermometer will be necessary to assure that requirements are met. Likewise, clipboards, pencils, and marking and tagging equipment (Section 20.5.1) are also necessary. Plastic or other bins provide a place to put top levels of produce as interior layers are inspected. Containers to hold ice removed from fresh poultry and fish help with the weighing task. Tools to open wooden, cardboard, plastic, and other containers are also necessary.

20.3   The Receiving Process

This section will outline in detail procedures important in assuring that incoming products are properly received.

20.3.1   Inspection Against Purchase Order/Purchase Record

There must be an in-house written record to describe products that have been ordered. This is referred to as a purchase order or purchase record (in Section 8.12.15). It is not correct to think of a purchase order only as a document that is *sent* to a supplier as the authority to ship or deliver products. This may be the case with large operations. However, even if orders are placed over the telephone the buyer must record important information to be used at time of receiving and payment. Therefore a copy of the purchase order/purchase record should be sent to receiving personnel who will then know:

What supplier is to deliver what product;

The amount (weight/count) to be delivered;

The size of purchase unit (case of six #10 cans, quart bottle, etc.) of the product;

Agreed-upon price (if receiving personnel perform arithmetic checks on invoices);

Basic specifications information (36-42 count frozen shrimp, U.S. Extra Fancy McIntosh apples, etc.);

Approximate delivery date.

As part of the receiving process the purchase order should be compared with the incoming shipment. Obviously foodservice management does not want to

Accept items it did not order;

Receive partial or no deliveries of necessary items;

Receive items of unacceptable quality.

If purchase order information is not available, receiving personnel cannot know if an incoming order is a correct one. Detailed information about the purchase order for large operations is found in Section 8.12.15. A discussion of the Purchase Record (for small properties) is presented in Section 20.7.

20.3.2 Inspection Against Specification

If a comparison of the incoming products with the purchase order indicates that the correct products have been delivered, quality assurance then becomes important. Products should be compared with the characteristics noted in the written specification. At this point specialized training to know and recognize quality determinants is important. This is also where care is required to assure that *all* incoming items meet the specifications. For example, "frozen" eggs or chicken that has thawed on the surface, a case of 6-ounce *rather* than 5-ounce meat patties, etc., must be detected by careful product review.

Pressure is sometimes exerted by delivery personnel ("we have a schedule to keep") because of the time required for a proper product inspection. Agreement can sometimes be made with the supplier to have products delivered at their risk with the invoice signed and mailed after thorough inspection. Arrangements for pickup of improper items, observed shortages, etc., would need to be considered when the agreement is reached.

Receiving clerks, at any rate, should not be rushed by delivery persons. The latter *may* be in a hurry. It is also possible however, that their haste will help hide attempts to steal from the foodservice operation. In any event, the foodservice buyer will pay the supplier for products delivered. He or she therefore has the right to assure that the foodservice facility is getting what is is paying for.

20.3.3 Inspection Against Delivery Invoice

After products have been checked against the purchase order and the specifications, they should be compared against the delivery invoice. This document originates from the supplier and will be used as the basis for calculating the bill owed to the supplier. It is obviously important that items be included on the delivery invoice in the correct quantity (see Section 20.5.2) and at the correct prices (see Section 20.3.1). If there are *no* corrections to the invoice, the receiving employee will be asked to sign the document. One copy will be retained by the foodservice operation (*see* Section 20.3.7). Remaining copies will be returned to the delivery person for supplier processing.

If there are corrections to the invoice (for example, recorded products are not received or only a partial delivery has been made) they *must* be recorded on the invoice *before* it is signed. Depending on the supplier's system, a credit memo (Section 20.4.3) may be used to reflect the correct amount owed to the supplier.

Signed copies of delivery invoices received will be turned in to the foodservice manager, accounting department, or other responsible person at least daily (see Section 20.3.7).

20.3.4   Acceptance of Products

When comparison of products with purchase order, specifications, and delivery invoice reveal no problems, or when observed problems are corrected or noted the signed delivery invoice indicates that:

> Products noted on the invoice were received in acceptable order (problems noted later may be difficult to reconcile).

> Payment will be due at the stipulated time for items noted on the delivery invoice.

Normally, products become the property of the foodservice operator at this point.

20.3.5   Receiving Clerk's Daily Report

Large operations have several uses for the receiving clerk's daily report. These include:

> It provides a record of all products received (including delivery date, supplier, quantity, and price). This can be a helpful check on the status of and payment for delivery invoices.

> It can provide a record of product transfer to storage in facilities when receiving and storage tasks are performed by different employees.

> It can be used as a partial basis for calculating food costs. Large operations frequently calculate daily food costs by considering "directs" from the receiving clerk's daily report to be items moved directly to preparation and, hence, used on the day of delivery. With this system "directs" and issues (from storage) plus or minus various adjustments equal daily food costs.

> The report, with invoices attached, can be used as the authorizing source for entry of information about received products in a perpetual inventory system (see Section 21.4.3).

A sample copy of two forms, Receiving Clerk's Daily Report: Food and Receiving Clerk's Daily Report: Beverage are found in Figures 20.1 and 20.2. Blank copies

FIGURE 20.1 Receiving Clerk's Daily Report: Food

Date ___8/1___

Name of Receiving Employee ___Joe___

Page No. _1_ of _1_

Supplier	Item	Amount	Purchase Unit	Unit Price	Total Value	Classification Direct	Classification Storage	Storage (√)
ace Supply	Applesauce	2 cases	case	15.45	30.90		30.90	✓
	B. Pepper	1 #	#	3.15	3.15		3.15	✓
	G. Beans	1 case	case	10.85	10.85		10.85	✓
Acme Bread	H. buns	30 doz.	dozen	1.10	33.00	33.00		

Totals **218.50** **465.15**

Receiving Employee ___Joe Jones___
(signature)

FIGURE 20.2   Receiving Clerk's Daily Report: Beverage

Date ___8/1/___

Name of Receiving Employee ___Joe___   Page No. __1__ of __1__

Supplier	Item	Amount	Purchase Unit	Unit Price	Classification				Storage (√)
					Beer	Liquor	Wine	Soda	
Smith Bev.	Smith Vodka	1 case	case	48.50		48.50			√
	Smith Scotch	1 case	case	57.35		57.35			√
	Smirnoff Red	6	Qts.	6.50		39.00			√
	House Chablis (gallon)	3 cases	case	23.50			23.50		√

Totals _____ 144.85 23.50 _____

Receiving Employee ___Joe Jones___
(signature)

which can be reproduced and instructions for completion of the forms are found in Sections 22.7 and 22.8.

Small foodservice operations may not have a need for the receiving clerk's daily report. Special procedures for these facilities are noted in Section 20.7.

20.3.6 Removal to Storage

After products have been received, they should *immediately* be removed to the proper, secure storage area. Products are now the property of the foodservice facility; security concerns to prevent employee theft and pilferage become important. Likewise, spoilage and quality deterioration of refrigerated or frozen products will occur if these items remain at room temperature. Therefore, removing items to storage should be considered as an integral part of the receiving system. Receiving personnel should not "wait until they have time" to perform this task.

As noted in Section 20.3.5, it may be helpful to require storage personnel to certify that items received are, in fact, delivered to storage. A column is provided on the receiving clerk's daily report for this purpose.

20.3.7 Processing of Receiving Documents

At least three types of forms used as part of the receiving process will be accumulated: purchase order, delivery invoice, and credit memo. Larger foodservice operations may additionally complete a receiving clerk's daily report. At the end of the receiving employee's shift these forms should be collected. Procedures for processing them include:

> The employee should match up applicable forms for each delivery. If he or she is to make an initial calculation of arithmetic extensions, this can be done at this time. Such figures will additionally be reviewed as part of the payment process (Section 9.5).

> These various forms should be given by the receiving employee to the official responsible for processing them for payment. In a small operation they would be turned in to the manager (if he or she did not receive the products). In a larger operation they would be turned in to an accounting office official. *Note:* Observe the security control which is in effect with this procedure. If the receiving documents were processed through the foodservice department, they could be altered before payment; there would be less assurance that all items on the invoice were actually received.

> The official who will subsequently be responsible for paying the bill represented by the invoice should file the documents together until time for payment (Section 9.5).

20.4 Rejecting Products

There will be times when problems are noted during the receiving process. This is, of course, the reason for use of careful procedures: the foodservice operator wants to note problems at time of delivery—before the items become the responsibility of foodservice management—so that the foodservice operation does not bear the cost of problems that are beyond its control. It is generally much easier to *reject* products *before* they are accepted than it is to *return* items *after* they are accepted.

20.4.1 Reasons to Refuse Products

There are several primary reasons why, from the perspective of the foodservice operation, products should be refused.

They were not ordered. The foodservice management does not want items that it cannot use.

They are not of required quality.

The price is not that quoted; often a call to the supplier can resolve the problem (note the need to record the correct quoted price on the purchase order).

They are not delivered on a timely basis. If products are delivered late, safety margins are affected; stockouts may occurs. This requires a reexamination of the supplier's eligibility. Products delivered early may not be desired either.

Storage costs increase.

Deterioration may occur if they remain in storage while older stock is used first.

There is an increased chance of theft and pilferage.

Bills must be paid sooner; this will affect cash flow.

20.4.2 Procedures to Refuse Items

If the receiving employee notes errors during the receiving process, several things should be done.

He or she should alert the buyer, chef, or other official. If, for example, a quality problem is noted but the product might be used to avoid a stockout, a price reduction might be negotiated with the supplier. The receiving employee can neither make the decision nor negotiate a price; a foodservice official must be contacted.

If only a partial amount is delivered or the required item is not available (such as when a supplier must "back order" an item), a foodservice official must be notified so that any necessary decisions can be made.

Delivery invoices should be changed to reflect items and prices, amounts of items, etc., which are actually received. Since foodservice officials have been notified, they—rather than the receiving employee—will assure that the revisions in the delivery invoice are made. (*Note*: The delivery person should sign any delivery invoice which is changed as part of the receiving inspection. This will confirm, from the supplier's perspective, that changes in the delivery were actually made.)

20.4.3 Credit Memos

Credit memos can be issued by suppliers for two purposes:

If suppliers bill foodservice operations on the basis of the original delivery invoice prepared before the driver leaves the supplier's warehouse a credit memo will be necessary to reduce the invoice because of problems observed during the receiving process.

If items are accepted and then returned, in almost all cases a credit memo will be issued by the supplier.

Special concerns in use of credit memo include:

Foodservice officials should personally contact their sales representative immediately to confirm that a credit memo will be issued to resolve problems noted during the delivery. They should not "assume" that the driver's copy will "make it" to the billing office.

Foodservice officials should always require that a credit memo be issued. They should not accept a "we'll deliver it next time" from the driver.

"Problem" invoices should not be filed for payment; they should be held in a separate file until the credit memo or its confirmation has been received from the supplier. It should then be filed for payment at the appropriate time.

If items are not delivered and a credit memo is issued, the items, when delivered, should be accompanied by another, separate delivery invoice.

When problems are not noted until after the delivery person has left, the supplier should be contacted immediately. Most reputable suppliers will correct occasional problems. The foodservice manager should use these occasions to learn why problems were not observed at time of delivery in order to further improve the receiving process.

A blank copy of a credit memo and instructions for completion of the form are found in Section 22.22.

20.5 Other Receiving Tasks

Several recurring tasks that affect control and security systems are highlighted in this section.

20.5.1 Marking and Tagging

The process of marking and tagging items that have been received involves making use of selected information on the delivery invoice for future use.

Marking. Information about delivery date and price can be written directly on the can, case, bottle, or other packaging unit before it is placed in storage. This is helpful for inventory and daily food cost calculations (the actual price can be easily recorded without having to look it up) and for sanitation/food cost reasons (a stock rotation plan can be easily policed; fewer products will spoil on the shelves).

Tagging. This system is used to keep track of expensive meats and fish. A two-part card is completed, and one part is attached to the item before it is placed in storage. The process then involves:

Sending the duplicate copy of the tag to the official who calculates food costs;

When the item is issued from storage to preparation, sending the tag to the food costing official who sums all tags to calculate daily the food cost for the item (such as meat or seafood);

Tags not "sent up" from the kitchen represent items that should still be in storage.

Advantages to the use of a tagging system include:

The receiving employee *must* weigh the product in order to fill in the tag.

It is easy to calculate a daily product cost.

Pilferage problems are noticed (tags represent products which should still be in storage).

Inventory counting and valuation are easy tasks; information is found on the tags.

Stock rotation can be monitored.

A copy of a storage tag is found in Figure 20.3, and is also duplicated in Section 22.16. These forms are also available from supply houses. They should be reproduced on very heavy "poster" type paper to withstand the handling to which they will be subjected during storage.

20.5.2 Verifying Weight/Count

Without exception the quantity of all items received must be verified. This must be done *before* the delivery invoice is signed. Special concerns include:

FIGURE 20.3 Sample Storage Tag

Tag Number __1005__	Tag Number __1005__
Date of Receipt __8/1__	Date Received __8/1__
Weight/Cost	Weight __35#__
$\underline{35}$ (×) $\underline{2.85}$ = $99\,\underline{75}$ No. of #s Price Cost	Price __2.85__
	Cost __99.75__
Name of Supplier: __Jacob Meats__	Supplier __Jacob__
Date of Issue: _____	Date Issued _____

Normally, if items are purchased by the count (6 cases of #10 cans, five 750 ml bottles of Canadian blend whiskey, etc.) they should be counted. If items are purchased by weight (50# of ground beef, 10 pounds of 6 oz. sirloin steaks, etc.), they should be weighed.

Portion control items (such as 6 oz. steaks) should be randomly weighed also. A previously established tare allowance should be policed. A one-ounce tare allowance on a steak portion means, for example, that an acceptable 6 oz. steak will weigh between 5.5 and 6.5 ounces.

Items weighing more or less than these limits will not be acceptable. Spot checking of portion control items should be a routine part of the receiving employee's job. Foodservice management officials would also be wise to do their own occasional check of these items.

Meats should be weighed separately. For example, 15 pounds of New York strip steaks and 15 pounds of ground beef will weigh 30 pounds when received. If 20 pounds of steak and ten pounds of ground beef were ordered, the foodservice operation will be paying a high steak price for ground beef.

Ice, packaging material, cardboard casing, etc., should be removed before products are weighed.

Individual items purchased by count (such as 96-count lemons, 36-42 count shrimp, etc.) should be counted on a "spot check" basis to assure that the proper size is received.

Cases of liquor and wine can be weighed to assure that no empty, broken, or partially filled bottles are being received.

20.5.3 Verifying Arithmetic Extensions

It is important that extensions (number of purchase units (x) price per purchase unit) be verified before bills are paid. This should be done even on computer printed bills. Use of a system in which this can be calculated at least two times seems advisable. This might easily be done when (1) verification is initially done by the receiving employee; and (2) a second verification is done as part of the payment process.

20.6 Security Concerns in Receiving*

There are many opportunities for employee and supplier theft when food and beverage products are received. Examples that management personnel should guard against include:

Receiving the wrong items (such as inexpensive foreign wines instead of higher quality wines or 70 percent fat content ground beef instead of 80 percent fat content beef) and paying a high price for low quality products.

Short weight or count: the foodservice operation pays for more product than was received.

Receiving, for example, thawed meat or seafood products, which are represented as fresh and for which a higher price is charged.

Grinding ice into ground meat products, adding fillers (such as soy products or nonfat dry milk extenders) in applicable products, selling meat with excess trim, etc.

Including the weight of ice and/or packaging in the amount of product for which a price is charged.

"Slack out" seafood: thawing frozen fish, packing in ice, and selling as fresh.

Combining expensive steaks and inexpensive meat items into one container, weighing the entire container and billing the operation for a greater poundage of expensive steaks and a lesser poundage of inexpensive meats.

Including one empty liquor bottle in a case of, for example, twelve quarts.

The list of possible ways that suppliers can steal from the property by overcharging for amount or quality of product received may be endless. Problems can occur with almost any product which is ordered.

---

*Section 20.6 is adapted from J. Ninemeier, Food and Beverage Security: A Systems Manual for Restaurants, Hotels, and Clubs (Boston, Mass.: CBI Publishing Co., 1981).

20.6.1 System Design for Security

To help guard against theft at the time products are received, basic principles should be followed to control product receiving. These include:

Receiving tasks should *not* be done by the same person who purchases (unless, of course, the owner-manager performs both these duties).

Someone *must* be trained to receive; receiving is important and should not be left to the dishwasher or whomever else is handy.

To the extent possible, product deliveries should be made at non-busy times so that receiving personnel (who may have other duties) will have time to correctly receive the products.

Deliveries should be made to a specified area of the facility. Receiving scales and other equipment should be available in the area.

After receipt, products should be immediately removed to storage. Chances for employee theft increase as products remain unattended.

Salesmen, delivery/route persons, etc., should *not* be permitted in the storage area. It is not proper for these personnel to have access to back-of-house production and storage areas. If possible, the receiving area should be located close to an outside exit and under view of management personnel.

The outside door should be locked. An audio signal can be installed to permit delivery personnel to signal when they have arrived. With this plan, delivery men are under visual supervision by receiving personnel during the entire time that they are present.

20.6.2 Review of Receiving System Requirements

Specific receiving procedures involving the verification of products delivered require the receiving personnel to:

Check all incoming goods against the purchase record (to determine that the amount and type of foods which were ordered were received).

Check all incoming goods against food purchase specification information to assure that the proper quality of items is received.

Check all incoming goods against the delivery invoice to assure that the type and amount of items that will be charged for were received.

Check the delivery invoice against the purchase record to assure that the price charged (per invoice) is the agreed price (as per purchase order).

Delivery date and price information should be marked (tagged) on containers at the time they are received and placed in inventory. This facilitates the taking of inventory and helps to assure that stock is rotated properly.

FIGURE 20.4 Purchase Record Form

Purchase Record *Ajax Meat, Shrimp, Produce Co.*
(supplier)

Date Ordered	Item Description	Unit	Price	Number Units Purchased	Total Purchase Cost	Invoice #	Comments
11/26	Stew Beef MBG #	#	1.69	25	42.25	385	OK
	Strip Stks MBG #	10oz.	2.92	25	73.00	305	10 Steaks damaged And refused *
					115.25		
	*Strip MBG#	10oz	2.92	[10]	[29.20]	305	
	2% (Discount)				86.05		
					(1.72)		
					84.33		Pd ck# 3792

All products should be weighed and/or counted. If, for example, fresh chicken is received, it should be removed from its case and ice to determine the correct product weight. It is also possible to weigh cases of liquor to assure that all bottles are full and present. Naturally, any beverage cases that are wet (or show signs of having been wet) should be opened; each bottle should be checked.

20.7 Control of Receiving in Small Operations

Section 20.2.1 noted one difficulty in designing the receiving process for small foodservice operations: it may not be possible to split the tasks of purchasing and receiving. When one official does both the purchasing and receiving, it makes sense to combine forms otherwise used for these purposes. A sample copy of a purchase record form appears in Figure 20.4.* Additionally, a version that can be reproduced and instructions for completion of the form are found in Section 22.21.

With use of the purchase record form, the buyer completes purchase information columns and uses the same form to complete information about receipt of the same products as they are delivered. Regardless of size of the foodservice operation, however, it is important that the basic procedures outlined in Section 20.3 be utilized.

---

*J. Ninemeier, and W. Quain, Unpublished Seminar Materials Developed for Louisiana Restaurant Association Seminars, 1979–1980.

21

INVENTORY AND STORAGE PRACTICES

After items have been properly received they must be placed in storage. The storage process can be considered a concluding task in the purchasing process. With the entry of materials into storage areas purchasing staff have obtained and provided user departments with necessary products. As items are withdrawn from storage they are utilized according to procedures established by user, rather than by purchasing, personnel.

21.1 The Purchase Decision and Inventory Management

Normally, food and beverage products are of two types:

Perishable products—These "directs" are not purchased for inventory but, rather, are used as soon as purchased. Examples are fresh produce and dairy products. While they may be stored for short periods of time, these items are generally purchased for immediate use. Thus, the purchase decision relates to determining the quantity needed for a time period of no more than several days. Inventory management involves both determining quantities to purchase and assuring that stock rotation and other processes to avoid spoilage and waste are practiced. While there may be some concern about theft and pilferage a larger concern is generally focused on minimizing costs due to mishandling.

Non-perishable products—These items, while obviously not purchased to "stockpile," are purchased to replace inventory levels. Examples include frozen food and grocery items. Since they are likely to be in storage for a longer time period inventory management decisions are necessary to determine:

Quantities to have on hand

Means to reduce theft and pilferage

Procedures to reduce quality deterioration

The purchase of both types of items must be done according to established inventory and storage policies.

21.1.1 Definition of Inventory and Storage Policy

The food and beverage operation must attempt to maintain a constant relationship between the quantity of products used and the amount of the item in inventory. Too much product money tied up in inventory can create cash flow problems. Too little product can cause stockouts—obviously also not desirable.

Regardless of the *amount* of product on hand inventory storage policies must be developed which guide the management of products in storage.

21.1.2 Components of an Inventory and Storage Policy

The following aspects of inventory and storage policies must be of concern:

Keeping products secure;
Retaining products' quality while in storage;
Knowing the amount of product used.

Each of these components will be discussed separately.

21.2 Procedures to Keep Inventory Secure*

Security concerns at time of storage must focus on:

Knowing how much product *should be* available

Knowing how much product *is* available in inventory (in order to determine the quantity of any missing items)

Preventing physical access to storage areas by unauthorized personnel.

In small food and beverage operations the amount of products that should be available is based on experience. Generally, products are purchased in predetermined amounts in order to bring inventory levels to preset levels; a count of the quantity of product available when a food and beverage order is put together suggests the amount necessary to be purchased. While this system is simple and is not time-consuming some basic element of control is lost since food and beverage officials do not really know how much product *should* be available.

Even small food and beverage facilities can use an inventory system for liquors, wines, meats, seafood, and other expensive items to provide a "running balance" at all times of the amount of such items in inventory. As items are added to storage the balance is increased; as items are withdrawn from storage (issued), the balance is reduced. This type of system is referred to as perpetual inventory and is reviewed in Section 21.4.3.

Either a physical inventory system (Section 21.4.2) or the perpetual inventory system already noted will suggest the amount of each item that *is* available in storage. This information not only helps to determine the quantity of products to be

---

Section 21.2 is adapted from: J. Ninemeier, Food and Beverage Security: A Systems Manual for Restaurants, Hotels, and Clubs (Boston, Mass.: CBI Publishing Co., 1982).

reordered; it is also a measure of the effectiveness of storage security control. An objective of storage control must be to reduce and eliminate inventory pilferage and theft (often referred to as inventory "shrinkage"). Procedures to help keep inventory items secure include:

There should be limited access. It is generally unwise to let anybody into storage areas. Only authorized personnel should enter storage areas. This policy is best met by keeping storage areas locked except during times when products are issued.

Storage areas should be lockable. It should be possible to lock the freezer and the dry storage and liquor storage areas. Additionally, a lockable walk-in refrigerator can protect wines and other expensive items. One or more compartments of a reach-in refrigerator should be lockable; expensive fresh meats, seafoods, etc., would, of course, be kept in these units.

Inventory control practices are used. Items judged expensive and "theft prone" should be controlled through use of a perpetual inventory system (discussed in Section 21.4.3). Items that are in work station, "broken case," or other storage areas in small operations may not be under perpetual inventory. However, expensive items should not be stored in these unlocked, unattended areas.

Items in work stations are placed under central inventory control at the end of each shift. For example, assume that the food and beverage manager expects to sell thirty New York strip steaks during the evening shift. Prior to the serving period this number of steaks are removed from locked inventory (and the perpetual inventory balance for steaks is reduced). At the end of each shift five steaks remain. These five steaks are returned to locked inventory (and the perpetual inventory balance is increased by five steaks).*

Items needed during a shift which are under locked storage should be retrieved by a management official with access to storage area keys.

The physical storage area must be designed with security in mind. While no facility can be made completely safe against a professional burglary, it can more easily be made secure from employee access. Locking up the area is a beginning. Doors must extend to the ceiling; lock clasps, door hinges, etc., must be reasonably secure. The ceiling also must be checked (to assure that employees cannot enter through the ceiling from another room). There should be no windows.

---

*Notice how easy total control of steaks becomes. For example, 25 steaks were sold (30 steaks at the start of the shift − 5 steaks left at the end of the shift = 25 steaks sold). A total of steaks sold is taken by guest check count. (This task is easily done if electronic register or other equipment with pre-set keys is used.) Adjustments in the total number of steaks used are made for burns and returns (which have been retained for management inspection). The physical count of number of steaks sold then equals the number of units sold by register or guest check tally. The chef must explain any difference between the number of steaks which should be and are remaining.

Some food and beverage operations store "precious" items under locked
storage within the locked storage areas. Examples of these valuable
items include liquor, sterling silver, or other serving ware, etc.

Adequate lighting in storage areas "robs" thieves of a place to hide; closed
circuit television systems can be used to keep an eye on storage
areas and building exits.

In many instances basic "common sense" coupled with the questioning "How
would I steal from my storage areas?" will provide sound, inexpensive ideas and
methods that can make food and beverage storage areas physically secure from
employee theft.

21.3 Procedures to Retain Product Quality

Items of proper quality are purchased and received. Quality can, of
course, be reduced if items are not stored under the proper conditions. Some food
and beverage storage practices recognize this concern.

Food must be rotated.   Foods in storage the longest should
be used first. This task is made easier when product packages are dated at the time
of delivery and when new products are placed under and behind those already in
storage.

**Foods must be stored at proper temperature and
humidity.**   Food and beverage officials should use accurate thermometers to
assure that temperatures for:

Refrigerated items are kept below 40°F;

Dry storage areas range from no less than 50°F to no more than 70°F;

Frozen items are kept between 0°F and −10°F.

Foods must be stored in clean storage areas.   Routine
cleaning for all frozen, refrigerated, and dry storage areas is very necessary.

**Effective storage practices require proper ventilation
and air circulation.**

On-going programs to control rodent and insect infestation are necessary;

Generally items should be stored in their original packing containers;

Items that absorb odors (such as flour) should be stored away from items
that give off odors (such as onions);

Many foods should be stored in airtight containers; all should be stored in
covered containers.

21.4　Procedures to Determine Quantity of Product Used

From a record-keeping perspective, inventory control involves "keeping track" of items in storage. There are at least three reasons for such systems. Knowledge of quantities of product in storage can help (1) control against theft; (2) aid in food and beverage costing procedures; and (3) determine additional quantities of product to purchase.

21.4.1　Need for Inventory Control System

It is simply not sufficient to "place products in storage, take them out when needed, and order more when necessary." There should be a planned, systematic process that regulates record-keeping control of items in storage. The two basic systems which incorporate required procedures for record keeping aspects of inventory control are the physical and perpetual inventory systems.

21.4.2　Physical Inventory System

A physical inventory system involves the periodic actual counting of products in inventory. This is routinely done at least once monthly in order to help assess the quantity of items on hand and to determine the actual cost of goods sold (a calculation necessary to develop financial statements when accrual accounting systems are used).

Many small food and beverage operations use this approach as the only means of keeping track of items in storage. With this plan, a once-a-month tally indicates the quantity of items on hand. Generally, an assumption is made that the value of low-cost items and those in process and in work station storage areas "average out"; that is, the value of these items remains approximately the same from month to month. Therefore, the value of items in storage is judged to be the cost represented by those products which are counted. The "constant value" of low-cost and other items which are not counted may be added to the total assessed cost of inventory items to determine the inventory value for the period.

The cost of inventory items is determined by multiplying the number of purchase units of each product by their cost. If products of the same type have two purchase prices because they were purchased at two different times the last cost is frequently used to assess value. (A detailed discussion regarding the assessment of inventory value is presented in Section 21.6.)

A sample physical inventory form is found in Figure 21.1. A blank copy which can be reproduced is found in Section 22.17. Instructions for use of the form are also included with the blank form.

The physical inventory form has two primary purposes:

Small food and beverage operations will find it useful to make periodic (usually monthly) inventory value assessments. This assessment is

FIGURE 21.1 Physical Inventory Form

Type of Product ___Dry___

Month ___April___   Month _____

Product	Unit	Amount in Storage	Purchase Price	Total Price	Amount in Storage	Purchase Price	Total Price
Applesauce	6-#10	42/6	15.85	68.68			
Ga. Beans	6-#10	35/6	18.95	72.65			
Flour	10# Bag	3	4.85	14.55			
Rice	50# Bag	1	12.50	12.50			

486.55

generally necessary to calculate the cost of goods sold for monthly income (profit and loss) statements in accrual accounting systems.

Larger food and beverage operations may find it to be a helpful supplement to their perpetual inventory system (Section 21.4.3). It is often easier to assess inventory *value* with the physical inventory form and to use the perpetual inventory system only to keep a running balance of the quantity of products on hand.

Advantages of a physical inventory system are:

It is easy, simple, and consumes minimal time.

It enables small food and beverage operations to make periodic calculations of product inventory values which are necessary for developing financial statements.

Disadvantages include:

Physical inventories only tell the quantity of product in storage; they do not tell the amount of product which *should be* in storage.

It is necessary to physically count items in storage each time an order is placed in order to determine the quantity to purchase. (With a perpetual inventory system this information will already be available.)

Small food and beverage operations should consider use of a physical inventory system to assess the quantity of most products in inventory. However, expensive items (meats, liquors and wines, seafood, etc.) might be controlled through use of a simplified perpetual inventory system as described below.

21.4.3 Perpetual Inventory System

A perpetual inventory system is one which keeps track of items in storage on a continuous basis. At any point in time the quantity of items under perpetual inventory is known. A "running balance" of the quantity in inventory is kept. As items are received and placed in storage the balance is increased; as items are withdrawn (issued) the balance is decreased. With this system it is possible to tell the quantity of products in storage at any point in time.

Some suggestions regarding use of perpetual inventory systems include:

All food and beverage operations can benefit from using a perpetual inventory for expensive items. In companion with limiting access and keeping storage areas secure this procedure will help to provide tight control over at least the highest cost items. Use of this idea is part of the "ABC Analysis System" which is reviewed in Section 21.5. Examples of products which might be controlled in *any* size of food and beverage operation through use of a perpetual inventory system include liquors and wines, meats, seafoods, and expensive frozen foods.

It is easier to use a perpetual inventory system when a record is kept only of the *quantity* rather than the *value* of products in inventory. A physical count must still be used to compare perpetual inventory records with the quantity of items actually available in storage. Therefore, inventory valuation (necessary for accounting—cost of goods-sold calculations) can be done at that time. This procedure would be identical to the system described in Section 21.4.2. The physical inventory form used for this purpose is presented in Section 22.17.

A sample perpetual inventory form is found in Figure 21.2. A blank copy which can be reproduced and instructions for completing the form are found in Section 22.18. The form is meant to be used in a binder. The form can be adapted to other sizes of cards or pages if desirable.

A perpetual inventory system enables the user to maintain one food and beverage control standard which is *not* possible when only a physical inventory system is used. The perpetual inventory system will indicate the quantity of product which *should* be available; this amount can be confirmed by a physical count. Any discrepancy between what *should be* and what *is* available becomes a measure of the effectiveness of the inventory/storage system.

Perpetual inventories must be verified. It is necessary to confirm the accuracy of the perpetual inventory with a monthly physical count. The quantity determined from physical count should be equal to the amount noted on the "balance" column of the perpetual inventory record.

Personnel who maintain the perpetual inventory should *not* normally be involved in taking the physical count since it then becomes easy to change the inventory records. This will, of course, defeat the purpose of taking the physical inventory. A food and beverage manager and, perhaps, someone from the accounting department (in a large facility) or from the foods area (as in a small food and beverage operation) can perform the physical count together. Steps in the process involve, first, arranging perpetual inventory sheets in the same sequence as the items are located in storage. One employee then counts the quantity of products in storage. The second person compares this quantity with the amount noted on the perpetual inventory form. Any differences must be explained. Note again that two people are used for this task to assure accuracy and honesty in the actual inventory count.

When quantities from the physical count and the perpetual inventory record agree, the costs of products in storage can be assessed.

Note has been made of the need to continually update the balance of items kept under the perpetual inventory system. The source of information concerning the addition of items to inventory is, of course, the signed delivery invoice and the receiving clerk's daily report.

This document, adjusted if necessary to account for credits or other problems, will indicate the number of additional items placed in storage.

FIGURE 21.2 Perpetual Inventory Form

Product Name *Applesauce*   Purchase Unit Size   *Case (6 #10)*

Date	In	Out	Balance Carried Forward *15*	Date	In	Out	Balance Carried Forward ____
5/16		3	12				
5/17		3	9				
5/18	6		15				
5/19		2	13				

21.4.4 Issues from Inventory

The source of information relating to the removal of items in inventory can be a formal issue requisition. Two sample copies of this form are noted in Figures 21.3 and 21.4. One form is used for the removal of food items under perpetual inventory. The second form applies to the withdrawal of beverages from central storage areas. Blank copies which can be reproduced and instructions for completion of the forms are located in Sections 22.5 and 22.9. If these documents are used the issue requisitions are collected during the several allowable times when issues are made; the storage area is otherwise kept locked so that removal of items is normally limited to only several times daily. At the end of the shift (or at another convenient time) the issue requisition forms are used to update (reduce) the balance of food and beverage items on the affected perpetual inventory form (Section 22.18).

Small food and beverage operations may not find it practical to utilize a formal issue requisition system for food products. These facilities might, however, be able to modify procedures:

To require that a management official be physically present at the time of any withdrawals from inventory (storage areas are otherwise kept locked).

To use a form with a format similar to that in Section 22.5 taped to the wall or door of each storage area. Personnel authorized to withdraw food items from storage then enter information on the form when products are removed. Management officials adopting this system are cautioned that close supervision is required to ensure that personnel adhere to this procedure.

In almost all cases, food and beverage operations, regardless of size, should utilize a perpetual inventory system, including some type of authorized withdrawal procedures for control of liquor, wine, and beer storage.

21.4.5 Bin Card System

Bin cards may also be used in an inventory control system. Briefly, this procedure involves attaching an index card to storeroom shelving units which house items for which additional control is desired. These normally will be fast-moving or expensive items. As products are shelved or removed changes in the number of units on the shelf are recorded on the bin card. The balance on the card can be quickly compared against both a physical count and against the balance noted on the perpetual inventory form to assure that all products are properly accounted for. A sample bin card form is shown in Figure 21.5. A blank form which can be reproduced and instructions for completing the form are found in Section 22.19.

FIGURE 21.3 Issue Requisition: Food

Storage _____ Date _3/18_

Refrigerated _____

Frozen _✓_

Dry _____

Item	Size of Package	Quantity Issued	Employee Initials	
			Withdrawn by	Approved by
NY Strips	portion cut	15 only	JN	CK
Shrimp (36-42)	5 #	2 pky.	JN	CK
Cheesecake	Box (cake)	1 cake	JN	CK

FIGURE 21.4 Issue Requisition: Beverage

Shift ___AM___   Date ___3/18___

Bar ___Main___   Bartender ___Joe___

Liquor	Bottles		Unit Cost	Total Cost
	Number	Size		
H. Brandy	3	750 mL	4.15	12.45
Tia Maria	1	1/5	13.75	13.75
H. Tequila	2	750 mL	4.80	9.60

Total Bottles ___17___   Total Cost ___107.50___

OK to issue ___CK___

Issued by ___BW___

Received by ___Joe___

$$\underbrace{107.50}_{cost} \div \underbrace{412.00}_{sales} = \underbrace{26\%}_{bev.\%}$$

FIGURE 21.5 Bin Card

Name of Item _House Rum_

Forward _15 Bottles_   Forward _____

Date	In	Out	Balance	Date	In	Out	Balance
8/3		4	11				
8/4		4	7				
8/5	12	3	16				

21.5 ABC Analysis System

Most food and beverage operations know that much of their investment in inventory is represented by a relatively small number of items. If a facility purchases 400 items which are necessary to produce its food and beverage products, perhaps only 100 of these items represent the largest cost. (For example, meats, seafoods, liquor, and wine are much more expensive than spices, cereal products, and baked items.)

The concept of ABC analysis suggests that food and beverage purchasers and management personnel:

Study their purchases to determine which products are most costly ("A" items), next costly ("B" items), and least costly ("C" items).

Categorizing items in this manner sets priorities on the need for control in the purchasing, receiving, and storage processes. For example, costly "A" items must be carefully controlled; less expensive "C" items need less control or, certainly, should not receive attention until proper procedures are developed for control of all "A" products.

The concept of ABC analysis has already been suggested in this handbook when food and beverage purchasers were told to

(1) develop perpetual inventory procedures for high-cost items; and

(2) keep expensive items under tight, secure storage control.

Advantages of thinking about purchased items in terms of their cost (and, therefore, relative importance) include:

Management time and effort will be better spent in controlling the most costly items.

Inventory investments can be minimized (since personnel will carefully consider minimum-maximum quantities of these products to carry in their inventory).

Specific policies will be developed for purchasing, receiving, and storing top-priority items.

21.6 Value of Inventory: A Special Word

Procedures must be developed to assign value to products in inventory. There are at least three commonly used methods:

First-In, First-Out (FIFO): The value of products in inventory is represented by the price paid for the product which has been purchased in the inventory most recently (since the first products placed in storage are used first). For example, if a case of applesauce in storage was purchased three weeks ago and cost $22.50 and if applesauce in a more recent delivery is valued at $23.75 cases in inventory are priced at the rate of $23.75.

Last-In, Last-Out (LIFO): The value of products is represented by the price paid for the product in the inventory the longest. In the example above, cases of applesauce would be valued at $22.50.

Weighted average: This method considers the actual cost of products in storage. If there are three cases of applesauce at the earlier price and five cases of product at the most recent price the value of a case of applesauce is $23.28 (three cases at $22.50 + five cases at $23.75 divided by eight cases).

Two very important points about methods to assess values of inventory must be noted:

The method used to assign inventory values affects financial statements. As methods are used which increase the cost of goods sold, profit is reduced; required taxes may be less.

Food and beverage officials should consult with their accountants about tax implications and other concerns for advice regarding the inventory valuation method they should utilize.

21.7 Ways to Reduce Inventory Costs

Cash-flow problems or, at the very least, minimized investment returns occur when inventory levels are too high. Procedures that might be utilized by purchasers and food and beverage personnel to reduce inventory costs include the following:

Reduce the quantities of products purchased; if stocks are too large the operation may be able to "live on inventory" for some length of time. One must be careful, however, to avoid frequent stockouts of required products.

Reduce requirements for delivery lead time and stockout safety levels. The minimum-maximum inventory system noted in Section 6.5 suggested that additional quantities of products be carried in inventory to allow for these factors. Inventory levels can, however, be lowered by reducing the quantities allowed for these factors.

Attempt to obtain more frequent deliveries of smaller quantities by negotiation with suppliers.

Be certain that the "par" levels of inventory are the correct size.

Standardize the types of products which are carried. For example, perhaps only two or three rather than four or five different sizes of shrimp need to be utilized (and therefore carried in inventory).

Refuse early deliveries (which must be paid for sooner than when payment would be due if products were delivered on an appropriate, timely delivery schedule).

22

SAMPLE FORMS

This section includes blank copies of all the forms which have been discussed in this manual. Their use can be a great help in implementing procedures which are necessary to attain the goal of obtaining and having available the *best* products at the *best* time and at the *best* price in an effective purchasing management system.

Instructions which detail how the forms are to be completed and used are also provided. If the forms are applicable, they can be easily reproduced for use in the food and beverage operation.

Helpful summaries of information for the purchase of specific foods are also included in this section. This information may be of assistance as purchasing specifications are developed. When used with the material presented in Section 15 (Purchase of Foods and Beverages), purchasers will have at least a background of necessary information to develop and communicate their product needs to eligible suppliers.

22.1 Instructions for Completing Form

Form Name: Purchase Specification

Objective: Used to describe the quality needs of products purchased by the food and beverage operation.

Developed/Used By: The form is developed by purchasing staff with input from suppliers and user department personnel (the latter must make the final decision regarding purchase specifications).

Source of Information: Information recorded on the form comes from interviews with suppliers and competitors, analysis of samples and trial order products, and from technical expertise of user and purchasing personnel.

When Developed/Used: The purchase specification is developed for products purchased for the foodservice operation and is provided to all eligible suppliers. Suppliers refer to the purchase specification in order to recall quality required of products as requests for prices are obtained. Prices quoted by suppliers should be for the quality of product required by the purchase specification.

Where Filed: Purchasing personnel should retain a copy of the form with files of other general purchase information. Copies should be sent to appropriate suppliers.

To Fill Out: The purchaser must go through a process to determine appropriate quality as noted in Section 5. Once determined, a specific quality description for each product should be written on the purchase specification form.

FIGURE 22.1 Purchase Specification

_____
(name of food and beverage operation)

1. Product name: _____

2. Product used for: _____

   _____

   _____

   _____

3. Product general description: _____

   _____

   _____

   _____

4. Detailed description: _____

   _____

   _____

   _____

5. Product test procedures: _____

   _____

   _____

   _____

6. Special instructions and requirements: _____

   _____

   _____

   _____

   _____

   _____

Copyright © by Jack D. Ninemeier.

22.2   Instructions for Completing Form

Form Name:	Petty Cash Voucher
Objective of Form:	To provide a written record of the amount and reason for purchases made from the petty cash fund.
Developed/Used By:	The petty cash voucher is developed by the foodservice manager and is used by the management official who is responsible for the petty cash fund.
Source of Information:	The supervisor who authorizes the purchase should indicate the purpose for the petty cash expense to the official who is responsible for the fund.
When Developed/Used:	The voucher is to be used each time a withdrawal is made from the petty cash fund.

FIGURE 22.2   Petty Cash Voucher

Date: _____   No. _____

Amount: _____

Purpose: _____

_____

_____

Authorized by: _____

Attach receipt
_____

Where Filed:	The completed form should remain with the petty cash fund until it is replenished. At that time vouchers should be withdrawn from the fund, should be summed, and then are used to support the amount of the check written to bring the fund back up to its authorized level.
To Fill Out:	The official responsible for the fund should complete the voucher, which is self-explanatory. A receipt given for the purchase should be attached to the voucher.

22.3 Instructions for Completing Form

Form Name:	Purchase Requisition
Objective:	Used by user department (such as food or beverage), storeroom personnel, or other staff to inform purchasing employees about the need to order additional quantities of necessary products.
Developed/Used By:	The form is developed by purchasing staff and used by employees with responsibility for determining when products in a specified quantity are to be ordered.
Source of Information:	Minimum-maximum inventory systems, physical count, study of perpetual inventory records, or other means might be used to determine the type and quantity of necessary products to be ordered.
When Developed/Used:	In larger operations the form is used each time products must be ordered. It is used to indicate to purchasing personnel the quantity and type of products to be ordered.
Where Filed:	The form is attached to the in-house copy of the purchase order/purchase record form as the authorization to purchase. It is filed in the bookkeeping/accounting office after bills (delivery invoices and/or monthly statements) are audited and processed for payment.
To Fill Out:	The department needing products (such as food, beverage, catering, etc.) must be indicated. Other information is essentially self-explanatory. Items needed, purchase unit size, number of purchase units, and specification number for applicable products should be indicated.

FIGURE 22.3 Purchase Requisition

Needed by _____ Requisition Number _____
_____(Department)_____
Date Needed _____ Date _____

Item	Purchase Unit	Number of Units	Specification Number

_____
(signature of authorizing staff member)

Copyright © by Jack D. Ninemeier.

22.4 Instructions for Completing Form

Form Name:	Supplier Performance Rating Sheet
Objective:	Provides a format to rate the performance of suppliers. The objective is to help determine whether vendor performance is acceptable relative to other suppliers. The food and beverage operation can then assess whether or not to continue to purchase from the specific supply source.
Developed/Used By:	The form is developed by purchasing staff after consideration of factors which define a "good" (or, at least, "acceptable") supplier for the property.
Source of Information:	The form is completed by recalling experience with the supplier being evaluated. It is also possible to keep a list, by dates, of problems with late deliveries, product quality, bill adjustments, etc. This technique permits the purchaser to assess objectively the number of problems that affect each performance rating.
When Developed/Used:	The supplier performance rating sheet is developed by considering the factors that are important in a "good" supplier. It should be used at least annually to assess and compare supplier performance. Study of the completed forms will suggest which suppliers are acceptable and also areas in which other suppliers' performance should be improved.
Where Filed:	The completed form should be filed along with other general information applicable to each supplier.
To Fill Out:	A separate rating sheet is used to evaluate each supplier. The purchasing staff who have contact with the supplier being rated should meet and jointly consider how frequently (consistently/ usually/sometimes) each of the listed desired activities is performed. A check mark (√) can be used to indicate the frequency.
Miscellaneous:	When rating sheets are completed for each supplier they can be compared. Suppliers who score low should be contacted and an effort should be made to resolve problems and to strengthen and improve the supplier/food and beverage operation relationship.

FIGURE 22.4 Supplier Performance Rating Sheet

Name of Supplier _____

Desired Activity	Frequency		
	Consistently	Usually	Sometimes
1. Delivers products of proper quality.			
2. Delivers products in right quantity.			
3. Charges reasonable price.			
4. Delivery schedules are right.			
5. Delivers in right place.			
6. Has good ideas about product use, tells about new products, and really wants to help my property.			
7. Will negotiate prices and services.			
8. Gives me "value" for my purchase dollar.			
9. Handles credit and other bill adjustments quickly and correctly.			
10. Salespersons are friendly and helpful.			
11. Delivery persons are friendly and helpful.			
12. Does not short-weight or count products being delivered.			
13. Have good working relationship with supplier.			
14. Supplier is honest and fair.			
15. Supplier "knows" his or her product and business.			
16. Supplier is easy to reach when there are problems.			
17. Supplier follows up on any problems.			

Instructions: Indicate with a check (√) how frequently the supplier performs each of the listed activities.

Copyright © by Jack D. Ninemeier.

22.5 Instructions for Completing Form

Form Name: Issue Requisition: Food
Objective of Form: Used to record the quantity of food products that are removed from inventory.

Developed/Used By: The form is developed by food and beverage officials and is completed by storeroom or management personnel as food items are removed from storage.

Source of Information: The form is completed by visual observation and count/weight of products as they are removed from various food storage areas.

When Developed/Used: The form is used during each of the routinely scheduled times when food products are to be removed from storage. It will additionally be used when "emergency" or special issues must be made. The form is only used when items kept under a perpetual inventory system are removed from storage areas.

Where Filed: The form should be kept with perpetual inventory information to substantiate the quantity of food products which have been issued.

To Fill Out: As issues are made the official enters the name of the item, the size of the package (such as 5# bale, #10 can, case of 6- #10 cans, etc.), and the quantity of each item for which a perpetual inventory is kept. Signatures (or initials) of the employee removing the food item(s) and the management official authorizing the withdrawal should also be included.

Miscellaneous: Normally, in small food and beverage operations, the form should be utilized to record only expensive items such as liquors, wines, meats, seafood items, etc., which are maintained under the perpetual inventory system and removed from the storage areas.

FIGURE 22.5 Issue Requisition: Food

Storage   Date _____

Refrigerated _____

Frozen _____

Dry _____

| Item | Size of Package | Quantity Issued | Employee Initials | |
			Withdrawal by	Approved by

22.6 Instructions for Completing Form

Form Name: Purchase Order
Objective: Used by large food and beverage operations to formally indicate type, quantity, price, and *all* other aspects of purchase agreement for an order placed with a supplier.

Developed/Used By: The form should be developed by the foodservice manager after consultation with an attorney (see "Miscellaneous" information below). It is used by the purchasing personnel as orders are placed.

Source of Information: In formal systems information about price of products may be assessed from request for price quotations (Section 22.23) received from eligible suppliers. Information about type and quantity of products to be ordered, delivery date, etc., are taken from in-house documents, such as purchase requisitions (Section 22.3).

When Developed/Used: The purchase order is used each time an order is placed. In some facilities a formal purchase order is only used for specified types of products or quantities or when high-dollar purchases are made.

Where Filed: One copy of the purchase order is sent to the supplier; a second copy is sent to receiving; a third copy is sent to accounting; a fourth copy is retained by purchasing. As part of the payment process all internal copies are matched up. They are then filed with other documents (delivery invoice, payment information, credit memos, if any, etc., relating to the order).

To Fill Out: The purchase order is given to the supplier awarded the order. Information relating to the supplier's address and delivery destination are self-explanatory. *Agreed-upon delivery date should be specified.* Information about product(s) ordered should be taken from request for price quotation, notes from telephone call, supplier meetings, etc.

Miscellaneous: It is important that an attorney be involved in drawing up necessary terms and conditions for orders. These are generally printed on the reverse side of the purchase order form. Possible topics to be considered* in a "terms and conditions" section include:

---

*Suggested by G. Aljian, editor, Purchasing Handbook, 3rd ed. (New York: McGraw-Hill, 1973).

FIGURE 22.6 Purchase Order

Purchase Order Number _____   Order Date _____

                                    Payment Terms _____

To _____   From/Ship to _____
        (supplier)   (name of foodservice)

_____   _____
                                              (address)

_____   Delivery Date _____
        (address)

Please Ship

Quantity Ordered	Description	√	Units Shipped	Unit Cost	Total Cost

Total Cost _____

IMPORTANT: This Purchase Order expressly limits acceptance to the terms and conditions stated above, noted on the reverse side hereof, and any additional terms and conditions affixed hereto or otherwise referenced. Any additional terms and conditions proposed by seller are objected to and rejected.

_____
(authorized signature)

Copyright © by Jack D. Ninemeier.

Sample Forms   307

Purchase Order to be exclusive agreement

Conditions of acceptance

Packaging/crating charges

Payment of invoices

Guarantees/warranties

Time of essence in performance

Buyer held harmless (patent/copyright infringement)

Compliance with purchase specifications

Right of change order

Right of inspection

Disposition of rejected products

Disclosure of information

Conditions of use, protection, liability for buyer's material/equipment

Rights of buyers to discoveries/developments from research/development work

Default

Termination

Conformance with laws

Order of precedence of documents, terms, conditions

Listing of applicable regulations

Assignments

Limitations on subcontracting

Limitations on buyer's liability

Quality tolerance

22.7 Instructions for Completing Form

Form Name:	Receiving Clerk's Daily Report: Food
Objective of Form:	Provides record of incoming food products, provides information regarding "directs" (for daily food cost calculations), and confirms that products delivered were placed in storage.
Developed/Used By:	The form is developed by the foodservice manager. It is used by the receiving employee and by the official who calculates daily food costs.
Source of Information:	All information for the form is taken from the confirmed delivery invoices for food products.

FIGURE 22.7   Receiving Clerk's Daily Report: Food

Date _____

Name of Receiving Employee _____   Page No. ____ of ____

Supplier	Item	Amount	Purchase Unit	Unit Price	Total Value	Classification		Storage (√)*
						Direct	Storage	

Totals _____ _____

Receiving Employee _____
(signature)

*The final column (Storage √) is used to confirm that the receiving employee has placed each delivered item in storage. If there are separate receiving and storage employees, the latter (storeroom clerk) should initial this column to confirm that he or she accepts responsibility for the items.

Copyright © by Jack D. Ninemeier.

When Developed/Used:	The "receiving clerk's daily report: food" is used to record each food delivery which is made. There is a separate report for beverages.
Where Filed:	The form is filed with other supportive information relating to daily food cost calculations.
To Fill Out:	All information necessary to complete the form is taken from the *confirmed* delivery invoices. Food items are classified as "direct" if they are perishable and are not purchased for inventory but rather immediate use. Examples are milk, fresh produce, and bakery products. Items such as frozen meats and canned goods would be classified as "storage" items. At the end of the day the "direct" and "storage" columns for all sheets are totaled. The sum of the "directs" is used in daily food cost calculations. The sum of the "storage" items should represent the amount by which the perpetual inventory value has *increased* for the day.

22.8   Instructions for Completing Form

Form Name:	Receiving Clerk's Daily Report: Beverage
Objective of Form:	Provides record of incoming beverage products, provides purchase cost information for each type of beverage (beer, liquor, wine, soda) and confirms that products delivered were placed in storage.
Developed/Used By:	The form is developed by the foodservice manager. It is used by the receiving employee and by the official who calculates the purchase cost of each beverage.
Source of Information:	All information for the form is taken from the *confirmed* delivery invoices for beverages.
When Developed/Used:	The *Receiving Clerk's Daily Report: Beverage* is used to record each beverage delivery. There is a separate report for food products.
Where Filed:	The form is filed with other supportive information relating to beverage cost calculations.
To Fill Out:	All information necessary to complete the form is taken from the *confirmed* delivery invoices. Beverage items are classified by type (beer, liquor, wine, soda). At the end of the day the four columns are summed for all sheets. This data,

FIGURE 22.8 Receiving Clerk's Daily Report: Beverage

Date _____

Name of Receiving Employee _____   Page No. ____ of ____

Supplier	Item	Amount	Purchase Unit	Unit Price	Beer	Liquor	Wine	Soda	Storage (√)*

The header "Classification" spans the Beer, Liquor, Wine, Soda columns.

Totals _____ _____ _____ _____

Receiving Employee _____
(signature)

The final column (Storage √) is used to confirm that the receiving employee has placed each delivered item in storage. If there are separate receiving and storage employees, the latter (storeroom clerk) should initial this column to confirm that he or she accepts responsibility for the items.

Copyright © by Jack D. Ninemeier.

totaled for the month, represents "purchases" information in the *Cost of Goods Sold: Beverage Calculations*.

22.9 Instructions for Completing Form

Form Name:	Issue Requisition: Beverage
Objective of Form:	This form is to record the number, type, and cost of all bottles issued to each bar at the end of each shift. It also provides the authorization for bottles to be removed (issued) from the central beverage storage area.
Developed/Used By:	The *Issue Requisition: Beverage* is developed by beverage management personnel at the end of each bartending shift. As noted above, it is used by central beverage storeroom personnel as the authorization to issue beverages in order to replenish bar inventory to necessary par levels.
Sources of Information:	Data for the form stems from (a) Number of empty bottles at the end of each shift; (b) Cost of beverages being issued to the bar (which is taken off delivery invoices less any discounts) and marked (tagged) on bottles. Cost information can also be obtained from purchase records or delivery invoices.
When Developed/Used:	This form is used at the end of each bartending shift. A separate form is used for each bar for each shift.
Where Filed:	The form is filed in the beverage manager's office. It can be used as the source of beverage costs under some beverage costing systems.
To Fill Out:	Information regarding shift number, bar, date, and name of bartender is filled in at the end of each bartending shift. A count is made, by type, of all empty bottles at the end of the shift. Cost is inserted in the appropriate column (see Sources of Information, above) and multiplied by the number of empty bottles to yield a total cost. (This total cost of all empties divided by sales generated from the shift can yield the beverage cost percent.) A beverage management official authorizes the reissue of full bottles to replenish bar inventory levels.

FIGURE 22.9 Issue Requisition: Beverage

Shift _____   Date _____

Bar _____   Bartender _____

Liquor	Bottles Number	Size	Unit Cost	Total Cost

Total Bottles _____   Total Cost _____

OK to issue _____

Issued by _____

Received by _____

_____ ÷ _____ = _____
Cost   Sales   Bev. %

Copyright © by Jack D. Ninemeier.

22.10 Instructions for Completing Form

Form Name: Purchasing Evaluation Guide

Objective: Used to obtain information about how the purchasing process can be improved.

Developed/Used By: The form should be developed by purchasing staff working closely with top management. Each of the activities judged to be important in the operation of a successful, effective purchasing department should be listed. It is used by staff members from purchasing, food and beverage departments, and by top management officials to confidentially indicate ideas about how purchasing might be improved.

Source of Information: The listing of activities can be those on the sample Purchasing Evaluation Guide or they can be amended by considering additional activities important to the specific operation. The remainder of the form is based only upon the knowledge and feeling of those who complete the form.

When Developed/Used: The Purchasing Evaluation Guide should be used in advance of the time when the formal purchasing evaluation process is undertaken.

Where Filed: After discussion the forms should be given to purchasing staff for their use. They can be filed, perhaps with accompanying recaps, with information applicable to prior purchasing evaluation forms.

To Fill Out: Each member of the purchasing and accounting departments and top management should be given a form to complete. Additionally, copies should be given to employees with receiving and storage duties. Management personnel and other interested employees in food and beverage departments can also complete copies. For each activity which is listed persons completing the form should:

Think about whether, from their perspective, improvements are needed (will assist purchasing staff to be more helpful to them).

Specific examples of problems or ideas/suggestions about how the activity can be performed more effectively.

When individual forms are completed they should be compiled and used to help evaluate the purchasing department's effectiveness. Problems that are consistently noted, of course, should receive first attention as plans to improve the task of purchasing are developed.

Date ―――――

Completed by
staff member in:

☐ Purchasing Dept.
☐ Food/Bev. Dept.
☐ Management
☐ Accounting Dept.

Instructions: For each of the following activities consider whether improvements can be made that will make purchasing more effective. Specific ideas/suggestions will be very helpful.

Activity	Improvements Needed		
	Yes	No	Comments
1. Organization of purchasing dept.			
2. Relations with user dept.			
3. Purchasing controls.			
4. Receiving controls.			
5. Storage controls.			
6. Make/buy analysis.			
7. Writing purchase specifications.			
8. Locating/working with suppliers.			
9. Personnel cooperation.			
10. Employee training.			
11. Document processing for payment.			
12. Policies.			
13. Standard operating procedures.			
14. "Paperwork."			
15. Product quality determination.			
16. Product quantity determination.			
17. Expediting/follow-up.			
18. Delivery timing.			
19. Other activities (list).			

22.11 Summary of Meat Grading Information

The purchase of meats can be made easier and an assurance of desired quality being purchased and received becomes more certain as U.S. Department of Agriculture grading standards are utilized. The following summary of meat grading information provides basic help to meat buyers as they consider quality grade distinctions as an added element in their purchase specifications.

Definitions*

a. Grading—Indicates the extent to which a specific meat product meets a quality standard established for it.
b. Type of meat—Refers to kind (beef, veal, lamb, pork).
c. Class—Refers to kind of animal (see below).

Part I—Quality Factors.   Grading refers to quality of the meat. The factors that determine meat quality are:

Finish—Fat that covers the carcass and is distributed inside the animal and between muscles.

Marbling—Amount of finish that appears in the muscle itself (more marbling will make the meat more juicy, flavorful, and tender).

Class—Type of animal (such as steer, cow, and bull distinctions for beef).

Sex of animal.

Shape—Conformation, which indicates the amount of preferred areas (such as loins, rounds, and chucks).

Firmness—Affected by the amount of fat, animal age, and other factors.

Age of animal.

Flesh—Color of the lean.

Part II—Class.   Class refers to the kind of animal.

Beef

Steer—Male with hormones removed at young age.

Heifer—Female without calf.

Cow—Female with one or more calves.

Bull—Male with male hormones.

Bullock—Young bull.

Stag—Male which is heavier or fatter than a bull.

Much of Section 22.11 is adapted from R. Pedderson, Specs: The Comprehensive Foodservice Purchasing and Specification Manual (Boston, Mass: CBI Publishing Co., Inc., 1977), pp. 76–99.

Veal

Veal—Bovine up to three months old.
Calf—Bovine older than three months.

Lamb

Lamb—Less than 1 year old.
Yearling—From 1 to 1¼ years old.
Mutton—More than 1¼ years old.

Pork

Barrow—Male without male hormones.
Gilt—Female without pigs.
Sow—Female with pigs.
Boar—Male with male hormones.
Stag—Male with male hormones removed after maturity.

Part III—Quality Grades. There are different names for quality grade for different meat types.

Name of USDA Grade	Beef			Veal		Lamb		Name of USDA Grade	Pork	
	Steer Heifer Bullock	Cow	Bull Stag	Veal	Calf	Lamb Yearling	Mutton		Barrow Gilt	Sow
Prime	x	—	—	x	x	x	—	U.S. No. 1	x	x
Choice	x	x	x	x	x	x	x	U.S. No. 2	x	x
Good	x	x	x	x	x	x	x	U.S. No. 3	x	x
Standard	x	x	—	x	x	—	—	U.S. No. 4	x	—
Commercial	x	x	x	—	—	—	—	Utility	x	—
Utility	x	x	x	x	x	x	x	Medium	—	x
Cutter	x	x	x	—	—	—	—	Cull	—	x
Canner	x	x	x	—	—	—	—			
Cull	—	—	—	x	x	x	x			

Part IV—Yield Grades. Yield grades show differences in yields of boneless, close trimmed, and retail cuts for beef and lamb. They also indicate differences in the general "fatness" of carcasses and cuts. There are no yield grade standards for veal or pork. Yield Grade 1 is the highest yield (least amount of trim); Yield Grade 5 is the lowest yield (highest amount of trim). Yield grades apply to all quality grades; however, the "X" indicates these grades in the largest supply.

USDA Quality Grades	Beef — Most Yield				Beef — Least Yield	Lamb — Most Yield				Lamb — Least Yield
	1	2	3	4	5	1	2	3	4	5
U.S. Prime			x	x	x			x^2	x^2	x^2
U.S. Choice		x	x	x				x	x	x
U.S. Good		x	x				x	x	x	
U.S. Standard	x	x	x			Not applicable				
U.S. Commercial		x	x	x	x	Not applicable				
U.S. Utility		x	x	x			x	x		
U.S. Cutter		x	x			Not applicable				
U.S. Canner		x	x			Not applicable				
U.S. Cull	Not applicable						x	x		

1. "x" indicates items in highest supply.
2. The prime grade is not applicable to mutton.

22.12 Summary of Purchase Information for Poultry

Detailed information about kind, class, and quality grading concerns are included here for the poultry buyer desiring more specific information as purchase specifications are developed.

Part I: Kinds and Classes of Poultry*

(a) Kind: Chicken. Classes are:

1. Cornish game hen—Chicken that is five to seven weeks old weighing less than two pounds.

*Information in Part I is adapted from R. Peddersen, Specs: The Comprehensive Food-service Purchasing and Specification Manual (Boston, Mass.: CBI Publishing Co., Inc. 1977), p. 240–241.

2. Broiler/fryer—Chicken nine to twelve weeks old of either sex.
3. Roaster—Chicken three to five months old of either sex.
4. Capon—Surgically unsexed male chicken less than eight months old.
5. Stag—Male chicken under ten months old.
6. Hen/stewing, Chicken/fowl—Female chicken more than ten months old.
7. Cock/Rooster—Mature, male chicken.

(b)   Kind: Turkey. Classes are:

1. Fryer - roaster turkey—Turkey under sixteen weeks of either sex.
2. Young hen turkey—Female turkey five to seven months old.
3. Young Tom turkey—Male turkey five to seven months old.
4. Yearling hen turkey—Female turkey under fifteen months old.
5. Yearling Tom turkey—Male turkey under fifteen months old.
6. Mature/old turkey (hen or tom)—Turkey more than fifteen months old.

(c)   Kind: Duck. Classes are:

1. Broiler/fryer duckling—Duck under eight weeks old of either sex.
2. Rooster duckling—Duck under sixteen weeks old of either sex.
3. Mature/old duck—Over six months old of either sex.

(d)   Kind: Goose. Classes are:

1. Young goose—Young goose of either sex (tender meated).
2. Mature/old goose—Mature goose of either sex (toughened meat).

Class (age) of products is a guide to meat tenderness.

Part II: Quality Grading Standards

Ready-to-cook poultry products are inspected for wholesomeness before being graded. Factors in the grading process include:

1. Conformation—Distribution of meat.
2. Fleshing—Amount of flesh over the back.
3. Fat—Amount of surface fat under the skin.
4. Lack of pinfeathers.
5. Freedom from exposed flesh caused by cuts, tears, or broken bones.
6. Lack of skin discoloration, blemishes, bruises.
7. Freedom from freezing defects.

Examination of birds for these factors will result in grades of A (highest quality), B, or C (lowest quality).

22.13 Summary of Grades and Standards for Canned Goods

Food and beverage purchasers may desire background information on Federal grades and standards that are important to consider in purchasing canned fruits and vegetables. The information which follows provides an overview of the topic.

Part I: Federal Grades*

Many canned products carry Federal grades, but the same names are not applied to the same grades for all products. Also, not all products use all grade levels. Grade names are:

U.S. Fancy *or* Grade A (highest quality).

U.S. Choice (fruits); (same as Grade B).

U.S. Extra Standard (vegetables); (same as Grade B).

U.S. Standard *or* Grade C (lowest graded quality).

Items not meeting Grade C standards must be so labeled.

In general, Grade A or Fancy products are selected for uniform size, color, maturity, tenderness, and freedom from defects. Buyers should specify this grade when flavor and appearance are very important.

Grade B (choice for fruits; extra standard for vegetables) is a good quality but scores lower on one or more of the factors noted above.

Grade C or standard products score lower than Grade B but are still of acceptable quality and are as nutritious and wholesome as the higher scoring grades. These products are most useful in recipes that require further cooking or additional ingredients.

Part II: Food Standards

The Food and Drug Administration (U.S. Department of Health, Education and Welfare) has established food standards that must be followed when products are to be shipped in interstate commerce.

Standards of Identity. These tell the nature and character of a food (what the food is). These standards concern:

---

*Part I is adapted from R. Peddersen, Specs: The Comprehensive Foodservice Purchasing and Specification Manual (Boston, Mass.: CBI Publishing Co., Inc. 1977), pp. 488—492.

The kinds and amount of ingredients that must go into a product.

For a specific food, what is in it, how it is made, and how the product looks; setting limits such as fat and moisture content. Standards exist for foods such as mayonnaise, fruit cocktail, and tomato catsup.

Standards of fill.   These regulate the quantity of the food in the container.

This standard indicates how full the container must be to avoid deceiving the buyer.

Generally, packages must contain the maximum quantity of food that can be sealed in the container and processed without damaging the food.

Standards apply to products that may shake down or settle after filling, or those which are made up of a number of units or pieces packed in a liquid.

Standards of fill have been developed for most canned fruits and vegetables.

Quality standards.   These apply chiefly to canned fruits and vegetables. They list the ingredients that go into the product.

These standards limit and describe the number and kinds of defects permitted.

Various tests indicate color, texture, tenderness, and freedom from defect.

Butter scoring is a familiar quality standard (92 = AA; 91 = A.)

If minimum quality standards are *not* met the product must be so labeled.

Part III: Can Labels

Standards also apply to labeling packages; a food is mislabeled if the label is false or misleading or if some information is missing. Labels must indicate:

The common name of the product and name and address of manufacturer, packer, or distributor.

Content weight.

Net contents of a serving (when the package declares contents in terms of servings).

List of ingredients in decreasing order by weight (foods with a "standard of identity" are exempt).

Statement which tells if artificial coloring, flavoring, or chemical preservatives are used.

Optional information may be included on a label:

    Brand name.

    Size and maturity of product.

    Illustration of product.

    Seasoning, if used.

    Contents of can measured by cups or number of pieces.

    Number of servings.

    Recipes and suggestions for use.

22.14　House Brand Liquor Selection Factors

Many specific factors affect the decision regarding the selection of house brand liquors. A listing of many of these concerns is supplied in this section.

Each of the following factors might need to be considered as house brands of liquor to be used are determined.*

    Price/quality (value) concerns

    Supplier services

    Supplier discounts (if any)

    Reciprocation between supplier and purchaser

    Opportunity buys

    Availability of product

    Type (reputation) of establishment

    Price structure of operation

    Reputation of label

    Clientele preference

    Owner's preference

    Liquor proof

    "Testing" results

    Brands used by competitive operations

    Suggestions from competent individuals

    Supplier payment plans (where laws permit options)

    Friendships with suppliers

---

*General selection criteria have been developed by K. A. Olschner in a class project for the University of New Orleans, School of Hotel, Restaurant and Tourism Administration, Summer, 1980. This is a partial listing of factors that were identified.

22.15 Review of Information Necessary for Food Purchases

The following are the most important points to consider as purchase specifications for food and beverage products are developed.

A. Meats.

Specifications for meat should include:

1. Product to be inspected.
2. Federal grade, if desired.
3. Federal yield grade, if product is to be graded (available for beef and lamb only).
4. Institutional Meat Purchasing Specification (IMPS) or Meat Buyers Guide (MBG) number.
5. Weight/thickness limitations.
6. Fat limitations.
7. State of refrigeration.
8. Miscellaneous information (method of tying, if applicable; boning procedures; packaging and marking instructions).

B. Seafoods

1. Fresh fish buyers must purchase what is available; they must know and be able to identify acceptable quality characteristics of fresh fish.
2. Specifications for frozen fish products should include:
    (a.) Type of fish.
    (b.) Weight limitations (if portion control product).
    (c.) Blast freezing; solid pack in shipping case.
    (d.) Protection by moisture and vapor proof materials.
    (e.) Ice glazing can also be specified to protect products such as shrimp and fish steaks.
    (f.) Breaded products must specify weight before and after breading.
    (g.) Headless frozen shrimp are generally purchased by count and size, as are shucked oysters and similar products.

C. Poultry.

Specifications for poultry should include:

1. Inspection to be required (if interstate commerce products are to be used).

2. Quality grade required (if desired, but most poultry specifications do indicate a grade designation).

3. Kind and class.

4. Style.

5. Size (weight).

6. State of refrigeration.

7. Breed.

D. Eggs.

Specifications should include:

1. Inspection to be required.

2. Quality grade.

3. Egg size.

4. Size/type of package.

5. Fresh or processed; if processed, market form.

6. Shell condition (fish, storage, processed storage).

E. Dairy Products.

Specifications will vary according to the product.

For Milk

1. Pasteurized homogenized milk (where applicable).

2. Kind.

3. Size/type of container.

4. Additives: Vitamins A and D are frequently added to milk products. Specify other additives as necessary.

5. Grade: milk should be Grade A.

For Cheese

1. Order cheese by name (when federal standards of identity exist or by experience with cheese types provided by eligible suppliers).

2. Container size/weight.

3. Federal Grades may also be specified for some common cheeses.

For Butter

1. Indicate grade.

2. Market form.

3. Classification (type) of butter.

F. For Cereal Products

Generally cereal products are sampled and acceptable brands are determined. The specification then indicates:

The name of product (such as flour).

Type of product (such as pastry flour).

Brand (if desired).

Size of purchase unit (such as 100# sack).

G. For Fruits and Vegetables

1. Name of product.
2. Grade (usually U.S. Grades A and B are preferred by food and beverage purchasers).
3. Additional quality requirements, if any.
4. Variety (not as important in the purchase of vegetables).
5. Size.
6. Quantity.
7. Brand (if desirable).
8. Growing area (less important in the purchase of vegetables).
9. Type of packaging required.
10. Count per container.

H. For Canned and Frozen Fruits and Vegetables

1. Name of product.
2. Style of product (such as "chunks").
3. Sieve size (as with the required diameter of peas).
4. Can or package size.
5. Number of cans or packages per case.
6. Source (geographic region of origin).
7. Grade.
8. Point score (if desired).
9. Packing medium.
10. Minimum required drain weight.

22.16 Instructions for Completing Form

Form Name: Storage Tag

Objective of Form: Identifies, by purchase unit (case, package, etc.) delivery date, weight, and cost of storage item.

Developed/Used By: The storage tag is developed by the foodservice manager. It is used by the receiving employee to identify, by delivered items, required information. At time of issue the tag is also used to help calculate daily food cost.

Source of Information:	Information for the tag is taken from the applicable delivery invoice *after* verification of weight and arithmetic extensions.
When Developed/Used:	The storage tag is used for all items on which stamped or handwritten information is not practical. Examples include fresh fish, irregular shapes of individual meat cuts, etc.
Where Filed:	One part of the tag is sent to the manager, cost controller, accountant, or other official responsible for food cost calculations. The second part of the tag is attached to the product while in storage. When the product is issued, the tag is sent to the food costing official for "matching up" with the original section of the tag.
To Fill Out:	Information for completing the tag is taken from the accompanying delivery invoice. Date of receipt will be date of placement in storage. Weight data is confirmed by use of an on-site scale. Price information should be confirmed from the purchase order or purchase record. Cost of product should be confirmed by checking the arithmetic extensions.

FIGURE 22.16 Storage Tag

Tag Number _____   Tag Number _____

Date of Receipt _____   Date Received _____

Weight/Cost   Weight _____

$$\frac{\qquad}{\text{No. of \#s}} (\times) \frac{\qquad}{\text{Price}} = \frac{\qquad}{\text{Cost}}$$ Price _____

Name of Supplier: Cost _____

_____   Supplier _____

Date of Issue: _____   Date Issued _____

22.17 Instructions for Completing Form

Name of Form:	Physical Inventory Form
Objective of Form:	Provides a format to calculate the value of items in inventory.
Developed/Used By:	The Physical Inventory form is developed by food and beverage officials and is used by the storeroom attendant (if available) and by a management official when the cost of items in inventory is assessed.
Source of Information:	A listing is made of each product in dry, refrigerated, and frozen storage which is to be included in the physical inventory count. Information regarding "amount in storage" is assessed from physical count; "purchase price" should be assessed from the price marked on the product case/can, etc., at the time of receipt.
When Developed/Used:	The form is used at least monthly to determine the cost of products in storage.
Where Filed:	The completed forms should be filed with other financial records used to support calculations for "cost of goods sold" on income (profit and loss) statements.
To Fill Out:	Two staff members (preferably one in management) should take the physical inventory. A listing of products to be counted is made in the column "product." The normal purchase unit (such as case, pounds, 10# bale, etc.) is noted in the second column. A physical count is taken to determine the amount (number) of purchase units actually in storage. The purchase price of one unit (generally based upon the *last* price paid when two or more prices are noted on containers) is multiplied by the number of units to determine the total price. The total price of all items for all sheets for each type of product (refrigerated, frozen, and dry) will represent the value of all items in inventory.
Miscellaneous:	The physical inventory process is necessary to control food and beverage products. Liquor, beer, and wine products should also be inventoried separately so that costs can be specifically assigned to each product.

The form is designed so that two months'

FIGURE 22.17 Physical Inventory Form

Type of Product _____

| | | Month _____ | | | Month _____ | | |
Product	Unit	Amount in Storage	Purchase Price	Total Price	Amount in Storage	Purchase Price	Total Price

Copyright © by Jack D. Ninemeier.

calculations can be performed on one form. This reduces the frequency of writing product name and purchase unit information on the forms. It is, of course, possible to write in the name of products and unit size, then to reproduce several copies of the form to reduce still further the need to write product names on the inventory forms.

22.18 Instructions for Completing Form

Form Name: Perpetual Inventory Form

Objective of Form: This form is used to keep a continual "running balance" of the quantity of product in inventory.

Developed/Used By: The Perpetual Inventory Form is developed by food and beverage management and is used by the storeroom employees or other individuals who are charged with the responsibility for maintaining inventory records.

Source of Information: Information regarding the quantity of product brought into storage is obtained from the supplier's delivery invoice *after* the receiving process is completed. Information regarding the quantity of product taken out of storage is obtained from the issue requisition or other forms used to authorize withdrawal from inventory.

When Developed/Used: At the end of each day the delivery invoices and issue requisitions can be used to update the "running balance" inventory. The form can then be used to "spot check" the record keeping— perpetual inventory balance against the quantity of product actually available on the storeroom shelf.

Where Filed: The form should remain in the storage area for use as needed.

To Fill Out: As products enter and leave the storage area the forms used to authorize these movements should be used to increase/decrease the "balance" column.

Miscellaneous: The Perpetual Inventory form collects information about the quantity, not the *cost,* of products in storage. As such, the form is used to control food storage. The value of stored items (which is needed for accounting purposes) is obtained through use of the physical inventory form (Section 22.17).

FIGURE 22.18 Perpetual Inventory Form

Product Name _____   Purchase Unit Size _____

Date	In	Out	Balance Carried Forward ____	Date	In	Out	Balance Carried Forward ____

22.19 Instructions for Completing Form

Form Name: Bin Card

Objective of Form: The Bin Card can be used to keep track of expensive and fast moving food and beverage items. It provides a checkpoint to assure that no products are misused or unaccounted for. The number of units in storage as noted on the bin card should equal the amount of product on the shelf *and* the quantity noted in the perpetual inventory records.

Developed/Used By: The bin card is developed by the food and beverage manager. It is completed by anyone authorized to place products in or to remove items from storage. It is also used by management personnel as they periodically compare the quantity of products in storage as noted on the bin card with the volume of items noted by physical count on the shelf.

Source of Information: A notation is made on the bin card *every* time that an item is placed in or taken out of storage. There are no forms or other documents that generate information needed on the bin card.

When Developed/Used: The bin card may be used for physical control of expensive and fast moving products. Examples of such items include liquors, wines, meats, seafoods, etc.

Where Filed: The forms should be secured directly to the shelving unit where the products are stored. There is a separate card for each product. When the card is filled it is replaced. After comparing it with the applicable perpetual inventory records the card can be discarded if it is not used in the specific food and beverage operation for another purpose.

To Fill Out: A separate bin card is completed for each item being controlled. A separate line is needed for each entry. Every time an item is placed in or taken out of storage an entry is made on the card. The amount placed in or taken out of storage is added to or subtracted from the "balance" so that a running total of the amount of items which *should* be inventory can be maintained.

FIGURE 22.19 Bin Card

Name of Item _____							
Forward _____				Forward _____			
Date	In	Out	Balance	Date	In	Out	Balance

22.20   Instructions for Completing Form

Form Name:	Checklist for Effective Supplier Relations
Objective of Form:	Provides means for food and beverage purchasers to evaluate their actions which impact on professional buyer-seller relations.
Developed/Used By:	Personnel with purchasing responsibilities should periodically review the checklist to assure that they are not consciously or subconsciously doing things that hinder effective relationships.
Source of Information:	Items on the list (perhaps with additions/deletions to make it specifically applicable to the property) are those which are thought to be important in maintaining good buyer-seller relationships. Purchasers may wish to ask suppliers about factors or to have a meeting on this topic at a local association session to develop the listing of important factors.

When Developed/Used:	The form should be given to newly employed personnel with purchasing duties and might be given to suppliers to affirm procedures which the food and beverage operation uses as it interacts with suppliers. Purchasing staff should review the listing of factors at least monthly and as "problems" with suppliers occur.
Where Filed:	The checklist for effective supplier relations should be filed in the purchasing department's office or with other general purchasing information.
To Fill Out:	In most instances the checklist can be used in its present format. Purchasing staff should read through the list to consider whether, in their actions and words, they routinely do things which foster good, rather than poor, buyer-seller relationships.

FIGURE 22.20 Checklist for Effective Supplier Relations

Food and beverage purchasers should attempt to consistently practice the following courtesies in their relationships with suppliers.

☐ Inform suppliers about purchasing policies.
☐ Give reasonable estimates of necessary product quantities.
☐ Suppliers are given sufficient advance notice about the need for price quotations and/or deliveries.
☐ Suppliers know about required delivery times and locations.
☐ Suppliers know when on-site visits for meetings with purchasing staff are permitted.
☐ Suppliers are asked about how their products might fit the needs of the food and beverage operation.
☐ Suppliers are thanked for advice and any other special assistance which is given.
☐ Sales managers are informed when their sales representatives do an especially good job.
☐ Suppliers are treated in a courteous, respectful manner during their visits.
☐ Suppliers' time is not wasted (as when they are led on about an order that they are not going to receive or when they are delayed an inordinate amount of time for a scheduled meeting).
☐ Suppliers are promptly told when the purchaser is too busy to meet with them for an unscheduled meeting.
☐ No favoritism is shown when suppliers are being interviewed; unless schedules have been prearranged they are seen on a "first-come, first served" basis.
☐ Suppliers are told the approximate length of time they will need to wait for an unscheduled meeting.
☐ Suppliers are notified about obvious mistakes in their bids/prices.
☐ All suppliers are asked for advice when purchase specifications are written or

FIGURE 22.20 Checklist for Effective Supplier Relations (cont.)

revised; all eligible suppliers receive copies of the specifications that apply to products they sell.

☐ Prices are solicited from all eligible suppliers.

☐ Unsuccessful bidders are informed when and why they did not receive an order.

☐ Rush orders are kept to an absolute minimum.

☐ Suppliers are allowed some leeway when they have an *occasional* problem completing an order for reasons beyond their control.

☐ Reasonable tolerances are allowed between product specifications and actual quality of products when delivery inspections are made.

☐ Reports of receiving personnel are verified before formal complaints are made to suppliers.

☐ Suggestions to improve delivery and service are given to suppliers.

☐ Misstatements are never given to suppliers.

☐ Food and beverage purchasers try to develop and maintain a reputation among suppliers for "fair dealing."

☐ Suppliers are not taken advantage of (even when there may be a "legal" right to do so).

☐ Suppliers are understood to need a "fair" profit for the products and services they supply.

☐ The food and beverage operation abides by all its agreements (written and verbal).

☐ A buyer-seller meeting is scheduled with the local restaurant or other professional association on an annual basis.

☐ Purchasers have the authority to make decisions about products and services offered by suppliers.

☐ Purchasers are attentive and good listeners in meetings with suppliers.

☐ Purchasers interact with suppliers in a professional, businesslike manner.

22.21 Instructions for Completing Form

Form Name: Purchase Record

Objectives of Form: The purchase record form has several uses. (a) It provides a format for recording purchase order information; that is, it provides a record of what the foodservice manager has agreed to purchase (food item, description, amount, purchase price). (b) It provides a reference for food receiving. Since one knows what has been ordered, it is possible to compare what is being received with what has been ordered. (c) It provides a means to determine the value of food items ordered and received during the financial period. This information is used to determine the value of "food purchases" when cost-of-goods-sold food calculations are made for the financial statement.

Developed/Used By: The purchase record is developed and used by the foodservice manager or other official(s) charged with responsibility for ordering and receiving food items.

Source of Information: Most of the information comes from the telephone conversation or purchase quotation from the supplier. One exception, invoice number, is taken from the delivery invoice which accompanies the food at the time of receiving. The "comments" section is only used in extraordinary cases (shortages, etc.) to explain unusual conditions. If changes are noted (for example, slight weight or count variations) when the order and receiving information is compared, a notation regarding *actual* product received (and invoiced for) should be made.

When Developed/Used: The purchase record is developed and used (a) each time a food purchase is made; (b) each time a food order is received; (c) at the end of the financial period when the value of food purchases is calculated.

Where Filed: The purchase record should be filed, with completed delivery invoices attached, in the foodservice manager's office. It may also be practical to provide a copy of order information to the individual responsible for food receiving so that comparison procedures (noted above) can be

To Fill Out:

carried out during the time of food receipt.
The date food is ordered should be indicated. The "item description" column should be completed (although when a written purchase specification has been agreed upon and given to the suppliers, this description task can be very brief). The unit (case of #10 cans; size of portion cut steak; container size or other quantitative description) price, and number of units purchased should be *carefully* written on the form. "Purchase cost" information is an extension of "price" × "number of units purchased." As noted above, any changes noted during delivery should be indicated on the purchase record so that, when completed, it represents a true statement of quantity and cost of all items purchased.

Miscellaneous:

Purchase order forms (with attached invoices) should be filed by the supplier and used as a source document for the accounting process.*
Discounts for prompt payment, quantity purchased, etc., should be listed on the form so that an accurate statement of food costs can be obtained.

The sum of food purchases (total of all purchase records, all suppliers, for the period) represents "purchases" value in calculations concerning the actual cost of food sold.

FIGURE 22.21 Purchase Record

_____ (supplier)

Date Ordered	Item Description	Unit	Price	Number Units Purchased	Total Purchase Cost	Invoice #	Comments

22.22 Instructions for Completing Form

Form Name: Credit Memo

Objective of Form: Provides authorized record of adjustments to be
                               made to delivery invoices.

Developed/Used By: The form is developed by the foodservice
                               manager and is used by the receiving person or
                               other staff member who notes problems requiring
                               credit adjustments.

Source of Information: When problems are noted information is taken
                               from the vendor's copy of the applicable delivery
                               invoice.

When Developed/Used: The form is completed each time a delivery
                               problem is noted which necessitates a change in a
                               delivery invoice. This will normally be at the time
                               delivery is made. However, problems (especially
                               with improper quality) may also be observed *after*
                               the delivery has been accepted. *If* the supplier will
                               then make an adjustment the form will be
                               completed by the food and beverage manager or
                               other official.

Where Filed: The completed form is attached to the top side of
                               the applicable delivery invoice and is processed
                               and filed with that document.

To Fill Out: The number and date of the affected invoice must
                               be noted. Products which are entered on the
                               delivery invoice but which are not accepted or
                               received for *any* reason are noted on the credit
                               memo. The reason for the adjustment is noted and
                               the form is signed by the delivery person and by
                               the receiving employee. One copy of the credit
                               memo is given to the delivery person; the
                               remaining copy is attached to the copy of the
                               applicable delivery invoice sent to bookkeeping for
                               payment.

FIGURE 22.22 Credit Memo

CREDIT MEMO

From _____

Number _____

To _____
(supplier)

_____

_____

_____

Invoice date _____

Credit should be given on the following:

Invoice number _____

Product	Unit	Number	Price/Unit	Total Price

Total _____

Reason: _____

_____
(delivery person)

_____
(authorizing signature)

(prepare in duplicate)

22.23 Instructions for Completing Form

Form Name: Request for Price Quotation

Objective: Used by large food and beverage operations to formally request prices from eligible suppliers for required products.

Developed/Used By: The form should be developed by purchasing personnel, approved by the food and beverage manager or other officials, and used by purchasing personnel as orders are being processed.

Source of Information: Type of product needed (product description) and quantity (unit/total) should be taken from the storeroom or user department purchase requisition or other forms. Suppliers wishing to quote a price for the order complete the last two columns of form (price per unit/total).

When Developed/Used: The form may be used each time orders are placed. It may be more practical, however, to use the form only when purchasing certain products, dealing with selected suppliers, purchasing in large quantities, purchasing high-dollar amounts, or other limitations established by management.

Where Filed: The form submitted by the accepted supplier should be filed with the purchase order that is issued.

To Fill Out: The form is self-explanatory. The form is designed so that copies can be sent to up to three suppliers without retyping most of the information required by the form. Only one "supplier/address" box is completed for the form sent to a specified supplier. The buyer need only indicate product, unit, total units required, and date of delivery information. The request form is sent to eligible suppliers with a return date noted.

When the forms are returned prices are compared and an order decision is made according to procedures outlined in Sections 8.12.3 and 8.12.4.

FIGURE 22.23 Request for Price Quotation

Date _____   Request Number _____

To
┌─────────────────────────────┐   Please quote your
│   │   price and delivery
│   │   on the following
│   │   products. Return to
│   │   this office by _____
└─────────────────────────────┘
        (supplier/address)   _____

| Product Description | Quantity | | Price | |
	Unit	Total	Per Unit	Total

Date of Delivery _____   Request by

Price Valid for _____   _____
                (number of days)   (company)

Signed _____   _____
              (supplier)

_____   _____
      (address)   (address)

_____   _____
 (authorized signature)   (authorized signature)

Copyright © by Jack D. Ninemeier.

22.24 Instructions for Completing Form

Form Name:	Quotation-Call Sheet
Objective:	Provides a format to list quoted prices for needed products from suppliers who are called or questioned during on-site visits.
Developed/Used By:	The form is developed by purchasing personnel and used as decisions about order placement are made.
Source of Information:	In informal systems information about products and quantities needed is obtained by a count of items available in inventory. Quantities needed are calculated and the difference between what is available and what is needed must be ordered. Suppliers who are called for prices are those eligible to provide products of a specified type (meats, produce, etc.) to the operation.
When Developed/Used:	The Quotation-Call Sheet is used by purchasing personnel who call suppliers for current prices or needed products.
Where Filed:	The Quotation-Call Sheet is attached to the purchase record, purchase order, or other form to indicate what has been ordered and the agreed price. After products are received all applicable documents will be used and filed as payments are processed.
To Fill Out:	The form is self-explanatory. Names of up to four suppliers are listed along the top of the form. Each supplier is called for a quote on his or her current price for needed products. After all suppliers are contacted, the form is analyzed and an order is placed. There are two possibilities:

The supplier with the lowest total price for products is awarded the entire order.

Each product is considered individually and the lowest price for each product is circled. Suppliers are awarded the order only for those products for which their quoted price was lowest. Minimum delivery poundage or dollar value restrictions placed by some suppliers on delivery may eliminate this possibility. Likewise, as more orders are placed with more suppliers, processing time for orders increases. Management personnel must make a careful analysis of the advantages and disadvantages to use of this method.

FIGURE 22.24 Quotation-Call Sheet

Date _____

Needed Product	Amt.	Supplier			

TOTAL: _____ _____ _____ _____ _____